Artificial Intelligence and Logic Programming

Artificial Intelligence and Logic Programming

Nishit Mathur

CENTRUM PRESS
NEW DELHI-110002 (INDIA)

CENTRUM PRESS
H.O.: 4360/4, Ansari Road, Daryaganj,
New Delhi-110002 (India)
Tel: 23278000, 23261597, 23255577, 23286875
B.O.: No. 1015, Ist Main Road, BSK IIIrd Stage,
IIIrd Phase, IIIrd Block, Bangalore-560085 (INDIA)
Tel: 080-41723429
Email: centrumpress@gmail.com
Visit us at: www.centrumpress.com

Artificial Intelligence and Logic Programming

First Edition, 2011

PRINTED IN INDIA

Printed at Tarun Offset Printers, Delhi-110053

Contents

Preface

Artificial Intelligence (AI) is the area of computer science focusing on creating machines that can engage on behaviors that humans consider intelligent. The ability to create intelligent machines has intrigued humans since ancient times, and today with the advent of the computer and 50 years of research into AI programming techniques, the dream of smart machines is becoming a reality.

Researchers are creating systems which can mimic human thought, understand speech, beat the best human chessplayer, and countless other feats never before possible. Find out how the military is applying AI logic to its hi-tech systems, and how in the near future Artificial Intelligence may impact our lives.

Author

1

Introduction

BACKGROUND

Artificial Intelligence is defined as the science of making computers do things that require intelligence when done by humans. AI has had some success in limited, or simplified, domains.

However, the five decades since the inception of AI have brought only very slow progress, and early optimism concerning the attainment of human-level intelligence has given way to an appreciation of the profound difficulty of the problem.Quite simple human behaviour can be intelligent yet quite complex behaviour performed by insects is unintelligent. Consider the behaviour of the digger wasp, *Sphex ichneumoneus*.

When the female wasp brings food to her burrow, she deposits it on the threshold, goes inside the burrow to check for intruders, and then if the coast is clear carries in the food. The unintelligent nature of the wasp's behaviour is revealed if the watching experimenter moves the food a few inches while the was is inside the burrow checking. On emerging, the wasp repeats the whole procedure: she carries the food to the threshold once again, goes in to look around, and emerges. She can be made to repeat this cycle of behaviour upwards of forty times in succession.

Mainstream thinking in psychology regards human intelligence not as a single ability or cognitive process but rather as an array of separate components. Research in AI has focussed chiefly on the following components of intelligence: learning, reasoning, problem-solving, perception, and language-understanding.

SIMPLEST LEARNING

The simplest is learning by trial-and-error. For example, a simple programme for solving mate-in-one chess problems might try out moves at random until one is found that achieves mate. The programme remembers the successful move and next time the computer is given the same problem it is able to produce the answer immediately.

The simple memorising of individual items—solutions to problems, words of vocabulary, etc.—is known as rote learning. Rote learning is relatively easy to implement on a computer. More challenging is the problem of implementing what is called generalisation. Learning that involves generalisation leaves the learner able to perform better in situations not previously encountered.

A programme that learns past tenses of regular English verbs by rote will not be able to produce the past tense of *e.g.* "jump" until presented at least once with "jumped", whereas a programme that is able to generalise from examples can learn the "add-ed" rule, and so form the past tense of "jump" in the absence of any previous encounter with this verb. Sophisticated modern techniques enable programmes to generalise complex rules from data.

REASONING

To reason is to draw inferences appropriate to the situation in hand. Inferences are classified as either deductive or inductive. An example of the former is "Fred is either in the museum or the cafe; he isn't in the cafe; so he's in the museum", and of the latter "Previous accidents just like this one have been caused by instrument failure; so probably this one was caused by instrument failure".

The difference between the two is that in the deductive case, the truth of the premises guarantees the truth of the conclusion, whereas in the inductive case, the truth of the premises lends support to the conclusion that the accident was caused by instrument failure, but nevertheless further investigation might reveal that, despite the truth of the premises, the conclusion is in fact false. There has been considerable success in programming computers to draw inferences, especially deductive inferences.

However, a programme cannot be said to reason simply in virtue of being able to draw inferences. Reasoning involves drawing inferences that are relevant to the task or situation in hand. One of the hardest problems confronting AI is that of giving computers the ability to distinguish the relevant from the irrelevant.

TYPES OF PROBLEMS

A huge variety of types of problem is addressed in AI. Some examples are: finding winning moves in board games; identifying people from their photographs; and planning series of movements that enable a robot to carry out a given task. Problem-solving methods divide into special-purpose and general-purpose. A special-purpose method is tailor-made for a particular problem, and often exploits very specific features of the situation in which the problem is embedded. A general-purpose method is applicable to a wide range of different problems.

One general-purpose technique used in AI is means-end analysis, which involves the step-by-step reduction of the difference between the current state and the goal state. The programme selects actions from a list of means--which in the case of, say, a simple robot, might consist of pickup, putdown, move forward, move back, move left, and move right-until the current state is transformed into the goal state.

ENVIRONMENTAL PERCEPTION

In perception the environment is scanned by means of various sense-organs, real or artificial, and processes internal to the perceiver analyse the scene into objects and their features and relationships. Analysis is complicated by the fact that one and the same object may present many different appearances on different occasions, depending on the angle from which it is viewed, whether or not parts of it are projecting shadows, and so forth. At present, artificial perception is sufficiently well advanced to enable a self-controlled car-like device to drive at moderate speeds on the open road, and a mobile robot to roam through a suite of busy offices searching for and clearing away empty soda cans.

LANGUAGE SYSTEM

A language is a system of signs having meaning by convention. Traffic signs, for example, form a mini-language, it being a matter of convention that, for example, the hazard-ahead sign means hazard ahead.

This meaning-by-convention that is distinctive of language is very different from what is called natural meaning, exemplified in statements like 'An important characteristic of full-fledged human languages, such as English, which distinguishes them from, *e.g.* bird calls and systems of traffic signs, is their productivity. A productive language is one that is rich enough to enable an unlimited number of different sentences to be formulated within it.

It is relatively easy to write computer programmes that are able, in severely restricted contexts, to respond in English, seemingly fluently, to questions and statements, for example the Parry and Shrdlu programmes described in the section Early AI Programmes. However, neither Parry nor Shrdlu actually understands language.

An appropriately programmed computer can use language without understanding it, in principle even to the point where the computer's linguistic behaviour is indistinguishable from that of a native human speaker of the language. What, then, is involved in genuine understanding, if a computer that uses language indistinguishably from a native human speaker does not necessarily understand?

There is no universally agreed answer to this difficult question. According to one theory, whether or not one understands depends not only upon one's behaviour but also upon one's history: in order to be said to understand one must have learned the language and have been trained to take one's place in the linguistic community by means of interaction with other language-users. In order to classify machines as "thinking", it is necessary to define intelligence. To what degree does intelligence consist of, for example, solving complex problems, or making generalizations and relationships? And what about perception and comprehension? Research into the areas of learning, of language, and of sensory perception have aided scientists in building intelligent machines. One of the most challenging approaches facing experts is building systems that mimic the behaviour of the human brain, made up of billions of neurons, and arguably the most complex matter in the universe. Perhaps the best way to gauge the intelligence of a machine is British computer scientist Alan Turing's test.

Artificial Intelligence has come a long way from its early roots, driven by dedicated researchers. The beginnings of AI reach back before electronics, to philosophers and mathematicians such as Boole and others theorizing on principles that were used as the foundation of AI Logic. AI really began to intrigue researchers with the invention of the computer in 1943.

The technology was finally available, or so it seemed, to simulate intelligent behaviour. Over the next four decades, despite many stumbling blocks, AI has grown from a dozen researchers, to thousands of engineers and specialists; and from programmes capable of playing checkers, to systems designed to diagnose disease. AI has always been on the pioneering end of computer science.

Advanced-level computer languages, as well as computer interfaces and word-processors owe their existence to the research into artificial intelligence. The theory and insights brought about by AI research will set the trend in the future of computing.

The products available today are only bits and pieces of what are soon tc follow, but they are a movement towards the future of artificial intelligence. The advancements in the quest for artificial intell:gence have, and will continue to affect our jobs, our education, and our lives.

REPRESENTATION

Another definition is concerned with the performance of machines which 'historically have been judged to lie within the domain of intelligence'. None of these definitions or the like have been universally accepted, perhaps because of their references to the word 'intelligence', which at present is an abstract and immeasurable quantity. A better definition of artificial intelligence, therefore, calls for formalization of the term 'intelligence'.

Psychologist and Cognitive theorists are of the opinion that intelligence helps in identifying the right piece of knowledge at the appropriate instances of decision making. A system capable of planning and executing the right task at the right time is generally called rational.

Thus, AI alternatively may be stated as a subject dealing with computational models that can think and act rationally 1, 2, 3, 4. A common question then naturally arises: A little thinking, however, reveals that a system that can reason well must be a successful planner, as planning in many circumstances is part of a reasoning process. Further, a system can act rationally only after acquiring adequate knowledge from the real world.

So, perception that stands for building up of knowledge from real world information is a prerequisite feature for rational actions. One step further thinking envisages that a machine without learning capability cannot possess perception. The rational action of an agent (actor), thus, calls for possession of all the elementary characteristics of intelligence. Relating artificial intelligence with the computational models capable of thinking and acting rationally, therefore, has a pragmatic significance.

APPROACH TO PROBLEMS

Problems dealt with in artificial intelligence generally use a common term called 'state'. A state represents a status of the solution at a given step of the problem solving procedure. The solution of a problem, thus, is a collection of the problem states. The problem solving procedure applies an operator to a state to get the next state.The process of applying an operator to a state and its subsequent transition to the next state, thus, is continued until the goal (desired) state is derived. Such a method of solving a problem is generally referred to as statespace approach. We will first discuss the state-space approach for problem solving by a well-known problem, which most of us perhaps have solved in our childhood.

TECHNIQES

The subject of artificial intelligence spans a wide horizon. It deals with the various kinds of knowledge representation schemes, different techniques of intelligent search, various methods for resolving uncertainty of data and knowledge, different schemes for automated machine learning and many others. Among the application areas of AI, we have Expert systems, Game-playing, and Theorem-proving, Natural language processing, Image recognition, Robotics and many others.

The subject of artificial intelligence has been enriched with a wide discipline of knowledge from Philosophy, Psychology, Cognitive Science, Computer Science, Mathematics and Engineering.

SUBJECT

The subject of artificial intelligence was originated with game-playing and theorem-proving programmes and was gradually enriched with theories from a number of parent disciplines. As a young discipline of science, the significance of the topics covered under the subject changes considerably with time.

Concept of Learning

The concept of learning is illustrated here with reference to a natural problem of learning of pronunciation by a child from his mother (fig above). The hearing system of the child receives the pronunciation of the character 'A' and the voice system attempts to imitate it. The difference of the mother's and the child's pronunciation, hereafter called the error signal, is received by the child's learning system auditory nerve, and an actuation signal is generated by the learning system through a motor nerve for adjustment of the pronunciation of the child. The adaptation of the child's voice system is continued until the amplitude of the error signal is insignificantly low. Each time the voice system passes through an adaptation cycle, the resulting tongue position of the child for speaking 'A' is saved by the learning process. The learning problem discussed above is an example of the well-known parametric learning, where the adaptive learning process adjusts the parametres of the child's voice system autonomously to keep its response close enough to the 'sample training pattern'.

The artificial neural networks, which represent the electrical analogue of the biological nervous systems, are gaining importance for their increasing applications in supervised (parametric) learning problems. Besides this type, the other common learning methods, which we do unknowingly, are inductive and analogy-based learning. In inductive learning, the learner makes generalizations from examples. For instance, noting that 'cuckoo flies', 'parrot flies' and 'sparrow flies', the learner generalizes that 'birds fly'. On the other hand, in analogy-based learning, the learner, for example, learns the motion of electrons in an atom analogously from his knowledge of planetary motion in solar systems.

Representation

The reasoning problem, one has to reach a pre-defined goal state from one or more given initial states. So, the lesser the number of transitions for reaching the goal state, the higher the efficiency of the reasoning system. Increasing the efficiency of a reasoning system thus requires minimization of intermediate states, which indirectly calls for an organized and complete knowledge base. A complete and organized storehouse of knowledge needs minimum search to identify the appropriate knowledge at a given problem state and thus yields the right next state on the leading edge of the problem-solving process. Organization of knowledge, therefore, is of paramount importance in knowledge engineering. A variety of knowledge representation techniques are in use in Artificial Intelligence. Production rules, semantic nets, frames, filler and slots, and predicate logic are only a few to mention. The selection of a particular type of representational scheme of knowledge depends both on the nature of applications and the choice of users.

Significance

The significant area of artificial intelligence is planning. The problems of reasoning and planning share many common issues, but have a basic difference that originates from their definitions. The reasoning problem is mainly concerned with the testing of the satisfiability of a goal from a given set of data and knowledge.

The planning problem, on the other hand, deals with the determination of the methodology by which a successful goal can be achieved from the known initial states. Automated planning finds extensive applications in robotics and navigational problems, some of which will be discussed shortly.

Acquisition of Knowledge

Acquisition of knowledge is equally hard for machines as it is for human beings. It includes generation of new pieces of knowledge from given knowledge base, setting dynamic data structures for existing knowledge, learning knowledge from the environment and refinement of knowledge. Automated acquisition of knowledge by machine learning approach is an active area of current research in Artificial Intelligence.

Intelligent Search: Search problems, which we generally encounter in Computer Science, are of a deterministic nature, *i.e.*, the order of visiting the elements of the search space is known. For example, in depth first and breadth first search algorithms, one knows the sequence of visiting the nodes in a tree. However, search problems, which we will come across in AI, are non-deterministic and the order of visiting the elements in the search space is completely dependent on data sets.

Logic Programming

One outgrowth of such attempts is propositional logic, which deals with a set of binary statements (propositions) connected by Boolean operators. The logic of propositions, which was gradually enriched to handle more complex situations of the real world, is called predicate logic. One classical variety of predicate logic-based programmes is Logic Programme. PROLOG, which is an abbreviation for PROgramming in LOGic, is a typical language that supports logic programmes. Logic Programming has recently been identified as one of the prime area of research in AI.

The ultimate aim of this research is to extend the PROLOG compiler to handle spatio-temporal models and support a parallel programming environment. Building architecture for PROLOG machines was a hot topic of the last decade.

Soft Computing

Soft computing is 'an emerging approach to computing, which parallels the remarkable ability of the human mind to reason and learn in an environment of uncertainty and imprecision'. It, in general, is a collection of computing tools and techniques, shared by closely related disciplines that include fuzzy logic, artificial neural nets, genetic algorithms, belief calculus, and some aspects of machine learning like inductive logic programming. These tools are used independently as well as jointly depending on the type of the domain of applications.

Imprecision and Uncertainty

Data and knowledgebases in many typical AI problems, such as reasoning and planning, are often contaminated with various forms of incompleteness. The incompleteness of data, hereafter called imprecision, generally appears in the database for i) lack of appropriate data, and ii) poor authenticity level of the sources. The incompleteness of knowledge, often referred to as uncertainty, originates in the knowledge base due to lack of certainty of the pieces of knowledge Reasoning in the presence of imprecision of data and uncertainty of knowledge is a complex problem.

Various tools and techniques have been devised for reasoning under incomplete data and knowledge. Some of these techniques employ i) stochastic ii) fuzzy and iii) belief network models. In a stochastic reasoning model, the system can have transition from one given state to a number of states, such that the sum of the probability of transition to the next states from the given state is strictly unity.

In a fuzzy reasoning system, on the other hand, the sum of the membership value of transition from the given state to the next state may be greater than or equal to one. The belief network model updates the stochastic/fuzzy belief assigned to the facts embedded in the network until a condition of equilibrium is reached, following which there would be no more change in beliefs. Recently, fuzzy tools and techniques have been applied in a specialized belief network, called a fuzzy Petri net, for handling both imprecision of data and uncertainty of knowledge by a unified approach.

APPLICATIONS

Almost every branch of science and engineering currently shares the tools and techniques available in the domain of artificial intelligence. However, for the sake of the convenience of the readers, we mention here a few typical applications, where AI plays a significant and decisive role in engineering automation.

Expert Systems

An expert system consists of a knowledge base, database and an inference engine for interpreting the database using the knowledge supplied in the knowledge base. The inference engine attempts to match the antecedent clauses (IF parts) of the rules with the data stored in the database. When all the antecedent clauses of a rule are available in the database, the rule is fired, resulting in new inferences. The resulting inferences are added to the database for activating subsequent firing of other rules.

In order to keep limited data in the database, a few rules that contain an explicit consequent (then) clause to delete specific data from the databases are employed in the knowledge base. On firing of such rules, the unwanted data clauses as suggested by the rule are deleted from the database.

Digital Imaging

A digital image can be regarded as az two-dimensional array of pixels containing gray levels corresponding to the intensity of the reflected illumination received by a video camera. For interpretation of a scene, its image should be passed through three basic processes: low, medium and high level vision.

The importance of low level vision is to pre-process the image by filtering from noise. The medium level vision system deals with enhancement of details and segmentation (*i.e.*, partitioning the image into objects of interest). The high level vision system includes three steps: recognition of the objects from the segmented image, labeling of the image and interpretation of the scene. Most of the AI tools and techniques are required in high level vision systems. Recognition of objects from its image can be carried out through a process of pattern classification, which at present is realised by supervised learning algorithms. The interpretation process, on the other hand, requires knowledge-based computation.

Speech and Natural Language Understanding

In speech analysis, the main probl em is to separate the syllables of a spoken word and determine features like ampli tude, and fundamental and harmonic frequencies of each syllable. The words then could be ident ified from the extracted features by pattern class ification techniques. Recently, artificial neural networks have been employed to class ify words from their features. The problem of understanding natural languages like English, on the other hand, includes syntactic and semantic interpretation of the words in a sentence, and sentences in a paragraph.

The syntactic steps are required to analyse the sentences by its grammar and are similar with the steps of compilation. The semantic analysis, which is performed following the syntactic analysis, determines the meaning of the sentences from the association of the words and that of a paragraph from the closeness of the sentences. A robot capable of understanding speech in a natural language will be of immense importance, for it could execute any task verbally communicated to it.

Scheduling

We assume that each job requires some operations to be done on all these machines in a fixed order say, M1, M2 and M3. Now, what should be the schedule of the jobs (J1-J2) or (J2 -J1), so that the completion time of both the jobs, called the make-span, is minimized? Let the processing time of jobs J1 and J2 on machines M1, M2 and M3 be (5, 8, 7) and (8, 2, 3) respectively. The gantt charts in fig. (a) and (b) describe the make-spans for the schedule of jobs J1 - J2 and J2 - J1 respectively. It is clear from these figures that J1-J2 schedule requires less make-span and is thus preferred.

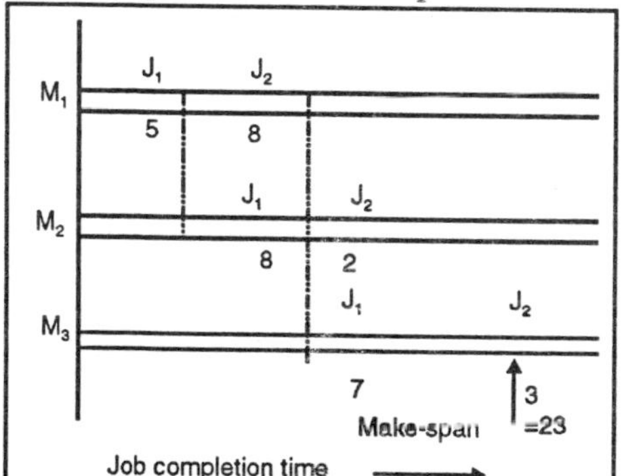

(a) The J_1-J_2 schedule

Fig. The Gantt Charts for the Flowshop Scheduling

Flowshop scheduling problems are a NP complete problem and determination of optimal scheduling (for minimizing the make-span) thus requires an exponential order of time with respect to both machine-size and job-size. Finding a sub-optimal solution is thus preferred for such scheduling problems.

Process Control

In process control, the controller is designed from the known models of the process and the required control objective. When the dynamics of the plant is not completelyknown, the existing techniques for controller design no longer remain valid. Rule-based control is appropriate in such situations. In a rule-based controlsystem, the controller is realised by aset of production rules intuitively set by an expert control engineer. The antecedent (premise) part of the rules in a rule-based system is searched against the dynamic response of the plant parametres. The rule whoseantecedent part matches with the plant response is selected and fired. When more than one rule is firable, the controller resolves the conflict by a set of strategies. On the other hand, there exist situations when the antecedent part of no rules exactly matches with the plant responses. Such situations are handled with fuzzy logic, which is capable of matching the antecedent parts of rules partially/approximately with the dynamic plant responses. Fuzzy control has been successfully used in many industrial plants. One typical application is the power control in a nuclear reactor. Besides design of the controller, the other issue in process control is to design a plant (process) estimator, which attempts to follow the response of the actual plant, when both the plant and the estimator are jointly excited by a common input signal. The fuzzy and artificial neural network-based learning techniques have recently been identified as new tools for plant estimation.

HISTORY

EVIDENCE

The term artificial intelligence was first coined in 1956,

at the Dartmouth conference, and since then Artificial Intelligence has expanded because of the theories and principles developed by its dedicated researchers. Through its short modern history, advancement in the fields of AI have been slower than first estimated, progress continues to be made.

ERA OF COMPUTERS

In 1941 an invention revolutionized every aspect of the storage and processing of information. That invention, developed in both the US and Germany was the electronic computer. The first computers required large, separate air-conditioned rooms, and were a programmers nightmare, involving the separate configuration of thousands of wires to even get a programme running.

The 1949 innovation, the stored programme computer, made the job of entering a programme easier, and advancements in computer theory lead to computer science, and eventually Artificial intelligence. With the invention of an electronic means of processing data, came a medium that made AI possible.

BEGINNING OF AI

Although the computer provided the technology necessary for AI, it was not until the early 1950's that the link between human intelligence and machines was really observed. Norbert Wiener was one of the first Americans to make observations on the principle of feedback theory feedback theory.

The most familiar example of feedback theory is the thermostat: It controls the temperature of an environment by gathering the actual temperature of the house, comparing it to the desired temperature, and responding by turning the heat up or down. Mechanisms that could possibly be simulated by machines.

This discovery influenced much of early development of AI. In late 1955, Newell and Simon developed *The Logic Theorist,* considered by many to be the first AI programme.

The programme, representing each problem as a tree model, would attempt to solve it by selecting the branch that would most likely result in the correct conclusion. The impact that the logic theorist made on both the public and the field of AI has made it a crucial stepping stone in developing the AI field. In 1956 regarded as the father of AI, organized a conference to draw the talent and expertise of others interested in machine intelligence for a month of brainstorming.

He invited them to Vermont for "The Dartmouth summer research project on artificial intelligence." From that point on, because of McCarthy, the field would be known as Artificial intelligence. Although not a huge success,the Dartmouth conference did bring together the founders in AI, and served to lay the groundwork for the future of AI research.

EXPANSION OF KNOWLEDGE

Although the field was still undefined, ideas formed at the conference were re-examined, and built upon. Centres for AI research began forming at Carnegie Mellon and MIT, and a new challenges were faced: further research was placed upon creating systems that could efficiently solve problems, by limiting the search, such as the Logic Theorist. And second, making systems that could learn by themselves.

In 1957, the first version of a new programme The *General Problem Solver*(GPS) was tested. The programme developed by the same pair which developed the Logic Theorist. The GPS was an extension of Wiener's feedback principle, and was capable of solving a greater extent of common sense problems. A couple of years after the GPS, IBM contracted a team to research artificial intelligence. While more programmes were being produced, McCarthy was busy developing a major breakthrough in AI history. In 1958 McCarthy announced his new development; the LISP language, which is still used today. LISP stands for LISt Processing, and was soon adopted as the language of choice among most AI developers. In 1963 MIT received a 2.2 million dollar grant from the United States government to be used in researching Machine-Aided Cognition (artificial intelligence).

Multitude of Programmes

SHRDLU was part of the microworlds project, which consisted of research and programming in small worlds. The MIT researchers headed by Marvin Minsky, demonstrated that when confined to a small subject matter, computer programmes could solve spatial problems and logic problems. Other programmes which appeared during the late 1960's were student, which could solve algebra story problems, and SIR which could understand simple English sentences. The result of these programmes was a refinement in language comprehension and logic.

Another advancement in the 1970's was the advent of the expert system. Expert systems predict the probability of a solution under set conditions. Because of the large storage capacity of computers at the time, expert systems had the potential to interpret statistics, to formulate rules.

And the applications in the market place were extensive, and over the course of ten years, expert systems had been introduced to forecast the stock market, aiding doctors with the ability to diagnose disease, and instruct miners to promising mineral locations. This was made possible because of the systems ability to store conditional rules, and a storage of information.

During the 1970's Many new methods in the development of AI were tested, notably Minsky's frames theory. Also David Marr proposed new theories about machine vision, for example, how it would be possible to distinguish an image based on the shading of an image, basic information on shapes, colour, edges, and texture. With analysis of this information, frames of what an image might be could then be referenced. another development during this time was the PROLOGUE language.

The language was proposed for In 1972, During the 1980's AI was moving at a faster pace, and further into the corporate sector. In 1986, US sales of AI-related hardware and software surged to $425 million. Expert systems in particular demand because of their efficiency. Companies such as Digital Electronics were using XCON, an expert system designed to programme the large VAX computers. DuPont, General Motors, and Boeing relied heavily on expert systems Indeed to keep up with the demand for the computer experts, companies such as Teknowledge and Intellicorp specializing in creating software to aid in producing expert systems formed. Other expert systems were designed to find and correct flaws in existing expert systems.

FROM LAB TO LIFE

The impact of the computer technology, AI included was felt. No longer was the computer technology just part of a select few researchers in laboratories. The personal computer made its debut along with many technological magazines. Such foundations as the American Association for Artificial Intelligence also started.

There was also, with the demand for AI development, a push for researchers to join private companies. 150 companies such as DEC which employed its AI research group of 700 personnel, spend $1 billion on internal AI groups. Other fields of AI also made there way into the marketplace during the 1980's. One in particular was the machine vision field. Although crude, these systems could distinguish differences shapes in objects using black and white differences.

The 1980's were not totally good for the AI industry. In 1986-87 the demand in AI systems decreased, and the industry lost almost a half of a billion dollars. Companies such as Teknowledge and Intellicorp together lost more than $6 million, about a third of there total earnings.

The large losses convinced many research leaders to cut back funding. Another disappointment was the so called "smart truck" financed by the Defence Advanced Research Projects Agency. The projects goal was to develop a robot that could perform many battlefield tasks. In 1989, due to project setbacks and unlikely success, the Pentagon cut funding for the project. Fuzzy logic, first pioneered in the US has the unique ability to make decisions under uncertain conditions. Also neural networks were being reconsidered as possible ways of achieving Artificial Intelligence. The 1980's introduced to its place in the corporate marketplace, and showed the technology had real life uses, ensuring it would be a key in the 21st century.

AI Testing

The military put AI based hardware to the test of war during Desert Storm. AI-based technologies were used in missile systems, heads-up-displays, and other advancements. AI has also made the transition to the home. With the popularity of the AI computer growing, the interest of the public has also grown.

Applications for the Apple Macintosh and IBM compatible computer, such as voice and character recognition have become available. Also AI technology has made steadying camcorders simple using fuzzy logic. With a greater demand for AI-related technology, new advancements are becoming available. Inevitably Artificial Intelligence has, and will continue to affecting our lives.

APPROACH

THEORIES

In the quest to create intelligent machines, the field of Artificial Intelligence has split into several different approaches based on the opinions about the most promising methods and theories. These rivaling theories have lead researchers in one of two basic approaches; bottom-up and top-down.

Bottom-up theorists believe the best way to achieve artificial intelligence is to build electronic replicas of the human brain's complex network of neurons, while the top-down approach attempts to mimic the brain's behaviour with computer programmes.

PARALLEL COMPUTATION

The human brain is made up of a web of billions of cells called neurons, and understanding its complexities is seen as one of the last frontiers in scientific research. It is the aim of

AI researchers who prefer this bottom-up approach to construct electronic circuits that act as neurons do in the human brain. Although much of the working of the brain remains unknown, the complex network of neurons is what gives humans intelligent characteristics. By itself, a neuron is not intelligent, but when grouped together, neurons are able to pass electrical signals through networks. The neuron "firing", passing a signal to the next in the chain.

Research has shown that a signal received by a neuron travels through the dendrite region, and down the axon. Separating nerve cells is a gap called the synapse. In order for the signal to be transferred to the next neuron, the signal must be converted from electrical to chemical energy. The signal can then be received by the next neuron and processed. Based on experiments with neurons, McCulloch and Pitts showed that neurons might be considered devices for processing binary numbers.

An important back of mathematic logic, binary numbers (represented as 1's and 0's or true and false) were also the basis of the electronic computer. A century earlier the true/false nature of binary numbers was theorized in 1854 by George Boole in his postulates concerning the Laws of Thought. Boole's principles make up what is known as Boolean algebra, the collection of logic concerning AND, OR, NOT operands.

Boole also assumed that the human mind works according to these laws, it performs logical operations that could be reasoned. Ninety years later, Claude Shannon applied Boole's principles in circuits, the blueprint for electronic computers. Boole's contribution to the future of computing and Artificial Intelligence was immeasurable, and his logic is the basis of neural networks.

McCulloch and Pitts, using Boole's principles, wrote a paper on neural network theory. The thesis dealt with how the networks of connected neurons could perform logical operations. It also stated that, one the level of a single neuron, the release or failure to release an impulse was the basis by which the brain makes true/false decisions. Using the idea of feedback theory, they described the loop which existed between the senses —> brain —> muscles, and likewise concluded that Memory could be defined as the signals in a closed loop of neurons. Although we now know that logic in the brain occurs at a level higher then McCulloch and Pitts theorized, their contributions were important to AI because they showed how the firing of signals between connected neurons could cause the brains to make decisions. McCulloch and Pitt's theory is the basis of the artificial neural network theory.

Using this theory, McCulloch and Pitts then designed electronic replicas of neural networks, to show how electronic networks could generate logical processes. They also stated that neural networks may, in the future, be able to learn, and recognize patterns. The results of their research and two of Weiner's books served to increase enthusiasm, and laboratories of computer simulated neurons were set up across the country. Two major factors have inhibited the development of full scale neural networks.

Because of the expense of constructing a machine to simulate neurons, it was expensive even to construct neural networks with the number of neurons in an ant. Although the cost of components have decreased, the computer would have to grow thousands of times larger to be on the scale of the human brain. The second factor is current computer architecture. The standard Von Neuman computer, the architecture of nearly all computers, lacks an adequate number of pathways between components. Researchers are now developing alternate architectures for use with neural networks.

Even with these inhibiting factors, artificial neural networks have presented some impressive results. Frank Rosenblatt, experimenting with computer simulated networks, was able to create a machine that could mimic the human thinking process, and recognize letters. But, with new top-down methods becoming popular, parallel computing was put on hold. Now neural networks are making a return, and some researchers believe that with new computer architectures, parallel computing and the bottom-up theory will be a driving factor in creating artificial intelligence.

EXPERT SYSTEMS

Because of the large storage capacity of computers, expert systems had the potential to interpret statistics, in order to formulate rules. An expert system works much like a detective solves a mystery. Using the information, and logic or rules, an expert system can solve the problem.

Games

On game with strong AI ties is chess. World-champion chess playing programmes can see ahead twenty plus moves in advance for each move they make. In addition, the programmes have an ability to get progress ably better over time because of the ability to learn.

Chess programmes do not play chess as humans do. In three minutes, Deep Thought (a master programme) considers 126 million moves, while human chess master on average considers less than 2 moves. Herbert Simon suggested that human chess masters are familiar with Favourable board positions, and the relationship with thousands of pieces in small areas.

Computers on the other hand, do not take hunches into account. The next move comes from exhaustive searches into all moves, and the consequences of the moves based on prior learning. Chess programmes, running on Cray super computers have attained a rating of senior master, in the range of Gary Kasparov, the Russian world champion.

Frames

On method that many programmes use to represent knowledge are frames. Pioneered by Marvin Minsky, frame theory revolves around packets of information. For example, say the situation was a birthday party. A computer could call on its birthday frame, and use the information contained in the frame, to apply to the situation. The computer knows that there is usually cake and presents because of the information contained in the knowledge frame. Frames can also overlap, or contain sub-frames.

APPLICATION AND USES

USING APPLICATIONS

We have been studying this issue of AI application for quite some time now and know all the terms and facts. But what we all really need to know is what can we do to get our hands on some AI today.

First, we should be prepared for a change. Our conservative ways stand in the way of progress. AI is a new step that is very helpful to the society. Machines can do jobs that require detailed instructions followed and mental alertness. AI with its learning capabilities can accomplish those tasks but only if the worlds conservatives are ready to change and allow this to be a possibility. It makes us think about how early man finally accepted the wheel as a good invention, not something taking away from its heritage or tradition.

Secondly, we must be prepared to learn about the capabilities of AI. The more use we get out of the machines the less work is required by us. In turn less injuries and stress to human beings. Human beings are a species that learn by trying, and we must be prepared to give AI a chance seeing AI as a blessing, not an inhibition.

Finally, we need to be prepared for the worst of AI. Something as revolutionary as AI is sure to have many kinks to work out. There is always that fear that if AI is learning based, will machines learn that being rich and successful is a good thing, then wage war against economic powers and famous people? There are so many things that can go wrong with a new system so we must be as prepared as we can be for this new technology.

Whatever we teach AI, they will suggest in the future if a positive outcome arrives from it. AI are like children that need to be taught to be kind, well mannered, and intelligent. If they are to make important decisions, they should be wise.

We as citizens need to make sure AI programmers are keeping things on the level. We should be sure they are doing the job correctly, so that no future accidents occur.

TEACHING COMPUTERS

The Artificial Intelligence Applications Institute has many project that they are working on to make their computers learn how to operate themselves with less human input. o have more functionality with less input is an operation for AI technology. If it isn't able or isn't reliable AUSDA will instruct you on finding alternative software which would better suit your needs.

According to AI, the software will try to provide solutions to problems like "identifying the root causes of incidents in which the use of computer software is involved, studying different software development approaches, and identifying aspects of these which are relevant to those root causes producing guidelines for using and improving the development approaches studied, and providing support in the integration of these approaches, so that they can be better used for the development and maintenance of safety critical software."

Well don't worry guys, because us nerds are looking out for you too! Just ask AIAI what they have for you and it turns up the EGRESS is right down your alley. This is a programme which is studying human reactions to accidents. It is trying to make a model of how peoples reactions in panic moments save lives. Although it seems like in tough situations humans would fall apart and have no idea what to do, it is in fact the opposite.

Quick Decisions are usually made and are effective but not flawless. These computer models will help rescuers make smart decisions in time of need. AI can't be positive all the time but can suggest actions which we can act out and therefor lead to safe rescues. So AIAI is teaching computers to be better computers and better people. AI technology will never replace man but can be an extension of our body which allows us to make more rational decisions faster.

APPLE COMPUTERS

Apple Computers may not have ever been considered as the state of art in Artificial Intelligence, but a second look should be given. Not only are today's PC's becoming more powerful but AI influence is showing up in them. Who else would go surfing with you on short notice- even if it is the net. Who else would care to tell you that you have a business appointment scheduled at 8:35 and 28 seconds and would notify you about it every minute till you told it to shut up.

Even with all the abuse we give today's PC's they still plug away to make us happy. We use PC's more not because they do more or are faster but because they are getting so much easier to use. And their ease of use comes from their use of AI. All Power Macintoshes come with Speech Recognition. This implication of AI in Personal computers is still very crude but it does work given the correct conditions to work in and a clear voice.

Not to mention the requirement of at least 16Mgs of RAM for quick use. Also Apple's Newton and other hand held note pads have Script recognition. Cursive or Print can be recognized by these notepad sized devices. With the pen that accompanies your silicon note pad you can write a little note to yourself which magically changes into computer text if desired. No more complaining about sloppy written reports if your computer can read your handwriting. If it can't read it though- perhaps in the future, you can correct it by dictating your letters instead.

Macros provide a huge stress relief as your computer does faster what you could do more tediously. Macros are old but they are to an extent, Intelligent. You have taught the computer to do something only by doing it once. In businesses, many times applications are upgraded. But the files must be converted.

All of the businesses records but be changed into the new software's type. Macros save the work of conversion of hundred of files by a human by teaching the computer to mimic the actions of the programmer. Thus teaching the computer a task that it can repeat whenever ordered to do so.AI is all around us all but get ready for a change. But don't think the change will be harder on us because AI has been developed to make our lives easier.

EXPERT SYSTEMS

As stated an expert system is able to do the work of a professional. Moreover, a computer system can be trained quickly, has virtually no operating cost, never forgets what it learns, never calls in sick, retires, or goes on vacation. Beyond those, intelligent computers can consider a large amount of information that may not be considered by humans. But to what extent should these systems replace human experts? Or, should they at all? For example, some people once considered an intelligent computer as a possible substitute for human control over nuclear weapons, citing that a computer could respond more quickly to a threat. and many

AI developers were afraid of the possibility of programmes like Eliza, the psychiatrist and the bond that humans were making with the computer. We cannot, however, over look the benefits of having a computer expert. Forecasting the weather, for example, relies on many variables, and a computer expert can more accurately pool all of its knowledge. Still a computer cannot rely on the hunches of a human expert, which are sometimes necessary in predicting an outcome.

In conclusion, in some fields such as forecasting weather or finding bugs in computer software, expert systems are sometimes more accurate than humans. But for other fields, such as medicine, computers aiding doctors will be beneficial, but the human doctor should not be replaced. Expert systems have the power and range to aid to benefit, and in some cases replace humans, and computer experts, if used with discretion, will benefit human kind.

GAME PLAYING

You can buy machines that can play master level chess for a few hundred dollars. There is some AI in them, but they play well against people mainly through brute force computation—looking at hundreds of thousands of positions. To beat a world champion by brute force and known reliable heuristics requires being able to look at 200 million positions per second.

SPEECH RECOGNITION

In the 1990s, computer speech recognition reached a practical level for limited purposes. Thus United Airlines has replaced its keyboard tree for flight information by a system using speech recognition of flight numbers and city names. It is quite convenient. On the the other hand, while it is possible to instruct some computers using speech, most users have gone back to the keyboard and the mouse as still more convenient.

Just getting a sequence of words into a computer is not enough. Parsing sentences is not enough either. The computer has to be provided with an understanding of the domain the text is about, and this is presently possible only for very limited domains.

The world is composed of three-dimensional objects, but the inputs to the human eye and computers' TV cameras are two dimensional. Some useful programmes can work solely in two dimensions, but full computer vision requires partial three-dimensional information that is not just a set of two-dimensional views. At present there are only limited ways of representing three-dimensional information directly, and they are not as good as what humans evidently use.

A "knowledge engineer" interviews experts in a certain domain and tries to embody their knowledge in a computer programme for carrying out some task. How well this works depends on whether the intellectual mechanisms required for the task are within the present state of AI. When this turned out not to be so, there were many disappointing results.

One of the first expert systems was MYCIN in 1974, which diagnosed bacterial infections of the blood and suggested treatments. It did better than medical students or practicing doctors, provided its limitations were observed. Namely, its ontology included bacteria, symptoms, and treatments and did not include patients, doctors, hospitals, death, recovery, and events occurring in time. Its interactions depended on a single patient being considered. Since the experts consulted by the knowledge engineers knew about patients, doctors, death, recovery, etc., it is clear that the knowledge engineers forced what the experts told them into a predetermined framework. In the present state of AI, this has to be true. The usefulness of current expert systems depends on their users having common sense.

HEURISTIC CLASSIFICATION

One of the most feasible kinds of expert system given the present knowledge of AI is to put some information in one of a fixed set of categories using several sources of information. An example is advising whether to accept a proposed credit card purchase.

Information is available about the owner of the credit card, his record of payment and also about the item he is buying and about the establishment from which he is buying it (*e.g.*, about whether there have been previous credit card frauds at this establishment).

BRANCHES

LOGICAL

The programme decides what to do by inferring that certain actions are appropriate for achieving its goals. The first article proposing this was [McC59]. [McC89] is a more recent summary.lists some of the concepts involved in logical aI. is an important text.

SEARCH

AI programmes often examine large numbers of possibilities, *e.g.* moves in a chess game or inferences by a theorem proving programme. Discoveries are continually made about how to do this more efficiently in various domains.When a programme makes observations of some kind, it is often programmed to compare what it sees with a pattern. For example, a vision programme may try to match a pattern of eyes and a nose in a scene in order to find a face. More complex patterns, *e.g.* in a natural language text, in a chess position, or in the history of some event are also studied.Facts about the world have to be represented in some way. Usually languages of mathematical logic are used.

INFERENCE

Mathematical logical deduction is adequate for some purposes, but new methods of *non-monotonic* inference have been added to logic since the 1970s. The simplest kind of non-monotonic reasoning is default reasoning in which a conclusion is to be inferred by default, but the conclusion can be withdrawn if there is evidence to the contrary.

For example, when we hear of a bird, we man infer that it can fly, but this conclusion can be reversed when we hear that it is a penguin. It is the possibility that a conclusion may have to be withdrawn that constitutes the non-monotonic character of the reasoning. Ordinary logical reasoning is monotonic in that the set of conclusions that can the drawn from a set of premises is a monotonic increasing function of the premises. Circumscription is another form of non-monotonic reasoning.

KNOWLEDGE AND REASONING

This is the area in which AI is farthest from human-level, in spite of the fact that it has been an active research area since the 1950s. While there has been considerable progress, *e.g.* in developing systems of *non-monotonic reasoning* and theories of action, yet more new ideas are needed. The Cyc system contains a large but spotty collection of common sense facts.

The approaches to AI based on *connectionism* and *neural nets* specialize in that. There is also learning of laws expressed in logic. [Mit97] is a comprehensive undergraduate text on machine learning. Programmes can only learn what facts or behaviours their formalisms can represent, and unfortunately learning systems are almost all based on very limited abilities to represent information. Planning programmes start with general facts about the world (especially facts about the effects of actions), facts about the particular situation and a statement of a goal. From these, they generate a strategy for achieving the goal. In the most common cases, the strategy is just a sequence of actions.

ONTOLOGY

Ontology is the study of the kinds of things that exist. In AI, the programmes and sentences deal with various kinds of objects, and we study what these kinds are and what their basic properties are. Emphasis on ontology begins in the 1990s.

HEURISTICS

A heuristic is a way of trying to discover something or an idea imbedded in a programme. The term is used variously in AI. *Heuristic functions* are used in some approaches to search to measure how far a node in a search tree seems to be from a goal. *Heuristic predicates* that compare two nodes in a search tree to see if one is better than the other, *i.e.* constitutes an advance towards the goal, may be more useful..

GENETIC PROGRAMMING

Genetic programming is a technique for getting programmes to solve a task by mating random Lisp programmes and selecting fittest in millions of generations.

FEATURES OF SIMULATION

MODELING

When designing complex devices such as integrated circuits and automobile engines, engineers routinely use computer simulation to predict how well the device would function if actually built. By helping to detect problems at an early stage in the design process, simulation postpones or eliminates the need for a physical prototype. Engineering costs decrease in numerous ways resulting in improved reliability, greater innovation, faster development time, and lower overall cost of development.While a routine part of the design process for some devices, simulation is hardly ever used to help design human-machine systems.

There are two main reasons for this, each stemming from difficulty modeling the human components of these systems. First, available frameworks for modeling human performance often prove unsatisfactory because they are incomplete in some crucial way, or cannot adequately predict design-relevant aspects of human performance.

Using such a framework requires spending a great deal of time and effort preparing application-specific elements of the simulation including models of newly designed devices and formal descriptions of "how-to" knowledge for operating in the domain of interest. The limitations of most human models often make it unlikely that this investment of time and effort will pay off.

Despite these limitations, human operator models have occasionally proven effective in practical terms. The most well-known example is project Ernestine which used the GOMS framework to predict how long, on average, a NYNEX telephone operator would require to handle a customer transaction using newly designed equipment and procedures. The model accurately predicted a time.63 seconds *greater* than that required with the old equipment. With each second of transaction time costing NYNEX three million dollars annually, purchasing this equipment would have been a costly mistake.

The value-added from a modeling effort depends on a number of factors. In this case, NYNEX did field trials that would have detected the problem even without modeling. In general, the cost-savings that results from modeling depend on how the modeling effort is integrated into the design process and on what evaluation methods would otherwise be employed.

For instance, models can be used at an early stage in the design process to detect problems that would otherwise be detected by later, more expensive evaluation. This reduces design costs both by minimizing the number of required design-test cycles and by reducing the average effort expended at each cycle before a problem is detected. Alternately, modeling can be used to direct empirical evaluations towards likely problems; this can be very useful when empirical data proves especially difficult or expensive to obtain.

To justify use of a simulation modeling framework in designing a human-machine system, engineers need to have some reasonable expectation that doing so will prove beneficial. For developers of modeling frameworks this presents two main challenges. First, the framework must be able to predict design-relevant aspects of human performance - *i.e.* it must be able to make predictions that designers care about.

Second, the time and expertise required to use the framework must be kept within practical limits. This paper will describe efforts to address these problems using the APEX modeling framework.

DESIGNING PREDICTIONS

Which aspects are relevant will vary depending on what constitutes good performance for the human-machine system as a whole. For example, in designing equipment for a telephone operator as described above, the important system performance variable was the average time required to complete a single transaction. Thus GOMS, whose traditional strength has been predicting completion time for brief, routine tasks, proved a useful and appropriate framework.

Other frameworks have been designed to predict, *e.g.*, how quickly skilled performance will emerge after learning a task whether a task is likely to impose excessive workload, whether the anthropometric properties of an interface (*e.g.* reach ability of controls) are human-compatible, and whether multiple operators are likely to cross-check one another's behaviour. APEX is a GOMS-like framework that incorporates mechanisms and methodologies for predicting certain forms of human error. The need for models that can predict error has often been mentioned in the literature on human modeling, but little progress has been made incorporating prediction capabilities into a practically useful modeling framework. At this time, research on human errors is still far from providing more than the familiar rough guidelines concerning the prevention of user error.

No prediction methodology, regardless of the theoretical approach, has yet been developed and recognized as satisfactory. In light of the apparent absence of adequate scientific theories, it is worth considering what engineers currently do to prevent design-induced operator error. Current practices can be divided into those that are applied at a late stage in the design process, and those applicable at an early stage.

At a late stage of the design process, engineers can test with live users on a physical prototype. This can be very effective but, like other late-stage techniques, also very expensive. At an early stage, designers must rely on a combination of informal "common sense" knowledge and explicit design guidelines found in any of a number of engineering handbooks. Research on error prevention generally focuses on improving techniques for user testing or on adding to and refining design guidelines. With APEX, we have tried the unusual approach of attempting to enhance the contribution of common sense knowledge in the design process.

In particular, people tend to apply their informal understanding of human error in an unsystematic way, causing them to overlook predictable problems. By incorporating this informal and relatively crude understanding in a model, APEX can apply that understanding systematically in a large number of simulated scenarios.

Design problems that might otherwise have been overlooked, and then seem obvious from hindsight, could thus be predicted early in the design process. For example, consider the task of withdrawing cash from an automatic teller machine (ATM). Withdrawals from most current ATMs involve a sequence of actions that begin with the user inserting a magnetic card, and end with collecting the requested cash and then retrieving the card. A well-known problem with the use of ATMs is the frequency with which users take their money but forget to retrieve their cards. ATMs avoid this problem by inverting the order of the final two steps, forcing users to retrieve their cards before the machine dispenses requested money. This way of compensating for human forgetfulness is what Donald Norman calls a "forcing function." By placing an easily omitted task step on the critical path to achieving a goal, the designer drastically reduces omission likelihood.

Failing to retrieve one's bank card from an ATM is an example of a *post completion error,* a general class of error in which a person omits a subtask that arises in service of a main task but is not on the critical path to achieving the main task's goal. These errors are common in all sorts of everyday tasks; other examples include failing to retrieve the original from a photocopier and failing to replace an automobile's fuel cap after refueling.

People with no training related to human factors or psychology recognize this pattern of error on the basis of common sense knowledge - *i.e.* their explanations of such errors resemble the definition given above. Despite some level of intuitive understanding, a number of factors make it easy for engineers to overlook these and other common forms of operator error.

For instance, a system may be used in a wide variety of operating conditions, only a small fraction of which invite error. Similarly, a complex system may have many associated modes, configurations and functions, greatly widening the range of situations in which error may be inadvertently facilitated by the design.

The potentially vast range of operating conditions and system states makes it difficult for engineers to consider potential errors systematically. Computer simulation makes it possible to overcome this difficulty, essentially by brute force. Rather than selecting a few test cases and hoping they are representative and revealing, the engineer uses simulation to explore many cases. The approach to predicting errors in APEX, described elsewhere in detail, consists mainly of two components. First, the model incorporates certain heuristic decision-making biases. Postcompletion errors, for example, emerge from a heuristic for ending ongoing tasks: a task is complete if the task's main goal is satisfied.

Such heuristics are generally good gambles, but prescribe incorrect behaviour in some situations. Second, the model incorporates a number of mechanisms that suppress reliance on fallible heuristics. For example, mentally rehearsing an intention (*e.g.* to retrieve one's ATM card) temporarily suppresses reliance on heuristics that prescribe behaviour inconsistent with the intention.

Building a modeling framework to make design-relevant predictions is, in many ways, a very different enterprise from that of building models to illustrate and explore psychological theories. Where psychological models attempt to show how some observed pattern of behaviour can emerge from lower-level processes, it is usually adequate in an engineering model to stipulate that pattern in the model without regard to how it arises. Similarly, there is less need to precisely characterize the pattern and its enabling conditions; crude generalizations might prove perfectly useful.

The described approach produces relatively crude, qualitative error predictions, focusing on circumstances in which a given form of error becomes especially likely. A fairly large rate of false positives (incorrect predictions of user error) is considered tolerable since engineers, relying on their own commonsense understanding, are expected to judge the predictions and reject those that seem improbable. In our view, user error is such a crucial design problem that methods for detecting design-facilitations for error must be judged on their practical value.

LOWEST COST

The emergence of powerful modeling frameworks promises a future in which modeling and simulation are a routine part of the design process for human-machine systems. But before this potential can be realised, measures must be taken to reduce time-cost and required expertise. To see how cost issues have been addresses in APEX, it is useful to consider where costs arise in the simulation modeling process. The process for preparing and using an APEX model. At the level of abstraction discussed here, the process and its associated costs are likely much the same for any simulation modeling framework.

- Construct a simulated world
- Do a task analysis
- Develop scenarios
- Run the simulation and analyse results

Step One

Is to write software that simulates the newly designed device and the task environment in which it will function. For instance, APEX has been used to simulate human air traffic controllers, emphasizing the effect of air traffic control (ATC) display design on controller performance.

The ATC *simworld* software models a display and associated devices along with an environment in which aircraft arrive in, depart from and move through controlled airspace. Constructing the simworld is the first step because choices about how to model the environment, including inevitable simplifications and emphases, strongly constrain subsequent steps.

Step Two

Is to represent the "how-to" knowledge the operator needs to carry out the task, including knowledge needed to operate newly designed devices. Modeling frameworks provide different formal notations for representing this knowledge. In GOMS, for example, the notation includes four structures: goals, operators, methods, and selection rules.

Step Three

The modeler completes the model preparation process by either specifying a set of simulation scenarios or by designing software that will generate scenarios at random. Whether a small number of hand-crafted scenarios or a large number of random ones is appropriate depends on what kind of predictions the model is supposed to make. For example, in the GOMS telephone operator model, the designer needed to know about small differences in performance at a few, very often repeated tasks. In such cases only a few scenarios are needed.

In contrast, a designer of ATC displays will be interested in large performance differences (errors) that might occur across a wide range of possible operating conditions. Scenarios corresponding to these many operating conditions are thus needed.

Step Four

One runs the simulation and analyses the simulation trace output that results. Analysis presents two main difficulties. First, the trace may include a vast amount of data, only a small portion of which may be of interest in a given situation. Second, it will often be necessary to process the raw trace data to reveal interesting, design-relevant patterns of performance.

These problems have not yet been adequately addressed in APEX. Currently, the simulation software includes a trace-control facility, allowing a user to specify what kinds of events are most interesting and should thus appear in the simulation trace. If the user knows just what to look for, this can be very helpful. Also, APEX can be run with the Cognition Simulation System which has mechanisms for gathering certain kinds of quantitative data from the model, esp. temporal data such as reaction times, and for representing the data in charts or graphs.

The main unmet need is the ability to specify general event patterns and recognize pattern instances in the trace.Our informal assessment, based on experience with APEX and other modeling frameworks, is that the main costs of modeling arise in steps 1 and 2. Efforts to reduce costs have thus focussed on these activities.

Simworld Construction Costs

In the worst case, constructing simworld software can require months of full-time effort from programmers familiar with both the modeling framework and with simulation programming in general. Although we see no way to entirely avoid the need for talented programmers, there are several ways to reduce the time and expertise simworld construction requires.

First, APEX incorporates a powerful and highly flexible simulation environment. Using this environment for APEX modeling requires almost no knowledge of simulation technology or theory. Second, APEX includes a simple and well-documented API (application programmer's interface) that we believe makes it unnecessary to know how APEX works when designing the simworld. We have tested this belief by having undergraduate interns with little programming experience apply APEX to novel (though simple) problems as a summer project. The few difficulties that were encountered have been remedied.

A good API and simulation environment not only reduce needed programmer expertise, but also save a great deal of time. A great deal more time could be saved by creating highly reusable simworld components. In particular, control elements such as switches, levers, dials, buttons, mice, keyboards, and so on will be needed in many different simworld domains. Similarly, display elements such as windows, menus, cursors, text-boxes, and maps are commonplace.

Rather than requiring the programmer to construct software representations of these device elements anew for each simworld, they can be provided in a component library. The process of building up this library has only just begun, but over time, this library should become a valuable programmer resource.

TASK ANALYSIS COSTS

APEX, like other human simulation models, consists of general-purpose components such as eyes, hands, and working memory; it requires the addition of domain-specific knowledge structures to function in any particular task domain. Task analysis is the process of *identifying* and *representing* the necessary knowledge. In highly reutilized task domains such as air traffic control, some part of the identification problem can be accomplished easily and fairly uncontroversial by reference to published procedures. For instance, to clear an airplane for descent to a given altitude, a controller uses a specific verbal procedure prescribed in the controller phraseology handbook.

"United two one inner, descend and maintain flight level five thousand." Other behaviours such as visually scanning the radar display to maintain awareness of current airspace conditions do not correspond to any documented procedure. For these, underlying "know-how" must be inferred from domain attributes and general assumptions about adaptive human learning processes.

Once identified, know-how must be formally represented. Every modeling framework provides a specialized notational scheme for this purpose. To compare different schemes, it is helpful to view them as specialized programming languages. Some task-analysis languages are like a computer assembly language in that they allow very fine control but require substantial time and expertise to use. Examples include the production-system notations used in frameworks such as SOAR Other task-analysis languages, particularly GOMS, are like high-level programming languages in that they allow the programmer/modeler to describe desired behaviours in relatively abstract and intuitive terms.

There are advantages and disadvantages to each approach. However, in our view, productions systems and other low-level languages are too unwieldy for describing behaviour in most task environments of practical interest. The air traffic control task, for example, involves many potentially interacting behaviours carried out over a lengthy interval in an environment which is complex, dynamic, time-pressured, and inherently uncertain. Performing effectively in such environments stretches the capabilities of the most sophisticated artificial intelligence techniques. In principle, these capabilities could be made to emerge from hand-crafted productions or other low-level structures. In practice, no modeling technique that demanded this kind of effort would make it outside the labouratory.

Our approach has been to develop PDL, a high-level language incorporates and extends the capabilities provided by GOMS. GOMS, as mentioned earlier, includes three notational structures. First, a user specifies *Goal* structures to describe the set of intentions the simulated human operator will have at the beginning of a scenario. Goals are decomposed into subgoals on the basis of *Method* structures; the set of these structures represent the operator's primary knowledge about how to get things done in the task domain. The modeler also declares a set of *Operators* - *i.e.* primitive goals that can be carried out without being decomposed into sub goals. If a sub goal matches one of the operators it is executed; otherwise it is recursively decomposed into lower-level sub goals. Finally, *Selection-Rules* are used to choose between

One PDL addition to GOMS is the *Wait for* structure, which specifies that a particular subgoal should not be carried out until some event has occurred. This has several uses, among them an increased ability to deal with uncertainty. For example, it allows one to specify that one should delay choosing between alternative elevators until ones. Other added capabilities make it possible to carry out and coordinate concurrent activities. Unlike GOMS, in which a Method's sub goals are carried out in sequence, sub goals specified in a PDL Procedure (the equivalent of a Method) are carried out concurrently. Watford are used to specify order.

The example PDL procedure above describes a set of steps (sub goals) for starting an automobile. Neither step *s1* for finding the ignition key or step *s2* for locating the slot to in which to insert the key have an associated wait for clause; thus both can be executed immediately and concurrently. These steps are logical preconditions for *s3* in which the hand containing the key is moved to the ignition slot. The wait for clause associated with s3 specifies that it should be delayed until these steps are complete. PDL includes numerous other extensions to GOMS capabilities. The *period* clause makes it possible to declare constraints on repetitive tasks. For example, watering a particular plant can be declared a recurrent (intentionally repetitive) task for which early repetition should be inhibited, but later should become increasingly urgent.

Perhaps the most significant set of extensions are those concerned with coordinating multiple potentially interacting tasks. PDL structures have been created to help detect tasks conflicts, determine whether ongoing tasks should be interrupted, manage task interleaving, and make use of slack-time in one task to make progress at another. In designing PDL, our intention has been to create an intuitive, elegant, and powerful language for expressing common elements of a task analysis.

The success of this effort, which we cannot yet judge, will be determined by how easy a modeler find it to express the behaviours identified in a preliminary task analysis. Designing and refining PDL with this goal in mind has been the primary way in which we have attempted to minimize the time and expertise required to perform a task analysis. However, we are also engaged in two related efforts. The first addresses the problem that not all common elements of a task analysis are appropriately handled with a specialized language construct.

Instead, modelers must specify the desired behaviour using existing constructs. For instance, one common behaviour is to attempt a goal by two different methods at the same time, stopping both efforts when any one succeeds. Rather than creating some kind of *do-in-parallel* construct (a viable idea with some disadvantages), a modeler can achieve this effect using the wait for clause in a fairly straightforward way. For example, a simulated air traffic controller might determine an aircraft's call sign by simultaneously trying to retrieve the information from memory and trying to find it on the radar display. The issue in this case is not so much that the behaviour is difficult to represent, but that a novice PDL user might not think of it. This problem is analogous to that of programmers having to learn "language idioms" and algorithms.

One final way to reduce time needed to perform task analysis is to create a library of "common sense" procedural knowledge. For instance, most people know how to flip a switch, turn a dial, use a mouse to position a pointer over a target, and so on. Moreover, such behaviours will be quite common in task environments of practical interest to designers.

Thus, by creating these procedures, we save APEX users from efforts they would very likely have to make. Not coincidentally, these behaviours are needed to read and operate device elements in the reusable simworld component library. The two efforts go together; for each standard simworld component, we create one or more associated "common sense" procedures.

The future of human-system simulation as an engineering tool clearly depends on whether the technology can be made sufficiently powerful and cost-effective. Achieving these practical goals requires recognizing and meeting a variety of challenges. Where an attempt to use a modeling framework in some novel way reveals the need for some new capability, that capability should be added.

Where the time and expertise needed to apply a modeling framework threaten to make the approach cost-ineffective, some way to reduce these costs must be found. In developing and applying APEX, we have discovered numerous sources of cost and complexity in the process of preparing a model for simulation. Ongoing efforts to reduce these costs promise to eventually make APEX a highly usable and cost-effective tool.

ROLE OF GAMES

INTRODUCTION

Game playing was one of the first tasks undertaken in

Artificial Intelligence. Game theory has its history from 1950, almost from the days when computers became programmable. The very first game that is been tackled in AI is chess. Initiators in the field of game theory in AI were Konard Zuse (the inventor of the first programmable computer and the first programming language), Claude Shannon, Norbert Wiener and Alan Turing.

Since then, there has been a steady progress in the standard of play, to the point that machines have defeated human champions (although not every time) in chess and backgammon, and are competitive in many other games.

TYPES OF GAME

Perfect Information Game: In which player knows all the possible moves of himself and opponent and their results. *E.g.* Chess. Imperfect Information Game: In which player does not know all the possible moves of the opponent. *E.g.*

Bridge since all the cards are not visible to player. Game playing is a search problem defined by following components: Initial state: This defines initial configuration of the game and identifies first payer to move. Successor function: This identifies which are the possible states that can be achieved from the current state.

This function returns a list of (move, state) pairs, each indicating a legal move and the resulting state. Goal test: Which checks whether a given state is a goal state or not. States where the game ends are called as terminal states. Path cost/utility/payoff function: Which gives a numeric value for the terminal states. In chess, the outcome is win, loss or draw, with values +1, -1, or 0. Some games have wider range of possible outcomes.

CHARACTERISTICS OF GAME PLAYING

Unpredictable Opponent: Generally we cannot predict the behaviour of the opponent. Thus we need to find a solution which is a strategy specifying a move for every possible opponent move or every possible state. Time Constraints: Every game has a time constraints. Thus it may be infeasible to find the best move in this time. How to Play A Game in AI?

Typical structure of the game in the AI is:

- 2- person game
- Players alternate moves
- Zero-sum game: one player's loss is the other's gain
- Perfect information: both players have access to complete information about the state of the game. No information is hidden from either player.
- No chance (e. g. using dice) involved

E.g. Tic- Tac- Toe, Checkers, Chess, Go, Nim, Othello

For dealing with such types of games, consider all the legal moves you can make from the current position. Compute the new position resulting from each move. Evaluate each resulting position and determine which is best for you. Make that move. Wait for your opponent to move and repeat the procedure. But for this procedure the main problem is how to evaluate the position? Evaluation function or static evaluator is used to evaluate the 'goodness' of a game position. The zero- sum assumption allows us to use a single evaluation function to describe the goodness of a position with respect to both players. Lets consider, f(n) is the evaluation function of the position 'n'.Then,

- f(n) >> 0: position n is good for me and bad for you
- f(n) << 0: position n is bad for me and good for you
- f(n) near 0: position n is a neutral position

e.g. evaluation function for Tic- Tac- Toe:

f(n) = [# of 3- lengths open for me] - [# of 3- lengths open for you]

where a 3- length is a complete row, column, or diagonal.

Games are represented in the form of trees wherein nodes represent all the possible states of a game and edges represent moves between them. Initial state of the game is represented by root and terminal states by leaves of the tree. In a normal search problem, the optimal solution would be a sequence of moves leading to a goal state that is a win. Even a simple game like tic-tac-toe is too complex for us to draw the entire game tree. Fig shows part of the game tree for tic-tac-toe.

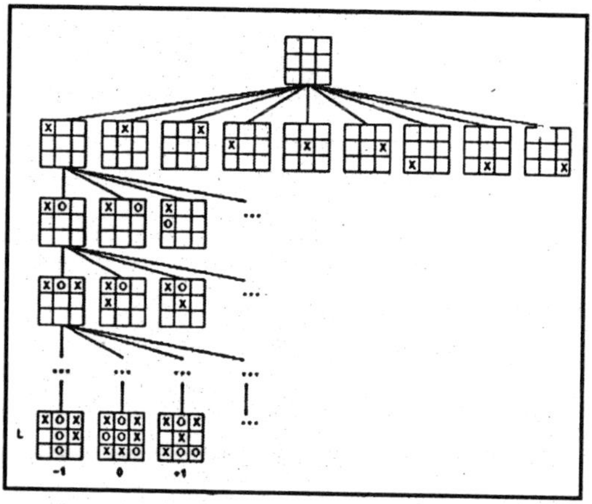

Fig. Game Tree for Tic-Tac-Toe

Let us represent two players by 'X' and 'O'. From the initial state, X has nine possible moves. Play alternates between X and O until we reach leaves. The number on each leaf node indicates the utility value of the terminal states from the point of view of X. High values are assumed to be good for X and bad for O.

Minimax Trees

Imagine a simple game that only has three moves, one move results in a win, another draw, and finally a loss. Therefore, we want to assess each node and figure what the outcome will be. Let us extend our game to one that allows you to make three moves per go, and only takes two goes to win. Therefore, we will want to look ahead to find out which move combination works for us. We can generate a game tree of all the possible moves.

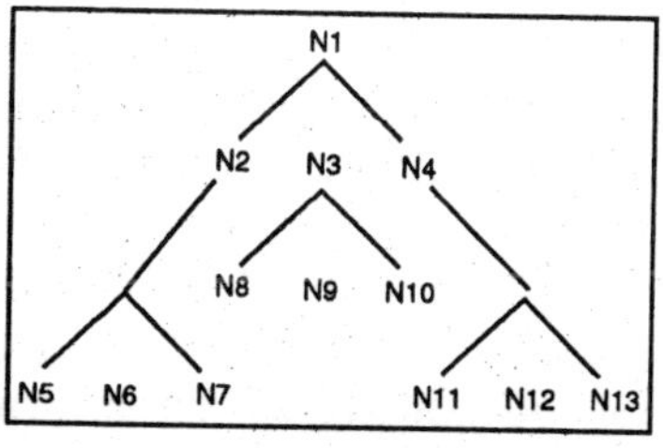

Fig. Game Tree

You can see how there are 9 final possible moves. Imagine that N11 is the winning situation; therefore our first move will have to be N4. How can we figure this out algorithmically? Let us assign values to a win, draw and loss. A win will be 1, a draw 0 and a loss -1. Say that N11 is the only winner, and the rest are drawing situations. So, what we'll want to do is evaluate the tree from the bottom-up propagating the *maximum* value for the nodes upwards. Therefore, for the N5-N7 group, 0 is the highest so this is applied to N2. N8-N10 also has 0 as the highest, which is taken on by N3. The N11-N13 group has 1 as the highest. The Programme knows to choose N4.

In our example, since the tree is only two layers deep this seems rather trivial. But imagine a tree 10 layers keep, this method would allow you to simply calculate which moves would lead to a winning situation. Most of you will already notice a large fault in this - trees this large are incredibly expensive in both memory and computational terms. A 10-layer tree that branches three times for each node would have 59,049 nodes. This is relatively simple - a Tic-tac-toe tree would have 362,880 nodes.

Therefore, we have to cut down the depth of our tree. This gives us a problem, though - if we limit the depth we are not guaranteed a winning scenario as one of the nodes. This is where the clever programming has to come in. You must create some sort of evaluation function that can assess how close to a winning situation the board is. Since the nodes are not so clear-cut (win, draw, loss) a more complicated numbering system has to be used. The system is completely dependent on the programmer and the board game in question.

Very few board games are one player, so how can we add this into our tree? When we are playing for ourselves, we are attempting to maximize our score, so our opponent will want to minimize our score. Here comes minimax into picture. In a two-player game, the first player moves with MAX score and the second player move with MIN score. A minimax search is used to determine all possible continuations of the game up to a desired level. A score is originally assigned to the leaf known as utility value and indicated by UTILITY(n). Then by evaluating each possible set of moves, a score is assigned to the upper level by the minimax algorithm. The minimax algorithm performs a preorder traversal and computes the scores on the fly. The same would be obtained by a simple recursive algorithm.

The rule is as follows:

```
Minimax_value(u)
{//u is the node you want to score if u is a
leaf return score of u;
else
if u is a min node
for all children of u: v1,.. vn ;
return min (Minimax_value(v1)...,
Minimax_value(vn))
else
for all children of u: v1,.. vn ;
return max (Minimax_value(v1)...,
Minimax_value(vn))
```

Let us take a look at a game tree. Here is our game tree with evaluations assigned to the final nodes:

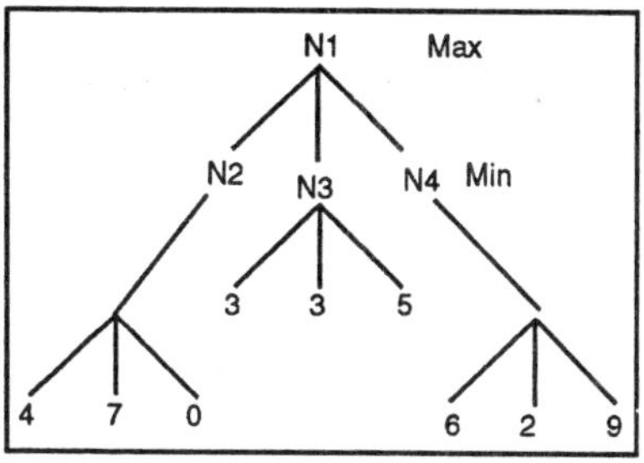

Fig. Minimax Tree with Evaluation Function Applied to Leaves

Now, assigned values are for boards representing our opponent's choice of boards. N1 stands for the current board, N2-N4 are our three possible moves and N5-N13 are the opponent's possible follow-up moves. Since our opponent will try to minimize our winning possibility, therefore will calculate the minimum value for each node and assign it to the parent. N2 will equal 0, N3 will equal 3, and N4 will equal 2. In making a choice for our best possible move, we look at the max of these values - which is 3 (N3).

Minimax Algorithm

Now let us put all this in the form of algorithm. Following is manimax algorithm, which takes current state as an input and returns a best possible operator to be applied to current state. Essentially this is same as what we have seen previously in recursive function. But this algorithm is written from the MAX player point of view.

```
Function MINIMAX-DECISION (state)
returns an operator
For each op in OPERATORS[game] do
VALUE [op] = MINIMAX-VALUE (APPLY (op, state),
game)
End
Return the op with the highest VALUE [op]
Function MINIMAX-VALUE (state, game)
returns a utility value
If TERMINAL-TEST (state) then
Return UTILITY (state)
Else If MAX is to move in state then
Return the highest MINIMAX-VALUE of SUCCESSORS
(state)
Else
Return the lowest MINIMAX-VALUE of SUCCESSORS
(state)
```

The minimax algorithm computes the minimax decision from the current state. It uses a simple recursive computation of the minimax values of each successor state, directly implementing the defining equations. The recursion proceeds all the way down to the leaves of the tree, and then the minimax values are backed up through the tree as the recursion unwinds.

In fig, a game with 2 plies is shown. One ply indicates one move of one player. MAX has three possible moves, which are followed by three possible moves each for MIN.

Tree shows these moves. Leaf nodes are evaluated and utility values are assigned to them. These values are propagated upward to assign the utility values to the parents.

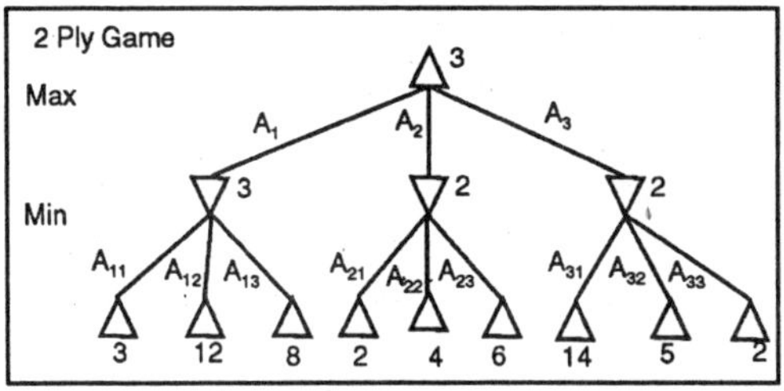

Fig. Minimax Game Tree

Summarizing, one can view in its entire form, the score values at each of the levels of the tree at any given point during the game. By viewing this tree, a player may be able to foresee which moves are more advantageous and beneficial for them.

The root of the tree represents the position of the current player, thus, depending on the number of levels that is to be searched, all odd levels represent the first player while the even levels represent the second player

Characteristics of minimax algorithm:

- *Completeness:* Minimax is complete if the tree is finite. *E.g* Chess has a very large but finite tree. Thus minimax is complete in case of chess.
- *Optimality:* If observed carefully, algorithm is optimal against an optimal player only. In fig.4, A1 is the optimal move if the opponent is also optimal. If opponent is not optimal then MAX can get more utility by selecting A3 if in turn MIN selects A31 giving utility of 14. But if opponent is optimal, he will select move A33 giving utility of 2 to MAX that is not optimal.
- *Time Complexity:* Algorithm performs a complete depth-first search exploration, time complexity is $O(b^m)$, where b is branching factor and m is depth of the tree.
- *Space Complexity:* Space complexity is O(bm).

For chess, b is approximately equal to 35 and m approximately equal to 100. Thus it is infeasible to find exact solution within given time limit. Thus one standard approach is applied called as depth limit search, in which search is limited to some depth from the current node. Nodes at that depth are assumed to be leaves and their utility values are estimated. Estimation function estimates desirability of the state. This is different for each game. There are different methods of estimation for a game. This is most interesting part of game theory.

Alpha-Beta Pruning

The problem with the minimax search is that the number of game states it has to examine is exponential in the number of moves. Unfortunately we can't eliminate the exponent, but we can effectively cut it in half. The trick is that it is possible to compute the correct minimax decision without looking at every node in the game tree. The particular technique we will examine is called alpha-beta pruning. When applied to the standard minimax tree, it returns the same move as minimax would, but prunes away branches that can't possibly influence the final decision.

Alpha and Beta

At each MAX node n, alpha(n) = maximum value found so far, At each MIN node n, beta(n) = minimum value found so far, The alpha values start at -infinity and only increase, while beta values start at +infinity and only decrease. Let us see an example. In fig. three possible moves of MIN corresponding to given move of MAX are evaluated. They have utility values of 3, 12 and 8. Thus MIN will select minimum of them *i.e.* 3.

Thus from this move of MAX, it can get utility value of 3. Here value of alpha becomes 3. Thus it is assured that utility value of MAX can no be less than 3. Now consider another move of MAX. That will lead to 3 possible moves of MIN. One of these moves has utility value of 2. Now this becomes beta value of MIN node.

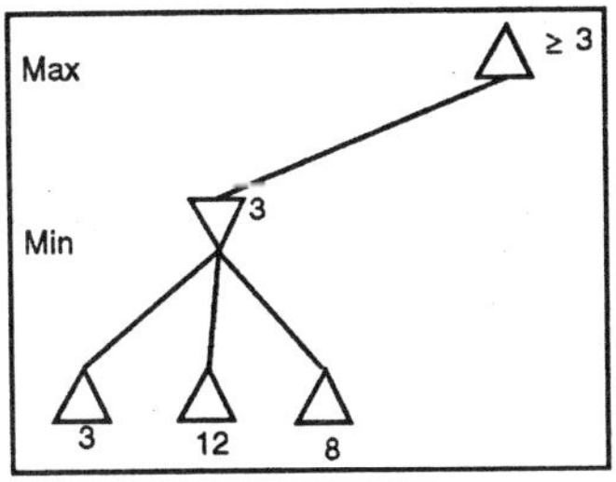

Fig. Alpha Pruning

Now whatever may be the utility values of other two children, utility value of MIN node cannot be grater than 2. Thus this MIN can propagate upward at the max value of 2. This 2 is less than current alpha of MAX node *i.e.* 3. Because MAX is assured with the utility value of at least 3, it will not consider any MIN node returning utility value less than 3. And thus it prunes the search there for this MIN node.

Applications

Game theory has vast applications in different fields. *Some of the important are mentioned below.*

- *Entertainment*: Game theory is used to define different strategies of different games.
- *Economics*: Each factor in the market, such as seasonal preferences, buyer choice, changes in supply and material costs, and other such market factors can be used to describe strategies to maximize the outcome and thus the profit.
- *Military*: Game theory can be useful in Military also. Military strategists have turned to game theory to play "war games". Usually, such games are not zero-sum games, for loses to one side are not won by the other.
- *Political science*: The properties of n-person non-zero-sum games can be used to study different aspects of political science and social science. Matters such as distribution of power, interactions between nations, the distribution of classes and their effects of government, and many other matters can be easily

investigated by breaking the problem down into smaller games, each of whose outcomes affect the final result of a larger game.

Conclusion

Game theory remained the most interesting part of AI from the birth of AI. Game theory is very vast and interesting topic. Game theory mainly deals with working in the constrained areas to get the desired results. They illustrate several important points about Artificial Intelligence like perfection can not be attained but we can approximate to it.

2

Business Process Planning

TECHNIQUES

ANALYSIS

Parsing of natural language utterances is still an active reasearch topic due to the inherent difficulties that make the problem much harder than *e.g.* parsing of programming languages. These difficulties include lexical and structural ambiguity of natural language utterances, complexities introduced by expressive grammar formalisms, the need to cope with illformed input or with deficiencies of the linguistic descriptions. The main goal of the web services is to have a collection of network-resident web services which can be accessed via standardised protocols. The functionality of these services can automatically be discovered and composed to form more complex services. This discovery and composition process is known as web service composition. Several standards have emerged to compose web service. One of the most prominent standards for composition is Business Process Execution Language.

The main drawback of this approach is its lack of modularity and dynamisms. This is because WS-BPEL only allows for off-line, or precompiled, composition. Consequently new composite services cannot be created on-the-fly. This restriction and WS-BPEL's lack of flexibility are the cause of various run-time failures and exceptions. Using AI planning techniques to generate composition process is a way to reduce errors and exceptions occur during run-time. AI planning is a way to reason about actions in composition. At each step of the composition, the current state participating services can be examined to ensure consistency. Peer surveys the current AI planning techniques and their application to web service composition.

PURPOSE

The purpose here is to evaluate and compare Hierarchical Task Network Planning and Planning as Model Checking in the web service composition domain. Even though comparisons of planners have been performed, they do not address the web service composition issues between different planning techniques. Examining planning techniques will in future help the developer to choose a better planner for composition purpose.

ROLE OF PLANNING TECHNIQUES

Explanation of Terms

This will provides an explanation of terms that are relevant to planning problems. These terms will be used through when dealing with planning techniques.

- *Plan:* A possible solution to a specified problem. A plan can be represented as a workflow.
- *Planning:* A process of generating and modifying plans.
- *Planner:* A system that performs planning.
- *Initial state description:* – Tells the planner the way is "right now", that is, the current state of the domain.
- *Goal state description:* Tells the planner the way we want the work to look when the plan has been executed, that is, the desired state of the domain on completion of the plan.
- *Action:* A special kind of events.

Focus of Planning

Planning focuses on selecting suitable actions and ordering them in an appropriate sequence so as to achieve some goal. It allows businesses and organizations to cut costs considerably while at the same time increasing their ability to handle the dynamic nature and complexity of today's business environment In general, a classical AI planning problem has the following components:

- An initial state description.
- A desired goal state description.
- A set of possible actions.

The objective of AI planning is to generate a plan, that is, a sequence of actions when executed from the initial state will result a goal state. A state is a snapshot of the state of the world at a particular point in time. States are represented by a set of ground literals in first-order language. The actions are expressions, which are described using some formal language. The expression consists of a name, parametre list, precondition list and effect list.

Often when formalising the initial state, we are confronted with the various problems ranging from incomplete information to fuzzy information. Incomplete information does not specify all knowledge relevant to the planning task. Fuzzy information implies that there exists a certain probability of being incorrect for each known fluent value.

The problems do not only occur during formalisation of initial state, but also during formalisation of goal state. For example, when planning for a round-trip from South Africa to Paris and then back to South Africa, we cannot distinguish between the initial state and the goal state. This implies that the initial state is equal to the goal state. Therefore, we need to add certain structures to split the planning into several distinct, consecutive phases.

MODEL CHECKING

In a full discussion of model checking is given by Clarke and Schlingloff. The fundamental concepts of model checking are described. In the following paragraphs model checking and its basic concepts will be discussed briefly, followed by planning as model checking. Model Checking is a formal verification technique used to determine whether or not a property holds in a finite state model. Model checkers and planners are normally used to perform verification. The model checker searches for a counter-example to falsify a given specification, and the planner searches for a sequence of actions to satisfy a goal. Labelled Transition System Analyser (LTSA) is an example system that uses model checking to verified final state of transition.

The main idea behind Planning as Model Checking paradigm is that planning problems should be solved model-theoretically. A planning domain is formalised as semantic models, which defines the states of the domain, the available actions and the state transitions caused by the execution of actions. The properties of planning domains are formalised as temporal formulas. The planning problem description includes planning domain, initial and goal states. Planning is done by verifying whether temporal formulas are true in a semantic model. At each step, the truth values of some suitable formulas in the model are check to ensure the correctness of plan at that time.

The main advantage of Planning as Model Checking is its ability to give clear and intuitive formalisation of planning problems. Its capability of dealing with nondeterministic, partial observability and extended goals allows it to solve generic problems. Moreover, Planning as Model Checking can also devise efficient algorithms that generate plans automatically and can deal with large size problems.

HIERARCHICAL TASK NETWORK PLANNING

Hierarchical Task Network (HTN) planning is a type of AI planning that allows for incorporating and exploiting domain-independent control knowledge. By incorporating domain-dependent control knowledge in a planner good performance in real world domains can be achieved. Planner such as TLPlan, TALplanner and SHOP2 are some examples of HTN planners that developed in the past decade. SHOP2 in particular was specifically designed for web service composition. Basically HTN planning is a type of problem reduction that decomposes tasks into subtasks, handle constraints, resolve interactions and in case of error, it will backtrack and try other decompositions.

The main objective of HTN planners is to produce a sequence of actions that perform some activity or task by using task decomposition. The planning domain description includes a set of operators and a set of methods. While the operators describe the effect of each primitive task, the methods tell how to recursively decompose the non-primitive tasks into smaller subtasks, until the planner reaches primitive tasks that can be performed directly using the planning operators.

According there are three types of tasks in HTN planning:

1. Goal tasks denote the desired properties of the final state;
2. Primitive tasks, which are tasks that can be execute directly by invoking atomic operations;
3. Compound tasks denote desired changes that involve several goal tasks and primitive tasks.

Followed from the formalisation of domain description is the problem description. The problem description includes domain description, initial state and initial task network. The main advantage of HTN planning lies in its ability to deal with very large problem domains by decomposing goal into smaller manageable subtasks, which can be solved directly. Hence, the computational cost of finding correct sequence of actions is reduced significantly. However, this technique requires experts to provide the planner with a task it needs to accomplish. Despite the disadvantage, HTN planning is still a good way to provide level abstraction. This means we do not need to poses complete knowledge about the service into order to do the selection.

SCENARIO

The scenario presented here will be used for analysis of planning techniques throughout the paper. The web service application scenario of an online purchase and delivery (OPD) service will be described in detail below.

Description

OPD offers a service that allows clients to directly purchase a given model of computer/laptop and have it delivered to a given location. To minimise the processes involved, we assume that payment will be done upon delivery. In order to form the OPD service we need to combine two existing separate, independent services, namely a computer supplier and a delivery service. These services are provided by their own service providers, which are providing web services that allow for queries about the products and services they offer.

Figure depicts the interaction between the user and the OPD service. The user sends a request by filling in a web form, which is the front-end of the OPD service. The purpose of this form is to capture the computer model and the delivery service that the user requires. The user's request is then send to the supplier process. The supplier will check the database for the availability of the model specified. If the specified model is not available, a notification will be send to the client and the rest of the process will terminate. The delivery service will only be activated only if it receives a confirmation from the supplier process stating the specified model is available.

When the processes are done, the OPD service will return the result of the search. The result can be successful or unsuccessful, depending on the availability of the service. When the result is successful, then the service will display information about pricing of the goods and the cost of the service to the user.

The client will then confirm whether or not they accept the offer. The supplier and delivery service will update their database accordingly. However, if the result is unsuccessful, the whole process will terminate and an appropriate error message will be displayed.

FAULT BEHAVIOUR

The discovery and binding of services will be done in run-time. In this section we discuss some of the fault behaviour posed by the scenario described.

Selection of Services

This is crucial to final composition, since wrong selection service can result in unexpected results. The selection can be based on the business rules, semantics and syntactic interface of the service. Which ever way the selection is based on depends on the nature the end result the composite service is trying to achieve. For example, as described in scenario, we might end up with thousands and thousands of suppliers that meet the requirement, but not all of them are equally suited to fulfilling them. The problem then breaks down to selecting the provider offering the most appropriate services.

Availability of Services

The other issue related to selection of service is availability. The service can become unavailable due to various factors. This can range from slow network traffic to server problems. The composition process needs to find out what exactly the cause of the problem is.

Consistency

The selected services may change during the composition. This can lead to unexpected behaviour. The ability to detect such changes and perform recovery is one of the goals of dynamic web service compositions.

Dependency

An example of dependency is delivery service depending on supplier service. The delivery service relies on the supplier to provide date when the computer will be available for delivery. If delivery service fails, one of the reasons might be due to failure on behalf of the supplier. Therefore, checking the dependencies between services is important.

Dealing with Non-deterministic

In the real world, there are various ways to perform the same action. Actions also have numerous possible outcomes. In web service composition, as in real world, our knowledge of the environment and services we are operating on is not complete. Due to this fact the result of composition process is difficult to determine. The service generated by the composition process may therefore be different from the service we specified as our goal state.

FORMALISATION

Model Checking

In this, we first provide WS-BPEL code of scenario described. To illustrate the relationship between WS-BPEL and Planning as Model Checking, the WS-BPEL code will then be translated into FSP. The software that used to translate WS-BPEL to FSP is a plug-in for Eclipse.

Formalising Planning Domain

The model defines the state of the domain, the available actions, and the state transitions caused by the execution of actions. In this scenario, our planning domain consists of three ground-level domains, namely the client, the supplier and shipping service while the main planning domain would be the OPD.

```
<process name="OPD"

<containers>
<container name="PO".../>
<container name="Invoice".../>
<container name="POFault".../>
<container name="shippingRequest".../>
<container name="shippingInfo".../>
<containers>

<partners>
<partner name="client".../>
<partner name="supplier".../>
<partner name="shippingProvider".../>
<partners>

<sequence>
```

```
<receive partner="client"
 operation="sendPurchaseorder">
</receive>

<flow>
<links>
<link name="ship-to-invoice"/>
</links>

<sequence>
<assignment>
<xpath>
<from container="PO" part="clientInfo"/>
<to container="shippingRequest"
 part="clientInfo"/>
</xpath>
</assignment>

<invoke partner="shippingProvider"
 operation="requestshipping"
 inputContainer="shippingRequest"
 outputContainer="shippingInfo">
<source linkName="ship-to-invoice"/>
</invoke>

</sequence>
<sequence>
<invoke partner="supplier"
 operation="initiatePriceCalculation"
 inputcontainer="PO">
</invoke>

<invoke partner="supplier"
 operation="sendshippingPrice"
 inputContainer="ship-to-invoice"/>
</invoke>

<receive partner="supplier"
```

```
  operation="sendInvoice"
  Container="Invoice"/>
</sequence>
```

BPEL CODE FOR OPD PROCESS

Planning as Model Checking relies heavily on finite-state programme verification. Thus, verification of WS-BPEL process is done by transforming WS-BPEL processes into transition states, and then verifies each state. However, LTSA-BPEL4WS plug-in does not address the issues relating to dynamic selection and matching between services. For this reason, it can only be used to check the validation of the composition workflow itself. In order to incorporate the selection and matching mechanism,

HIERARCHICAL TASK NETWORK PLANNING

Since our OPD is a non-primitive task, we first need to decompose it until a primitive task network is obtained. To perform this decomposition, appropriate methods must be selected and applied. The consistency and completeness of the primitive task network is guaranteed through the use of correct methods. Consider method $m = (t, d)$ where t represents the task and d represents the task network.

The method will only be considered correct if and only if d is the correct implementation of t. In the simplest case, d is a complete and consistent plan which produces the effects of t. Moreover, we can add a precondition to ensure everything is correctly executed up to the point before the start of the current method. Such precondition of tasks in d is established through the preconditions of t or within d itself. If the desired complex task (*i.e.* OPD) is decomposed into a set of primitive tasks without violating any of the given conditions (*i.e.* preconditions and post-conditions) then the planning problem is considered to be successful.

PLANNING AS MODEL CHECKING

As was mentioned, selection of services is the most important step in the whole composition process. Planning as Model Checking selects services using type matching algorithm. To ensure that the selected services are able to composite in a coherent manner, the composition capabilities between services are also checked. Availability of services and dependency between services are closely linked with selection of services. They are checked and verified using type matching algorithm and composition capability.

In terms of consistency of services, in the dynamic world, the properties of services change due to various reasons. To detect and compensate for these changes, Planning as Model Checking uses state-transition to check each state at a particular time during composition to ensure the properties of the services is consistent with respect to the requirement. The overall consistency of the composition is checked for safety, violation and deadlocks to ensure that the composition is in a working manner.

The correctness in selection of services, checking for availability, dependency and consistency contribute to ensure the correctness of the overall composition. However, just examining each state itself will not solve the problems introduced by non-deterministic actions. The approach Planning as Model Checking takes to deal with such problems is the use of weak, strong and strong-cyclic plan graphs. The weak and strong plans are set of state-action pairs which may (is guaranteed to) achieve the goal. The weak plan will have at least one execution path that reaches a goal, while every single execution path in strong plan will reaches a goal. A strong-cyclic plan is a plan whose executions always have a possibility of terminating and, when they do, they are guaranteed to achieve the goal.

The issue of dealing with non-deterministic actions have been tackled by the Planning as Model Checking. However, planning with extended goals and partial observability is a very important issue and has not been addressed until recent research is done. The algorithm they developed was built on the techniques developed in the Planning as Model Checking framework for the restricted problems of extended goals and of partial observability. Up to this stage we see Planning as

Model Checking possesses a high level of accuracy as it verifies all actions and the overall composition as a whole. However, all these verification steps are very time consuming to perform on a large set, because in worst case it have O(n!) complexity.

TASK NETWORK PLANNING

HTN planning may be domain-specific or domain configurable. Domain-configurable means that it is domain-independent with the ability to allow configuration to suite ones need. Such ability is very convenient for web service composition to adapt from different composition to composition.

Different levels of abstraction provided by HTN planning avoid tyranny of detail that would result from planning at the most primitive level. Such abstraction level is necessary in real world domains, because it significantly reduces the search space by forming abstract plans and then expanding these into more detailed plans. For example, in our scenario, during the selection of shipping service, we only need to know we want a service that can provide delivery and there is no need to consider how they perform the actual shipping until later stage. In this way together with it support for parallel interaction between tasks, the time that needs to spend on discovery and selection of services reduced significantly.

Henceforth, the key benefit of HTN planning is the computation cost of finding the correct way to arrange activities for the current problem is small. In the worst case if have O((n/k)!?k).The planning process in HTN is fully automated, but human intervention is allowed when required. Human can intervene while the plan is being set up and/or when the process cannot decompose tasks anymore, providing that not all the primitive tasks have been reached. In terms of accuracy, the planner considers the entire execution path and it has the opportunity to minimise various types of failures or unexpected occurrences. This is done by incorporating backtracking mechanism and integrating complex precondition reasoning, post-condition checks and performing evaluation of arbitrary code at plan time. The backtracking mechanism is used on checking discovered services to ensure suitability, as well as during execution. During execution, the methods pre- and post condition are checked to ensure consistency. If failures or unexpected events have occurred, it will backtrack to where the problem is and try to correct the method or select alternatives. The way HTN planning deals with non-deterministic actions is by defining and implementing methods which can handle non-deterministic actions. For example: In the best case, hierarchical methods can result in linear-time instead of exponential-time planning algorithms.

Almost all planners for large-scale applications are HTN planners, because HTN planning allows the human expert to provide the crucial knowledge about how to perform complex tasks so that large plans can be constructed with little computational effort. Planners such as SHOP2 an HTN planner used in web service composition, are based on HTN planning.

It is evident that for web service composition to reach its full potential, it should have the ability to automatically compose web services. To this end a planning technique can be used to automated web service composition. A list of current planning techniques used in web services is presented. Planning as Model Checking and HTN Planning presented in this paper are just two of the approaches that incorporate control knowledge.

These approaches were considered and analysed according to a set of criteria described. The result of the analysis shows that HTN planning has various advantages over Planning as Model Checking. However, the analysis conducted on planning as model checking and HTN planning presented in section 5.1 and 5.2 respectively, is not complete. It can serve as a starting point for future research in analysing such planning techniques. Even with planning techniques, we still need a framework to map the planning techniques onto the relevant standards, where composition can take place. Such mapping between Planning as Model Checking and WS-

BPEL have been done by Bertoli, *et al.* in [3], and the mapping between HTN planning and OWL-S using SHOP2. However, the mapping between HTN planning and BPEL is still an open issue. Furthermore, even with the planning technique in place, there is no way of ensuring that the planning process will execute as expected without proper control mechanisms in place. Therefore, in order to ensure proper execution of the planning process, a control mechanism is required.

Planning without control is meaningless and any good planning system should ensure that it has a control mechanism in place. Future works include more depth analysis of Planning as Model Checking and HTN planning in relation to the fault behaviours of web service composition. Having all the information on hand, we then need to examine how control mechanism is applied according to ensure proper execution of composition.

CONTEXTUAL GRAMMAR

TRANSFORMATIONAL GRAMMARS

A generic term for any generative grammar which uses transformations. In a narrower sense, the theory developed The goal of this theory is to illustrate the implicit knowledge of language. based on current language use, by a system of explicit rules.

Differing from the taxonomic structuralism of Harris, Bloomfield, and others, which is based on the segmentation and classification of concrete language data, Chomsky's model refers to the ability of competent speakers and to the linguistic intuitions which a competent speaker can make explicit about his/her language.

Historically, Chomsky belongs to the tradition of rationalism of Leibniz and Descartes. By elabourating the concept of 'innate ideas,' Chomsky turns against the behaviourist approaches of the American structuralists and expands his theory to a theory of language acquisition. The development of competence is explained by the innate language acquisition device on the basis of grammar universals. Therefore the formulation of the theory takes precedence over the analysis of data, and transfor-mational grammar proceeds deductively by laying down hypotheses about the linguistic generation mechanism, taking the creative aspects of linguistic ability into account. This is true of Chomsky's first theory, which appeared in book Syntactic structures: an infinite set of kernel sentences, produced by context-free phrase structure rules, forms the basis for the application of transformational rules, which ensure an infinite set of sentences by finite means.

In the second phase of transformational grammar, documented in Chomsky'sAspects of the theory of syntax in 1965, the original syntactic theory is expanded to a general theory of grammar which includes phonology and semantics. The following revisions are characteristic of the so-called 'aspects model' (also known as the standard theory, ST): the grammar, in the sense of a comprehensive linguistic theory, consists of a generative, syntactic component as well as interpretive, semantic, and phonological components.

The basis of the syntax is the deep structure which is formed by context-free phrase structure rules and lexical rules. The context-free phrase structure rules guarantee recursive ness by self-embedded constructions; recursive ness was achieved by generalizing transformations in the earlier model. The deep structure contains all semantically relevant information at an abstract basic level of structure and is the point of departure for the semantic interpretation of sentences. The works of Katz in the area of interpretive semantics are relevant here.

The corresponding surface structure is derived from meaning-neutral transformations such as deletion. The surface structure forms the basis for the phonological-phonetic representation. Criticism of this conception was, above all, based on the role of semantics, since the semantic interpretation of a sentence is dependent on surface structure phenomena such as intonation, word order, and thetheme-rheme division. This led to the development of two competing approaches in the 1960s and 1970s: generative semantics and the extended standard theory. Revisions of the standard theory were instigated by Jackendoff and Chomsky and lie in a restriction on the range of transformations through universal constraints and in semantic interpretation, which refers to the deep structure and surface structure.

Changes occurring since 1973 have led to the introduction of the term Revised Extended Standard theory (=REST), which differs from the extended standard theory in the following ways:

- The exact delimiting and definition of the individual grammatical components, especially the strict division between syntax and semantics (as well as phonology, stylistics, and pragmatics);
- The application of marked ness theory, which was developed in phonology;
- The reduction of transformations to structure-preserving transformations, especially move-?;
- The universal formulation of constraints, which correspond to psychologically interpretable universals and which are specified by language-specific parametres;
- The introduction of traces as abstract empty category nodes in the surface structure, which mark and make accessible the former position of transposed NP-constituents;
- The semantic interpretation can only operate on a single level of the surface structure which encodes semantic information from deep structure.

In theory, the term government takes on a central meaning; within core grammar, a strong modularization of the syntax is attempted; phenomena of individual languages are captured by suitable parametreization.

EXPLANATION

Transformational grammar is an approach to the use of grammar in communications that involves a logical and analytical process to fully grasp the meaning behind the words selected. From this perspective, transformational grammar goes beyond the process of structural grammar, which tends to focus on the proper construction of sentences as the device for communication. Along with sentence structure, transformational grammar will also attempt to explore the thought behind the words. Sometimes referred to as TG grammar, transformational grammar attempts to apply logic to the task of looking into the deeper meanings of the structure of sentences, and to analyse both the surface and the underlying intent of the words used.

This means employing more than just a visual approach to the words that make up the sentence. Syntax also plays a role in the logical process of transformational grammar, as will context. To a degree, transformational grammar will call upon most of the tools of linguistics in an attempt to fully analyse the spoken or written word. One of the main proponents of the idea of transform-ational grammar was Noam Chomsky.

During the middle portion of the 20th century, Chomsky worked to develop a logical approach to analysing the syntax of structural grammar within the setting of the English language. As a result of his efforts, Chomsky developed and promoted the concept of grammar as being a broader theory regarding language structure, rather than simply defining a method for developing the structure for sentences. This approach had been inherent for centuries in the broader concepts of universal grammar. But due to the work of Chomsky, linguists and grammarians began to understand transformational grammar as a discipline all its own.

People engage in the task of approaching grammar from a transformational approach every day. In some cases, it is a matter of employing transformational grammar as a means of comprehending a grouping of words within the setting or context, rather than focusing on the actual structure of the words. At other times, the idea of transformational grammar is utilized as a means of conveying more than one meaning. The double-entendre may be thought of as a limited example of transformational grammar, as the device provides both a surface and a hidden conveyance of ideas.

NETS

MODEL

A Predicate Transition Net model of expert systems with fuzzy logic is proposed as a means for dealing with uncertainty. Attention is focused on consultant expert systems which use the production rules formalism to represent knowledge. Models of the basic fuzzy logical operators are presented base on the Predicate Transition Nets formalism. The combination of these operators allows to represent the links among the rules of a knowledge base and to simulate dynamically the behaviour of an expert system in its search for a solution to a problem in its domain to expertise. Finally, two applications of this model are described: assessment of parallelism in a knowledge base and the evaluation of time-related measures for expert systems.

CASE GRAMMAR

In this the interpretation of language we considered what is referred to as syntactic knowledge.

Roughly speaking, syntactic knowledge includes knowledge about:

- Syntactic categories such as noun, verb, verb phrase, and
- And how these categories may co-occur and may be ordered.

More abstractly, syntactic knowledge may be defined as linguistic knowledge that can be stated without any reference to whatever the words may refer. Semantic knowledge is linguistic knowledge that does depend on properties of a word's referent.

Correct Sequencing

Stones can't sing beautifully; in fact, they can't sing at all! This is semantic knowledge because it states a regularity that depends on the referent of the word stones. If the referent of stones was the Welsh people, then many would not find the sentence semantically anomalous. Charles Fillmore was one of the first linguists to introduce a representation of linguistic knowledge that blurred this strong distinction between syntactic and semantic knowledge of a language. He introduced what was termed case structure grammar and this representation subsequently had considerable influence on psychologists as well as computational linguists.

We see that, linguistic knowledge is organized around verbs or more precisely, a verb sense. (A verb may have more than one sense or meaning and these are represented separately. For example, to run for office is a different sense of run than to run to first base, and these would be two different representations in a case grammar.) Associated with each verb sense is a set of cases. Some of the cases are obligatoryand others are optional. A case is obligatory if the sentence would be ungrammatical if it were omitted.

There are two notable features that are illustrated in the example representation. First, the cases associated with a verb seem to be associated with questions that we one would naturally ask about an event. Who did what to whom when? The representation seems well adapted to the retrieval of the information provided in a sentence. This feature was particularly appealing to psychologists and computational linguists.

A second interesting feature is that the same representation is provided to both the active and passive forms of the sentence. In the figure the active form is shown above the representation and the passive form below. This feature would be consistent with a finding that we rarely recall the exact syntactic form of the sentence but do recall the basic information provided by the sentence.

In the next figure to the right, the green portion illustrates the basic case structure representation of the sentence information. But, when we hear this sentence we also know the set of inferences shown; namely, that John had a book at some time b andJim has the book at some time a and timeb is before time. The blue box illustrates the way in which these inferences can be linked to the case structure representation. The case structure representation served to inspire the development of what was termed a frame-based representation in AI research. Within a frame-base architecture it is quite natural to have these type of inferences triggered by the representation of the sentence. (For those familiar with certain types of Object Oriented programming language; the frame-based architecture in AI was a somewhat more complicated and elabourated programming environment.)

One of the consistent findings in human sentence understanding is that we seem to draw these inferences automatically. And, we rarely remember whether or not such information was explicitly stated in the sentence. This observation is consistent with some of the features of a frame-based representation as suggested by case structure grammar

Another aspect of the case grammar representation is that it can be effectively used to parse incomplete or noisy sentences. For example, while John gave book is not grammatical, it is still possible to create an appropriate case grammar parse of this string of words. However, case grammar is not a particularly good representation for use in parsing sentences that involve complex syntactic constructions.

3

Digital Signal Processing

BACKGROUND

In 15 years, the power of personal computers has increased by a factor of nearly one-thousand. By all accounts, it will increase by another factor of one-thousand in the next 15 years. This tremendous power has changed the way science and engineering is done, and there is no better example of this than Digital Signal Processing. In the early 1980s, DSP was taught as a graduate level course in electrical engineering. A decade later, DSP had become a standard part of the undergraduate curriculum.

Today, DSP is a basic skill needed by scientists and engineers in many fields. Unfortunately, DSP education has been slow to adapt to this change. Nearly all DSP textbooks are still written in the traditional electrical engineering style of detailed and rigorous mathematics. DSP is incredibly powerful, but if you can't understand it, you can't use it. Digital Signal Processing is one of the most powerful technologies that will shape science and engineering in the twenty-first century.

Revolutionary changes have already been made in a broad range of fields: communications, medical imaging, radar and sonar, high fidelity music reproduction, and oil prospecting, to name just a few. Each of these areas has developed a deep DSP technology, with its own algorithms, mathematics, and specialized techniques. This combination of breath and depth makes it impossible for any one individual to master all of the DSP technology that has been developed. DSP education involves two tasks: learning general concepts that apply to the field as a whole, and learning specialized techniques for your particular area of interest. This chapter starts our journey into the world of Digital Signal Processing by describing the dramatic effect that DSP has made in several diverse fields. The revolution has begun.

Digital Signal Processing is distinguished from other areas in computer science by the unique type of data it uses: signals. In most cases, these signals originate as sensory data from the real world: seismic vibrations, visual images, sound waves, etc. DSP is the mathematics, the algorithms, and the techniques used to manipulate these signals after they have been converted into a digital form. It includes a wide variety of goals, such as: enhancement of visual images, recognition and generation of speech, compression of data for storage and transmission, etc. Suppose we attach an analog-to-digital converter to a computer and use it to acquire a chunk of real world data.

The roots of DSP are in the 1960s and 1970s when digital computers first became available. Computers were expensive during this era, and DSP was limited to only a few critical applications. Pioneering efforts were made in four key areas: radar and sonar, where national security was at risk; oil exploration, where large amounts of money could be made; space exploration, where the data are irreplaceable; and medical imaging, where lives could be saved. The personal computer revolution of the 1980s and 1990s caused DSP to explode with new applications.

Rather than being motivated by military and government needs, DSP was suddenly driven by the commercial marketplace. Anyone who thought they could make money in the rapidly expanding field was suddenly a DSP vender. DSP reached the public in such products as: mobile telephones, compact disc players, and electronic voice mail. DSP has revolutionized many areas in science and engineering. A few of these diverse applications are shown here. This technological revolution occurred from the top-down. In the early 1980s, DSP was taught as a graduate level course in electrical engineering. A decade later, DSP had become a standard part of the undergraduate curriculum. Today, DSP is a basic skill needed by scientists and engineers in many fields. As an analogy, DSP can be compared to a previous technological revolution: electronics. While still the realm of electrical engineering, nearly every scientist and engineer has some background in basic circuit design. Without it, they would be lost in the technological world. DSP has the same future.

This recent history is more than a curiosity; it has a tremendous impact on your ability to learn and use DSP. Suppose you encounter a DSP problem, and turn to textbooks or other publications to find a solution. What you will typically find is page after page of equations, obscure mathematical symbols, and unfamiliar terminology. It's a nightmare! Much of the DSP literature is baffling even to those experienced in the field. It's not that there is anything wrong with this material, it is just intended for a very specialized audience. State-of-the-art researchers need this kind of detailed mathematics to understand the theoretical implications of the work.

APPLICATIONS

TELECOMUNICATIONS

Telecommunications is about transferring information from one location to another. It includes many forms of information: telephone conversations, television signals, computer files, and other types of data. To transfer the information, you need a channel between the two locations. This may be a wire pair, radio signal, optical fibre, etc. Telecommunications companies receive payment for transferring their customer's information, while they must pay to establish and maintain thc channcl.

The financial bottom line is simple: the more information they can pass through a single channel, the more money they make. DSP has revolutionized the telecommunications industry in many areas: signaling tone generation and detection, frequency band shifting, filtering to remove power line hum, etc. Three specific examples from the telephone network will be discussed here: multiplexing, compression, and echo control.

Multiplexing

There are approximately one billion telephones in the world. At the press of a few buttons, switching networks allow any one of these to be connected to any other in only a few seconds. The immensity of this task is mind boggling! Until the 1960s, a connection between two telephones required passing the analog voice signals through mechanical switches and amplifiers. One connection required one pair of wires. In comparison, DSP converts audio signals into a stream of serial digital data. Since bits can be easily intertwined and later separated, many telephone conversations can be transmitted on a single channel. For example, a telephone standard known as the T-carrier system can simultaneously transmit 24 voice signals.

Each voice signal is sampled 8000 times per second using an 8 bit companded (logarithmic compressed) analog-to-digital conversion. This results in each voice signal being represented as 64,000 bits/sec, and all 24 channels being contained in 1.544 megabits/sec. This signal can be transmitted about 6000 feet using ordinary telephone lines of 22 gauge copper wire, a typical interconnection distance. The financial advantage of digital transmission is enormous. Wire and analog switches are expensive; digital logic gates are cheap.

Compression

When a voice signal is digitized at 8000 samples/sec, most of the digital information is redundant. That is, the information carried by any one sample is largely duplicated by the neighbouring samples. Dozens of DSP algorithms have been developed to convert digitized voice signals into data streams that require fewer bits/sec. These are called data compression algorithms. Matching uncompression algorithms are used to restore the signal to its original form. These algorithms vary in the amount of compression achieved and the resulting sound quality. In general, reducing the data rate from 64 kilobits/sec to 32 kilobits/sec results in no loss of sound quality.

When compressed to a data rate of 8 kilobits/sec, the sound is noticeably affected, but still usable for long distance telephone networks. The highest achievable compression is about 2 kilobits/sec, resulting in sound that is highly distorted but usable for some applications such as military and undersea communications.

Echoes

Echoes are a serious problem in long distance telephone connections. When you speak into a telephone, a signal representing your voice travels to the connecting receiver, where a portion of it returns as an echo. If the connection is within a few hundred miles, the elapsed time for receiving the echo is only a few milliseconds. The human ear is accustomed to hearing echoes with these small time delays, and the connection sounds quite normal. As the distance becomes larger, the echo becomes increasingly noticeable and irritating.

The delay can be several hundred milliseconds for intercontinental communications, and is particularity objectionable. Digital Signal Processing attacks this type of problem by measuring the returned signal and generating an appropriate antisignal to cancel the offending echo. This same technique allows speakerphone users to hear and speak at the same time without fighting audio feedback (squealing). It can also be used to reduce environmental noise by canceling it with digitally generated antinoise.

Audio Processing

The two principal human senses are vision and hearing. Correspondingly, much of DSP is related to image and audio processing. People listen to both music and speech. DSP has made revolutionary changes in both these areas.

Music

The path leading from the musician's microphone to the audiophile's speaker is remarkably long. Digital data representation is important to prevent the degradation commonly associated with analog storage and manipulation. This is very familiar to anyone who has compared the musical quality of cassette tapes with compact disks. In a typical scenario, a musical piece is recorded in a sound studio on multiple channels or tracks. In some cases, this even involves recording individual instruments and singers separately. This is done to give the sound engineer greater flexibility in creating the final product.

The complex process of combining the individual tracks into a final product is called mix down. DSP can provide several important functions during mix down, including: filtering, signal addition and subtraction, signal editing, etc. One of the most interesting DSP applications in music preparation is artificial reverberation. If the individual channels are simply added together, the resulting piece sounds frail and diluted, much as if the musicians were playing outdoors. This is because listeners are greatly influenced by the echo or reverberation content of the music, which is usually minimized in the sound studio.

DSP allows artificial echoes and reverberation to be added during mix down to simulate various ideal listening environments. Echoes with delays of a few hundred milliseconds give the impression of cathedral like locations. Adding echoes with delays of 10-20 milliseconds provide the perception of more modest size listening rooms.

Speech Generation

Speech generation and recognition are used to communicate between humans and machines. Rather than using your hands and eyes, you use your mouth and ears. This is very convenient when your hands and eyes should be doing something else, such as: driving a car, performing surgery, or (unfortunately) firing your weapons at the enemy. Two approaches are used for computer generated speech:

digital recording and vocal tract simulation. In digital recording, the voice of a human speaker is digitized and stored, usually in a compressed form. During playback, the stored data are uncompressed and converted back into an analog signal. An entire hour of recorded speech requires only about three megabytes of storage, well within the capabilities of even small computer systems. This is the most common method of digital speech generation used today.

Vocal tract simulators are more complicated, trying to mimic the physical mechanisms by which humans create speech. The human vocal tract is an acoustic cavity with resonate frequencies determined by the size and shape of the chambers. Sound originates in the vocal tract in one of two basic ways, called voiced and fricative sounds. With voiced sounds, vocal cord vibration produces near periodic pulses of air into the vocal cavities. In comparison, fricative sounds originate from the noisy air turbulence at narrow constrictions, such as the teeth and lips. Vocal tract simulators operate by generating digital signals that resemble these two types of excitation.

The characteristics of the resonate chamber are simulated by passing the excitation signal through a digital filter with similar resonances. This approach was used in one of the very early DSP success stories, the Speak and Spell, a widely sold electronic learning aid for children.

Speech Recognition

Speech recognition is a classic example of things that the human brain does well, but digital computers do poorly. Digital computers can store and recall vast amounts of data, perform mathematical calculations at blazing speeds, and do repetitive tasks without becoming bored or inefficient. Unfortunately, present day computers perform very poorly when faced with raw sensory data. Teaching a computer to send you a monthly electric bill is easy. Teaching the same computer to understand your voice is a major undertaking. Digital Signal Processing generally approaches the problem of voice recognition in two steps: feature extraction followed by feature matching. Each word in the incoming audio signal is isolated and then analysed to identify the type of excitation and resonate frequencies. These parametres are then compared with previous examples of spoken words to identify the closest match.

Often, these systems are limited to only a few hundred words; can only accept speech with distinct pauses between words; and must be retrained for each individual speaker. While this is adequate for many commercial applications, these limitations are humbling when compared to the abilities of human hearing. There is a great deal of work to be done in this area, with tremendous financial rewards for those that produce successful commercial products.

Echo Location

A common method of obtaining information about a remote object is to bounce a wave off of it. For example, radar operates by transmitting pulses of radio waves, and examining the received signal for echoes from aircraft. In sonar, sound waves are transmitted through the water to detect submarines and other submerged objects. Geophysicists have long probed the earth by setting off explosions and listening for the echoes from deeply buried layers of rock. While these applications have a common thread, each has its own specific problems and needs. Digital Signal Processing has produced revolutionary changes in all three areas.

Radar

Radar is an acronym for Radio Detection And Ranging. In the simplest radar system, a radio transmitter produces a pulse of radio frequency energy a few microseconds long. This pulse is fed into a highly directional antenna, where the resulting radio wave propagates away at the speed of light.

Aircraft in the path of this wave will reflect a small portion of the energy back towards a receiving antenna, situated near the transmission site. The distance to the object is calculated from the elapsed time between the transmitted pulse and the received echo. The direction to the object is found more simply; you know where you pointed the directional antenna when the echo was received. The operating range of a radar system is determined by two parametres: how much energy is in the initial pulse, and the noise level of the radio receiver. Unfortunately, increasing the energy in the pulse usually requires making the pulse longer. In turn, the longer pulse reduces the accuracy and precision of the elapsed time measurement.

This results in a conflict between two important parametres: the ability to detect objects at long range, and the ability to accurately determine an object's distance. DSP has revolutionized radar in three areas, all of which relate to this basic problem. First, DSP can compress the pulse after it is received, providing better distance determination without reducing the operating range. Second, DSP can filter the received signal to decrease the noise. This increases the range, without degrading the distance determination. Third, DSP enables the rapid selection and generation of different pulse shapes and lengths. Among other things, this allows the pulse to be optimized for a particular detection problem.

Now the impressive part: much of this is done at a sampling rate comparable to the radio frequency used, at high as several hundred megahertz! When it comes to radar, DSP is as much about high-speed hardware design as it is about algorithms.

Sonar

Sonar is an acronym for Sound NAvigation and Ranging. It is divided into two categories, active and passive. In active sonar, sound pulses between 2 kHz and 40 kHz are transmitted into the water, and the resulting echoes detected and analysed. Uses of active sonar include: detection and localization of undersea bodies, navigation, communication, and mapping the sea floor.

A maximum operating range of 10 to 100 kilometres is typical. In comparison, passive sonar simply listens to underwater sounds, which includes: natural turbulence, marine life, and mechanical sounds from submarines and surface vessels. Since passive sonar emits no energy, it is ideal for covert operations. You want to detect the other guy, without him detecting you. The most important application of passive sonar is in military surveillance systems that detect and track submarines.

Passive sonar typically uses lower frequencies than active sonar because they propagate through the water with less absorption. Detection ranges can be thousands of kilometres. DSP has revolutionized sonar in many of the same areas as radar: pulse generation, pulse compression, and filtering of detected signals. In one view, sonar is simpler than radar because of the lower frequencies involved. In another view, sonar is more difficult than radar because the environment is much less uniform and stable.

Sonar systems usually employ extensive arrays of transmitting and receiving elements, rather than just a single channel. By properly controlling and mixing the signals in these many elements, the sonar system can steer the emitted pulse to the desired location and determine the direction that echoes are received from. To handle these multiple channels, sonar systems require the same massive DSP computing power as radar.

Reflection Seismology

As early as the 1920s, geophysicists discovered that the structure of the earth's crust could be probed with sound. Prospectors could set off an explosion and record the echoes from boundary layers more than ten kilometres below the surface. These echo seismograms were interpreted by the raw eye to map the subsurface structure. The reflection seismic method rapidly became the primary method for locating petroleum and mineral deposits, and remains so today.

In the ideal case, a sound pulse sent into the ground produces a single echo for each boundary layer the pulse passes through. Unfortunately, the situation is not usually this simple. Each echo returning to the surface must pass through all the other boundary layers above where it originated. This can result in the echo bouncing between layers, giving rise to echoes of echoes being detected at the surface. These secondary echoes can make the detected signal very complicated and difficult to interpret. Digital Signal Processing has been widely used since the 1960s to isolate the primary from the secondary echoes in reflection seismograms. How did the early geophysicists manage without DSP? The answer is simple: they looked in easy places, where multiple reflections were minimized. DSP allows oil to be found in difficult locations, such as under the ocean.

Image Processing

Images are signals with special characteristics. First, they are a measure of a parametre over space (distance), while most signals are a measure of a parametre over time. Second, they contain a great deal of information.

For example, more than 10 megabytes can be required to store one second of television video. This is more than a thousand times greater than for a similar length voice signal. Third, the final judge of quality is often a subjective human evaluation, rather than an objective criteria. These special characteristics have made image processing a distinct subgroup within DSP.

DSP FUNDAMENTALS

DSP techniques are based on a divide-and-conquer strategy called superposition. The signal being processed is broken into simple components, each component is processed individually, and the results reunited. This approach has the tremendous power of breaking a single complicated problem into many easy ones. Superposition can only be used with linear systems, a term meaning that certain mathematical rules apply. Fortunately, most of the applications encountered in science and engineering fall into this category.

This chapter presents the foundation of DSP: what it means for a system to be linear, various ways for breaking signals into simpler components, and how superposition provides a variety of signal processing techniques.

Signals and Systems

A signal is a description of how one parametre varies with another parametre. For instance, voltage changing over time in an electronic circuit, or brightness varying with distance in an image. A system is any process that produces an output signal in response to an input signal.Continuous systems input and output continuous signals, such as in analog electronics.

Discrete systems input and output discrete signals, such as computer programmes that manipulate the values stored in arrays.

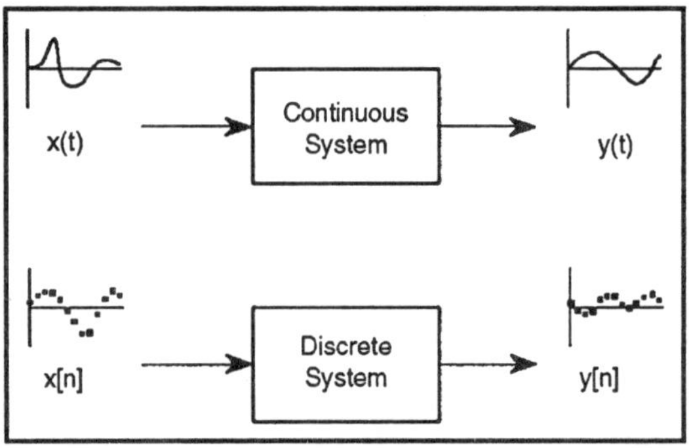

Terminology for signals and systems. A system is any process that generates an output signal in response to an input signal. Continuous signals are usually represented with parentheses, while discrete signals use brackets. All signals use lower case letters, reserving the upper case for the frequency domain. Unless there is a better name available, the input signal is called: x(t) or x[n], while the output is called: y(t) or y[n].

Signals and systems are frequently discussed without knowing the exact parametres being represented. This is the same as using x and y in algebra, without assigning a physical meaning to the variables. This brings in a fourth rule for naming signals. If a more descriptive name is not available, the input signal to a discrete system is usually called: x[n], and the output signal: y[n]. For continuous systems, the signals: x(t) and y(t) are used.There are many reasons for wanting to understand a system. For example, you may want to design a system to remove noise in an electrocardiogram, sharpen an out-of-focus image, or remove echoes in an audio recording. In other cases, the system might have a distortion or interfering effect that you need to characterize or measure.

For instance, when you speak into a telephone, you expect the other person to hear something that resembles your voice. Unfortunately, the input signal to a transmission line is seldom identical to the output signal. If you understand how the transmission line (the system) is changing the signal, maybe you can compensate for its effect. In still other cases, the system may represent some physical process that you want to study or analyse. Radar and sonar are good examples of this. These methods operate by comparing the transmitted and reflected signals to find the characteristics of a remote object. In terms of system theory, the problem is to find the system that changes the transmitted signal into the received signal.

At first glance, it may seem an overwhelming task to understand all of the possible systems in the world. Fortunately, most useful systems fall into a category called linear systems. This fact is extremely important. Without the linear system concept, we would be forced to examine the individual characteristics of many unrelated systems. With this approach, we can focus on the traits of the linear system category as a whole. Our first task is to identify what properties make a system linear, and how they fit into the everyday notion of electronics, software, and other signal processing systems.

Requirements for Linearity

A system is called linear if it has two mathematical properties: homogeneity and additivity. If you can show that a system has both properties, then you have proven that the system is linear. Likewise, if you can show that a system doesn't have one or both properties, you have proven that it isn't linear. A third property, shift invariance, is not a strict requirement for linearity, but it is a mandatory property for most DSP techniques. When you see the term linear system used in DSP, you should assume it includes shift invariance unless you have reason to believe otherwise.

These three properties form the mathematics of how linear system theory is defined and used. Later in this chapter we will look at more intuitive ways of understanding linearity. For now, let's go through these formal mathematical properties. Homogeneity means that a change in the input signal's amplitude results in a corresponding change in the output signal's amplitude. In mathematical terms, if an input signal of x[n] results in an output signal of y[n], an input of k x[n] results in an output of k y[n], for any input signal and constant, k.

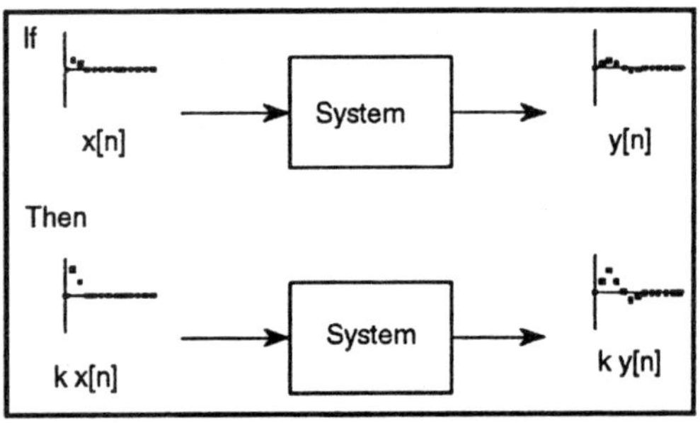

Definition of homogeneity. A system is said to be homogeneous if an amplitude change in the input results in an identical amplitude change in the output. That is, if x[n] results in y[n], then kx[n] results in ky[n], for any signal, x[n], and any constant, k.

A simple resistor provides a good example of both homogenous and nonhomogeneous systems. If the input to the system is the voltage across the resistor, v(t), and the output from the system is the current through the resistor, i(t), the system is homogeneous. Ohm's law guarantees this; if the voltage is increased or decreased, there will be a corresponding increase or decrease in the current.

Now, consider another system where the input signal is the voltage across the resistor, v(t), but the output signal is the power being dissipated in the resistor, p(t). Since power is proportional to the square of the voltage, if the input signal is increased by a factor of two, the output signal is increase by a factor of four. This system is not homogeneous and therefore cannot be linear.

Consider a system where an input of x1[n] produces an output of y1[n]. Further suppose that a different input, x2[n], produces another output, y2[n]. The system is said to be additive, if an input of x1[n]+x2[n] results in an output of y1[n]+y2[n], for all possible input signals. In words, signals added at the input produce signals that are added at the output.

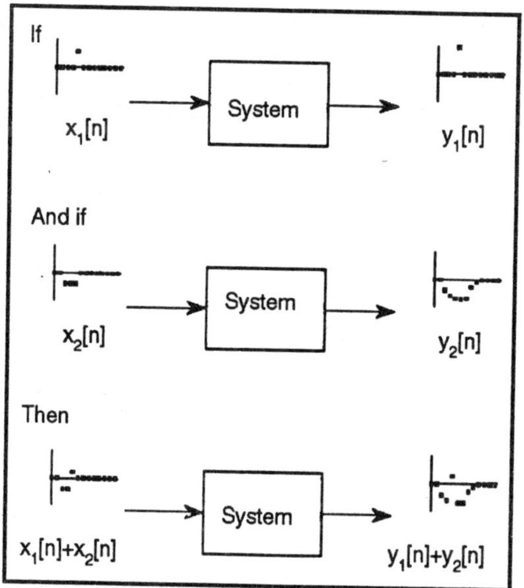

Definition of additivity. A system is said to be additive if added signals pass through it without interacting. Another important definition is shift invariance, shift invariance means that a shift in the input signal will result in nothing more than an identical shift in the output signal. In more formal terms, if an input signal of x[n] results in an output of y [n], an input signal of x[n+s] results in an output of y[n+s], for any input signal and any constant, s.

Pay particular notice to how the mathematics of this shift is written, it will be used in upcoming chapters. By adding a constant, s, to the independent variable, n, the waveform can be advanced or retarded in the horizontal direction. For example, when s=2, the signal is shifted left by two samples; when s=-2, the signal is shifted right by two samples.

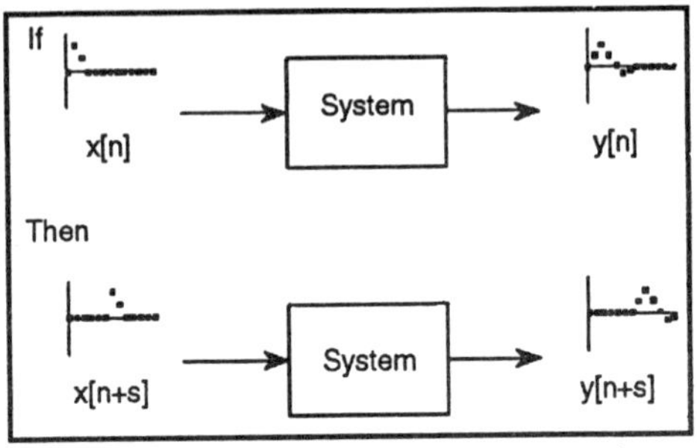

Static Linearity and Sinusoidal Fidelity

Static linearity defines how a linear system reacts when the signals aren't changing, *i.e.*, when they are DC or static. The static response of a linear system is very simple: the output is the input multiplied by a constant. That is, a graph of the possible input values plotted against the corresponding output values is a straight line that passes through the origin.

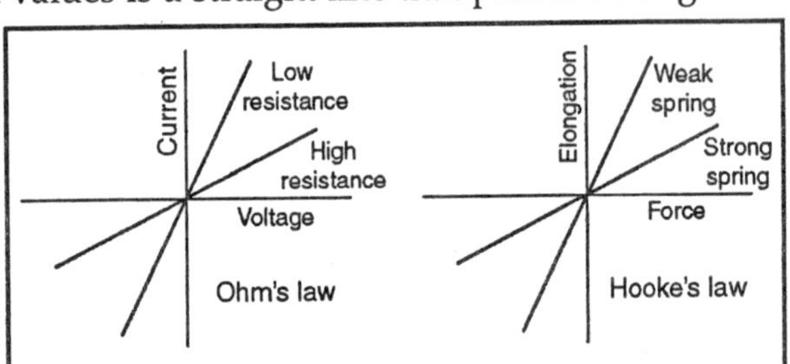

In (a), Ohm's law: the current through a resistor is equal to the voltage across the resistor divided by the resistance. In (b), Hooke's law: The elongation of a spring is equal to the applied force multiplied by the spring stiffness coefficient.

All linear systems have the property of static linearity. The opposite is usually true, but not always. There are systems that show static linearity, but are not linear with respect to changing signals. However, a very common class of systems can be completely understood with static linearity alone. In these systems it doesn't matter if the input signal is static or changing. These are called memoryless systems, because the output depends only on the present state of the input, and not on its history. For example, the instantaneous current in a resistor depends only on the instantaneous voltage across it, and not on how the signals came to be the value they are. If a system has static linearity, and is memoryless, then the system must be linear. This provides an important way to understand (and prove) the linearity of these simple systems.

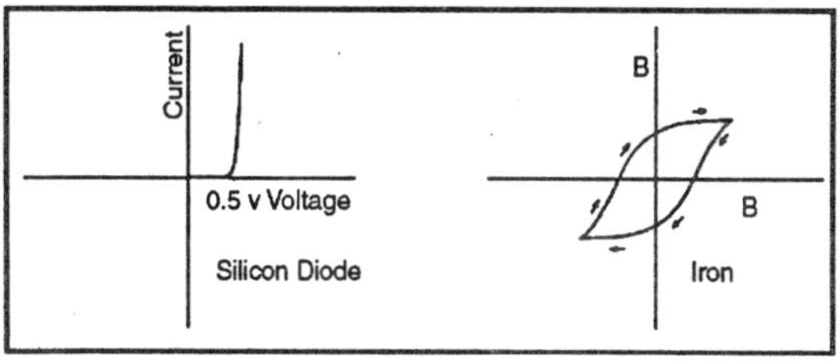

Two examples of DC nonlinearity. In (a), a silicon diode has an exponential relationship between voltage and current. In (b), the relationship between magnetic intensity, H, and flux density, B, in iron depends on the history of the sampl a behaviour called hysteresis.

An important characteristic of linear systems is how they behave with sinusoids, a property we will call sinusoidal fidelity: If the input to a linear system is a sinusoidal wave, the output will also be a sinusoidal wave, and at exactly the same frequency as the input. Sinusoids are the only waveform that have this property. For instance, there is no reason to expect that a square wave entering a linear system will produce a square wave on the output.

Although a sinusoid on the input guarantees a sinusoid on the output, the two may be different in amplitude and phase. This should be familiar from your knowledge of electronics: a circuit can be described by its frequency response, graphs of how the circuit's gain and phase vary with frequency.

Now for the reverse question: If a system always produces a sinusoidal output in response to a sinusoidal input, is the system guaranteed to be linear? The answer is no, but the exceptions are rare and usually obvious. For example, imagine an evil demon hiding inside a system, with the goal of trying to mislead you. The demon has an oscilloscope to observe the input signal, and a sine wave generator to produce an output signal. When you feed a sine wave into the input, the demon quickly measures the frequency and adjusts his signal generator to produce a corresponding output. Of course, this system is not linear, because it is not additive. To show this, place the sum of two sine waves into the system. The demon can only respond with a single sine wave for the output. This example is not as contrived as you might think; phase lock loops operate in much this way.

Convolution

Convolution is a mathematical way of combining two signals to form a third signal. It is the single most important technique in Digital Signal Processing. Using the strategy of impulse decomposition, systems are described by a signal called the impulse response.

Convolution is important because it relates the three signals of interest: the input signal, the output signal, and the impulse response. This chapter presents convolution from two different viewpoints, called the input side algorithm and the output side algorithm. Convolution provides the mathematical framework for DSP.

The Delta Function and Impulse Response

An impulse is a signal composed of all zeros, except a single nonzero point. In effect, impulse decomposition provides a way to analyse signals one sample at a time. The previous chapter also presented the fundamental concept of DSP: the input signal is decomposed into simple additive components, each of these components is passed through a linear system, and the resulting output components are synthesized (added).

The signal resulting from this divide-and-conquer procedure is identical to that obtained by directly passing the original signal through the system. While many different decompositions are possible, two form the backbone of signal processing: impulse decomposition and Fourier decomposition. When impulse decomposition is used, the procedure can be described by a mathematical operation called convolution. In this chapter (and most of the following ones) we will only be dealing with discrete signals. Convolution also applies to continuous signals, but the mathematics is more complicated.

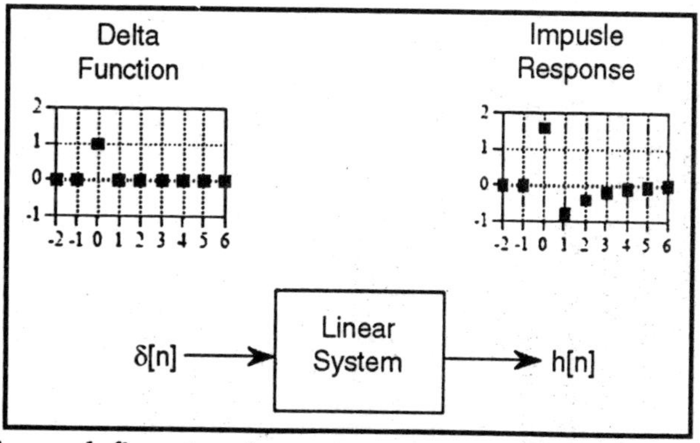

Figure defines two important terms used in DSP. The first is the delta function, symbolized by the Greek letter delta, [n]. The delta function is a normalized impulse, that is, sample number zero has a value of one, while all other samples have a value of zero. For this reason, the delta function is frequently called the unit impulse.

Let's summarize this way of understanding how a system changes an input signal into an output signal. First, the input signal can be decomposed into a set of impulses, each of which can be viewed as a scaled and shifted delta function. Second, the output resulting from each impulse is a scaled and shifted version of the impulse response. Third, the overall output signal can be found by adding these scaled and shifted impulse responses.

In other words, if we know a system's impulse response, then we can calculate what the output will be for any possible input signal. This means we know everything about the system. There is nothing more that can be learned about a linear system's characteristics. The impulse response goes by a different name in some applications. If the system being considered is a filter, the impulse response is called the filter kernel, the convolution kernel, or simply, the kernel. In image processing, the impulse response is called the point spread function. While these terms are used in slightly different ways, they all mean the same thing, the signal produced by a system when the input is a delta function

Convolution is a formal mathematical operation, just as multiplication, addition, and integration. Addition takes two numbers and produces a third number, while convolution takes two signals and produces a third signal. Convolution is used in the mathematics of many fields, such as probability and statistics.

In linear systems, convolution is used to describe the relationship between three signals of interest: the input signal, the impulse response, and the output signal.

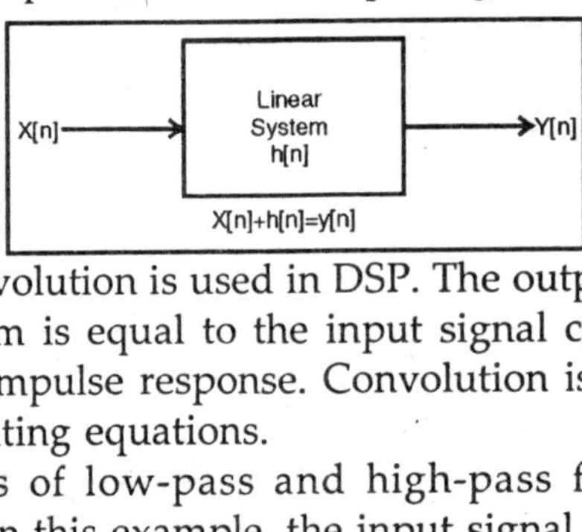

How convolution is used in DSP. The output signal from a linear system is equal to the input signal convolved with the system's impulse response. Convolution is denoted by a star when writing equations.

Examples of low-pass and high-pass filtering using convolution. In this example, the input signal is a few cycles of a sine wave plus a slowly rising ramp. These two components are separated by using properly selected impulse responses. Figure shows convolution being used for low-pass and high-pass filtering.

The example input signal is the sum of two components: three cycles of a sine wave (representing a high frequency), plus a slowly rising ramp (composed of low frequencies). In (a), the impulse response for the low-pass filter is a smooth arch, resulting in only the slowly changing ramp waveform being passed to the output. Similarly, the high-pass filter, (b), allows only the more rapidly changing sinusoid to pass.

The Input

Convolution using the input side algorithm:

```
DIM X[80] 'The input signal, 81 points
DIM H[30] 'The impulse response, 31 points
DIM Y[110] 'The output signal, 111 points
GOSUB Mythical subroutine to load X[] and
    H[]
FOR I% = 0 TO 110 'Zero the output array
Y(I%) = 0
NEXT I%
FOR I% = 0 TO 80 Loop for each point in X[]
FOR J% = 0 TO 30 Loop for each point in H[]
Y[I%+J%] = Y[I%+J%] + X[I%]*H[J%]
NEXT J% NEXT I% '(we must remember * is also
    denoted as convolution! but in this case
    is multiplication)
GOSUB Mythical subroutine to store Y[]
END
```

The Output

$$y[i] = \sum_{j=0}^{M-1} h[j]x[i-j]$$

This equation is called the convolution sum. It allows each point in the output signal to be calculated independently of all other points in the output signal. The index, i, determines which sample in the output signal is being calculated, and therefore corresponds to the left-right position of the convolution machine. In computer programmes performing convolution, a loop makes this index run through each sample in the output signal. To calculate one of the output samples, the index, j, is used inside of the convolution machine.

Convolution using the output side algorithm:

```
DIM X[80] 'The input signal, 81 points
DIM H[30] 'The impulse response, 31 points
DIM Y[110] 'The output signal, 111 points
GOSUB Mythical subroutine to load X[] and
    H[]
```

```
FOR I% = 0 TO 110 Loop for each point in Y[]
Y[I%] = 0 Zero the sample in output array
FOR J% = 0 TO 30 Loop for each point in H[]
IF (I%-J% < 0) THEN GOTO 240
IF (I%-J% > 80) THEN GOTO 240
Y(I%) = Y(I%) + H(J%) t X(I%-J%)
NEXT J%
NEXT I%
GOSUB Mythical subroutine to store Y[]
END
```

GENETIC ALGORITHMS

INTRODUCTION

Genetic Aalgorithms has three major applications, namely, intelligent search, optimization and machine learning. Currently, Genetic Algorithms is used along with neural networks and fuzzy logic for solving more complex problems. Because of their joint usage in many problems, these together are often referred to by a generic name: 'soft-computing'.

A Genetic Algorithms operates through a simple cycle of stages:

- Creation of a 'population' of strings,
- Evaluation of each string,
- Selection of best strings and
- Genetic manipulation to create new population of strings.

The cycle of a Genetic Algorithms is presented below,

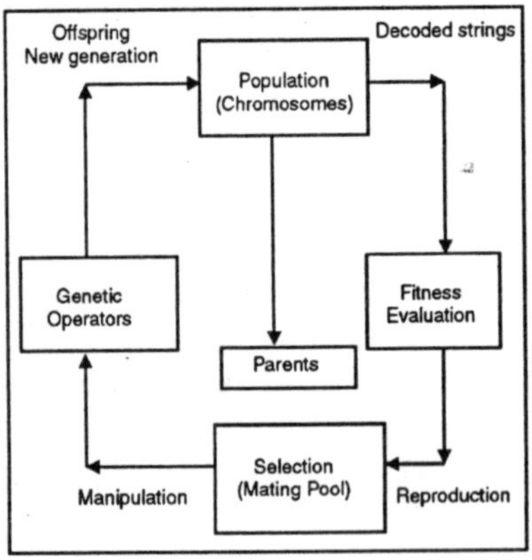

Each cycle in Genetic Algorithms produces a new generation of possible solutions for a given problem. In the first phase, an initial population, describing representatives of the potential solution, is created to initiate the search process. The elements of the population are encoded into bit-strings, called chromosomes.

The performance of the strings, often called fitness, is then evaluated with the help of some functions, representing the constraints of the problem. Depending on the fitness of the chromosomes, they are selected for a subsequent genetic manipulation process. It should be noted that the selection process is mainly responsible for assuring survival of the best-fit individuals.

After selection of the population strings is over, the genetic manipulation process consisting of two steps is carried out. In the first step, the crossover operation that recombines the bits (genes) of each two selected strings (chromosomes) is executed. Various types of crossover operators are found in the literature. The single point and two points crossover operations are illustrated.

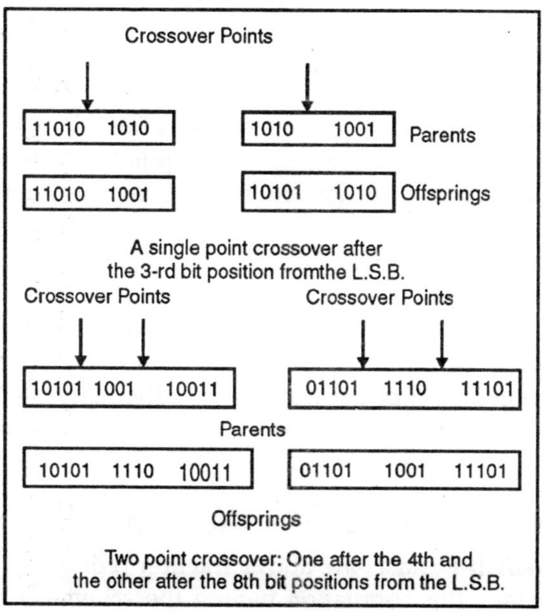

A single point crossover after the 3-rd bit position fromthe L.S.B.

Two point crossover: One after the 4th and the other after the 8th bit positions from the L.S.B.

The crossover points of any two chromosomes are selected randomly. The second step in the genetic manipulation process is termed mutation, where the bits at one or more randomly selected positions of the chromosomes are altered. The mutation process helps to overcome trapping at local maxima. The offsprings produced by the genetic manipulation process are the next population to be evaluated.

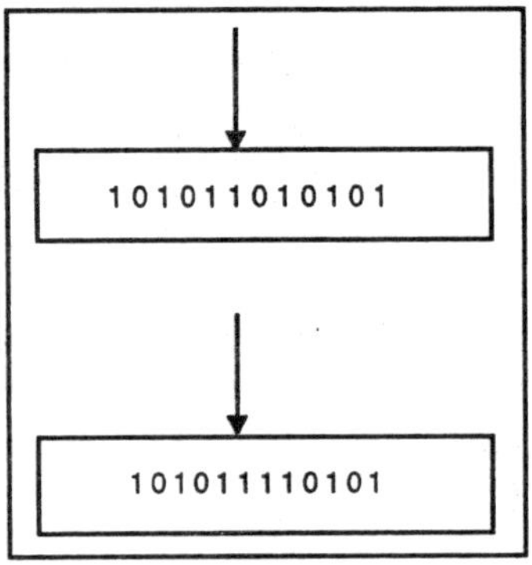

Fig. Mutation of a Chromosome at the 5th Bit Position

EXPLANATION

To explain Holland's observation in a deterministic manner let us presume the following assumptions.

- There are no recombination or alternations to genes.
- Initially, a fraction f of the population possesses the schema S and those individuals reproduce at a fixed rate r.
- All other individuals lacking schema S reproduce at a rate $s < r$.

Thus with an initial population size of N, after t generations, we find Nf r t individuals possessing schema S and the population of the rest of the individuals is N(1 - f) st. Therefore, the fraction of the individuals with schema S is given by,

$$\left(Nfr^t\right)/[N(1-f)s^t + Nfr^t] = f(r/s)^{t/}[1+f\{(r/s)^t - 1\}$$

For small t and f, the above fraction reduces to f (r/s) t, which means the population having the schema S increases exponentially at a rate (r/s). A stochastic proof of the above property will be presented shortly, vide a well-known theorem, called the fundamental theorem of Genetic algorithm.

GENETIC ALGORITHMS

For presentation of the fundamental theorem of Genetic Algorithms, the following terminologies are defined in order.

Definition

The order of a schema H, denoted by O(H), is the number of fixed positions in the schema.

Fundamental Theorem of Genetic Algorithms

Let the population size be N, which contains mH (t) samples of schema H at generation t. Among the selection strategies, the most common is the proportional selection. In proportional selection, the number of copies of chromosomes selected for mating is proportional to their respective fitness values. Thus, the principles of proportional selection, a string i is selected with probability,

$$f_i / \sum_{i=1}^{n} f_i$$

where fi is the fitness of string i. Now, the probability that in a single selection a sample of schema H is chosen is described by

$$\sum_{i=1}^{m_H(t)} f_i / \sum_{i=1}^{n} f_i$$

$$= m_H(t) f_H / \sum_{i=1}^{n} f_i$$

where f H is the average fitness of the mH (t) samples of H. Thus, in a total of N selections with replacement, the expected number of samples of schema H in the next generation is given by

$$m_H(t+1) = N\, m_H(t) f_H / \sum_{i=1}^{n} f_i$$

$$= m_H(t) f_H / f_{av}$$

$$\text{where } f_{av} = \sum_{i=1}^{n} f_i / N$$

Where fav is the population average fitness in generation t. The last expression describes that the Genetic algorithm allocates over an increasing number of trials to an above average schema. The effect of crossover and mutation can be incorporated into the analysis by computing the schema survival probabilities of the above average schema.

In crossover operation, a schema H survives if the cross-site falls outside the defining length d(H). If pc is the probability of crossover and L is the word-length of the chromosomes, then the disruption probability of schema H due to crossover is,

$$p_c\, d(H)/(L-1)$$

A schema H, on the other hand, survives mutation, when none of its fixed positions is mutated. If pm is the probability of mutation and O(H) is the order of schema H, then the probability that the schema survives is given by

$$(1-p_m)^{O(H)}$$

$$= 1 - p_m O(H)$$

Therefore, under selection, crossover and mutation, the sample size of schema H in generation (t + 1) is given by,

$$m_H(t+1) \geq \left(m_H(t) f_H / f_{av}\right)$$

$$[1 - p_c\, d(H)/(L-1) - p_m O(H)]$$

The above theorem is called the fundamental theorem of GA or the Schema theorem. It is evident from the Schema theorem that for a given set of values of d(H), O(H), L, pc and pm, the population of schema H at the subsequent generations increases exponentially when fH > fav.

This, in fact, directly follows from the difference equation:

$$m_H(t+1) - m_H(t) \geq (f_H / f_{av} - 1/K) K\, m_H(t)$$

$$\text{where } K = 1 - p_c\, d(H)/(L-1) - p_m O(H)$$

$$\Rightarrow \Delta m_H(t) \geq K(f_H / f_{av} - 1/K)\, m_H(t)$$

Replacing Δ by (E -1), where E is the extended difference operator, we find

$$(E-1-K_1)m_H(t) \geq 0$$

$$\text{where } K_1 = K(f_H / f_{av} - 1/K)$$

Since m H (t) in equation (E-1-K1)mH(t)≥0 is positive, E ≥ (1 +K1).

Thus, the solution of (15.12) is given by,

$$m_H(t) \geq A(1+K_1)^t$$

where A is a constant.

Setting the boundary condition at t = 0, and substituting the value of K1 by therein, we finally have:

$$m_H(t) \geq m_H(0)(K f_H / f_{av})^t$$

Since K is a positive number, and f H/fav > 1, mH (t) grows exponentially with iterations. The process of exponential increase of mH (t) continues until some iteration r, when fH approaches fav. This is all about the proof of the schema theorem.

MARKOV MODEL

For the sake of understanding, let us now consider the population size = 3 and the chromosomes are 2-bit patterns, as presumed earlier.

The set S now takes the following form:

S = {(00, 00, 00), (00, 00, 01), (00, 00, 10), (00, 00, 11),
(00, 01, 00), (00, 01, 01), (00, 01, 10), (00, 01, 11),
....
....
(11, 11, 00), (11, 11, 01), (11, 11, 10), (11, 11, 11) }

It may be noted that the number of elements of the last set S is 64. In general, if the chromosomes have the word length of m bits and the number of chromosomes selected in each Genetic Algorithm cycle is n, then the cardinality of the set S is 2 ^ mn.

The Markov transition probability matrix P for 2-bit strings of population size 2, thus, will have a dimension of (16 x 16), where the element pij of the matrix denotes the probability of transition from i-th to j-th state. A clear idea about the states and their transitions can be formed from fig.

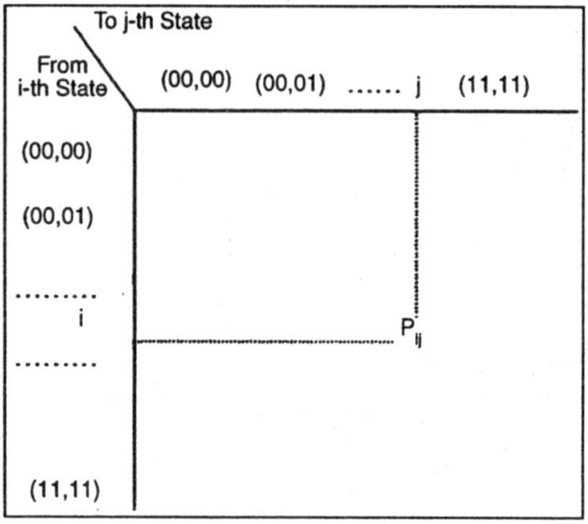

It needs mention that since from a given i-th state, there could be a transition to any 16 j-th states, therefore the row sum of P matrix must be 1. Formally,

$$\sum_{\forall j} P_{ij} = 1$$

for a given i.

Now, let us assume a row vector πt, whose k-th element denotes the probability of occurrence of the k-th state at a given genetic iteration (cycle) t; then πt + 1 can be evaluated by

$$\pi_{t+1} = \pi_t P$$

Thus starting with a given initial row vector π0, one can evaluate the state probability vector after n-th iteration πn by

The behaviour of Genetic Algorihms without mutation can be of the following three types:

1. The GA may converge to one or more absorbing states (*i.e.*, states wherefrom the GA has no transitions to other states).
2. The GA may have transition to some states, wherefrom it may terminate to one or more absorbing states.
3. The GA never reaches an absorbing state.

Taking all the above into account, we thus construct P as a partitioned matrix of the following form:

$$P = \left(\begin{array}{c|c} 1 & 0 \\ \hline R & Q \end{array}\right)$$

where I is an identity matrix of dimension (a x a) that corresponds to the absorbing states; R is a (t x a) transition sub-matrix describing transition to an absorbing state; Q is a (t x t) transition sub-matrix describing transition to transient states and not to an absorbing state and 0 is a null matrix of dimension (t x t). It can be easily shown that Pn for the above matrix P can be found to be as follows.

$$P^n = \begin{pmatrix} 1 & 0 \\ N_n R & Q^n \end{pmatrix}$$

where the n-step transition matrix Nn is given by

$$N_n = 1 + Q + Q^2 + Q^3 + \ldots\ldots + Q^{n-1}$$

As n approaches infinity,

$$\underset{n \to \infty}{Lt} \; N_n = (1 - Q)^{-1}$$

Consequently, as n approaches infinity,

$$\underset{n \to \infty}{Lt} P^n = \begin{pmatrix} 1 & 0 \\ (1-Q)^{-1} R & 0 \end{pmatrix}$$

Goodman has shown that the matrix (I - Q) -1 is guaranteed to exist. Thus given an initial probability vector p 0, the chain will have a transition to an absorbing state with probability 1. Further, there exists a non-zero probability that ab sorbing state will be the globally optimal state.

Since the first 'a' columns for the matrix Pn, for $n \to \infty$, are non-zero and the remaining columns are zero, therefore, the chain must have transition to one of the absorbing states. Further, note that the first 'a' columns of the row vector p n for $n \to \infty$ denote the probability of absorption at different states, and the rest of the columns denote that the probability of transition to nonabsorbing states is zero. Thus probability of transition to absorbing states is one. Formally,

$$\sum_{i=1}^{a} \underset{n \to \infty}{Lt} (\pi_n)_i$$

$$= \sum_{i=1}^{a} \underset{n \to \infty}{Lt} (\pi_0 P^n)_i$$

$$= \sum_{i=1}^{a} \underset{n\to\propto}{\mathrm{Lt}}(\pi_0 \cdot \left(\frac{1}{(1-Q)^{-1}R}\right))i$$

$$=1$$

PROBLEM SOLVING

SEARCH

Problem solving requires two prime considerations: first representation of the problem by an appropriately organized state space and then testing the existence of a well-defined goal state in that space. Identification of the goal state and determination of the optimal path, leading to the goal through one or more transitions from a given starting state.

Thus we can start with some well-known search algorithms, such as the depth first and the breadth first search, with special emphasis on their results of time and space complexity. It then gradually explores the 'heuristic search' algorithms, where the order of visiting the states in a search space is supported by thumb rules, called heuristics, and demonstrates their applications in complex problem solving. It also discusses some intelligent search algorithms for game playing. Common experience reveals that a search problem is associated with two important issues: first 'what to search' and secondly 'where to search'.

The first one is generally referred to as 'the key', while the second one is termed 'search space'. In AI the search space is generally referred to as a collection of states and is thus called state space. Unlike common search space, the state space in most of the problems in AI is not completely known, prior to solving the problem.

So, solving a problem in AI calls for two phases: the generation of the space of states and the searching of the desired problem state in that space. Further, since the whole state space for a problem is quite large, generation of the whole space prior to search may cause a significant blockage of storage, leaving a little for the search part. To overcome this problem, the state space is expanded in steps and the desired state, called 'the goal', is searched after each incremental expansion of the state space. Depending on the methodology of expansion of the state space and consequently the order of visiting the states, search problems are differently named in AI. For example, consider the state space of a problem that takes the form of a tree. Now, if we search the goal along each breadth of the tree, starting from the root and continuing up to the largest depth, we call it breadth first search.

On the other hand, we may sometimes search the goal along the largest depth of the tree, and move up only when further traversal along the depth is not possible. We then attempt to find alternative offspring of the parent of the node (state) last visited. If we visit the nodes of a tree using the above principles to search the goal, the traversal made is called depth first traversal and consequently the search strategy is called depth first search. We will shortly explore the above schemes of traversal in a search space. One important issue, however, needs mention at this stage.

We may note that the order of traversal and hence search by breadth first or depth first manner is generally fixed by their algorithms. Thus once the search space, here the tree, is given, we know the order of traversal in the tree. Such types of traversal are generally called 'deterministic'. On the other hand, there exists an alternative type of search, where we cannot definitely say which node will be traversed next without computing the details in the algorithm. Further, we may have transition to one of many possible states with equal likelihood at an instance of the execution of the search algorithm. Such a type of search, where the order of traversal in the tree is not definite, is generally termed 'nondeterministic'. Most of the search problems in AI are non-deterministic.

APPROACHES

The simplest among them is the generate and test method. The algorithm for the generate and test method can be formally stated as follows:

- Procedure Generate and Test
  - Begin

a. Repeat
   1. Generate a new state and call it current-state;
b. Until current-state = Goal;
- End.

It is clear from the above algorithm that the algorithm continues the possibility of exploring a new state in each iteration of the repeat-until loop and exits only when the current state is equal to the goal. Most important part in the algorithm is to generate a new state. This is not an easy task. If generation of new states is not feasible, the algorithm should be terminated. In our simple algorithm, we, however, did not include this intentionally to keep it simplified.To formalize this, we define a four tuple, called state space, denoted by,

{ nodes, arc, goal, current },

where nodes represent the set of existing states in the search space; an arc denotes an operator applied to an existing state to cause transition to another state; goal denotes the desired state to be identified in the nodes; and current represents the state, now generated for matching with the goal. We will now present two typical algorithms for generating the state space for search. These are depth first search and breadth first search.

Initial Search

The breadth first search algorithm visits the nodes of the tree along its breadth, starting from the level with depth 0 to the maximum depth. It can be easily realised with a queue. For instance, consider the tree, given in figure.In this, the nodes in the tree are traversed following their ascending ordered labels.

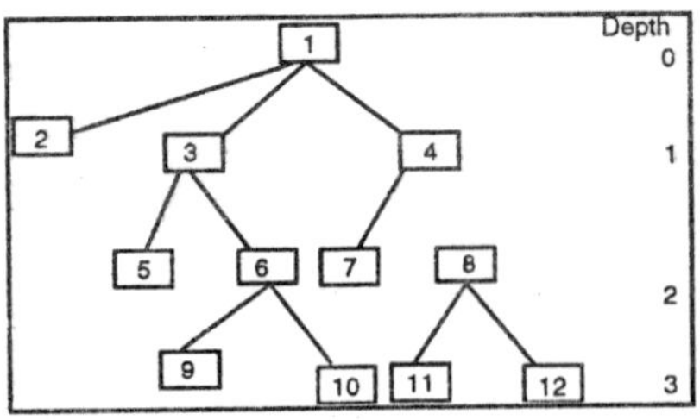

The order of traversal in a tree of depth 3 by breadth first manner. The algorithm for traversal in a tree by depth first manner can be presented with a queue as follows:

Procedure Breadth-first-search

- Begin
- Place the starting node in a queue;
- Repeat
  - Delete queue to get the front element;
  - If the front element of the queue = goal,
  - Return success and stop;
  - Else do
  - Begin
    a. Insert the children of the front element,
    b. If exist, in any order at the rear end of
    c. The queue;
  - End
- Until the queue is empty;
- End.

The breadth first search algorithm, presented above, rests on a simple principle. If the current node is not the goal add the offspring of the current in any order to the rear end of the queue and redefine the front element of the queue as the current. The algorithm terminates, when the goal is found.

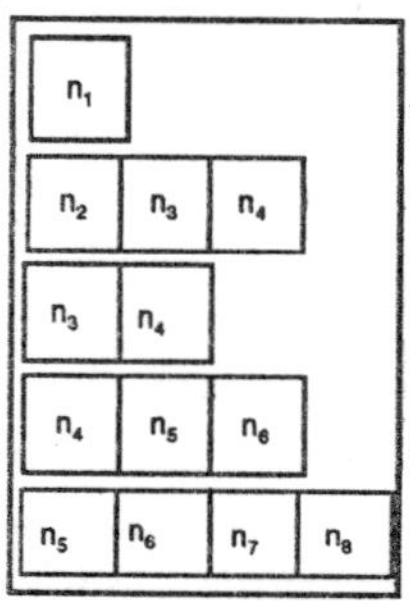

First few steps of breadth first search on the tree of fig.

Time Complexity

For the sake of analysis, we consider a tree of equal branching factor from each node = b and largest depth = d.

Since the goal is not located within depth (d-1), the number of false search is given by,

$$1 + b + b^2 + b^3 + \ldots + b^{d-1} = \left(b^d - 1\right)/(b-1),\ b >> 1$$

Further, the first state within the fringe nodes could be the goal. On the other hand, the goal could be the last visited node in the tree. Thus, on an average, the number of fringe nodes visited is given by

$$\left(1 + b^d\right)/2$$

Consequently, the total number of nodes visited in an average case becomes,

$$\left(b^d - 1\right)/(b-1) + \left(1 + b^d\right)/2$$

$$\cong b^d (b+1)/2(b-1)$$

Since the time complexity is proportional to the number of nodes visited, therefore, the above expression gives a measure of time complexity.

Space Complexity

The maximum number of nodes will be placed in the queue, when the leftmost node at depth d is inspected for comparison with the goal. The queue length under this case becomes bd. The space complexity of the algorithm that depends on the queue length, in the worst case, thus, is of the order of bd. In order to reduce the space requirement, the generate and test algorithm is realised in an alternative manner, as presented below.

Depth First Search

The depth first search generates nodes and compares them with the goal along the largest depth of the tree and moves up to the parent of the last visited node, only when no further node can be generated below the last visited node. After moving up to the parent, the algorithm attempts to generate a new offspring of the parent node. The above principle is employed recursively to each node of a tree in a depth first search. One simple way to realise the recursion in the depth first search algorithm is to employ a stack. A stackbased realisation of the depth first search algorithm is presented below.

Procedure Depth first search

- Begin
  - Push the starting node at the stack,
  - Pointed to by the stack-top;
  - While stack is not empty do
- Begin
  - Pop stack to get stack-top element;
  - If stack-top element = goal, return
  - Success and stop
  - Else push the children of the stack-top
  - Element in any order into the stack;
- End
  - End while;
- End

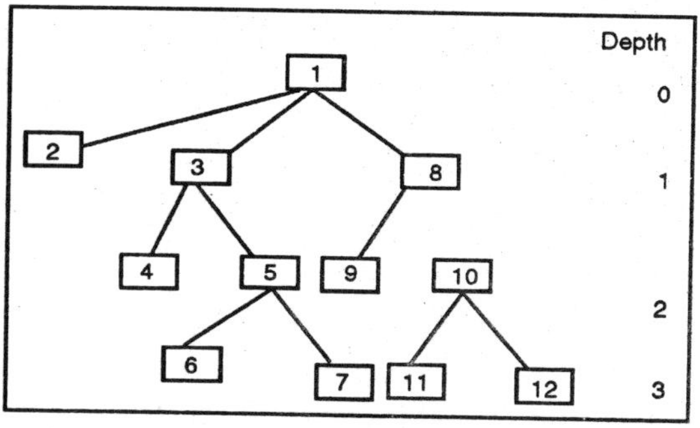

Fig. A Depth First Search on a Tree

In the above algorithm, a starting node is placed in the stack, the top of which is pointed to by the stack-top. For examining the node, it is popped out from the stack. If it is the goal, the algorithm terminates, else its children are pushed into the stack in any order.

The process is continued until the stack is empty. The ascending order of nodes in fig. A represents its traversal on the tree by depth first manner. The contents of the stack at the first few iterations are illustrated below in fig. The arrowhead in the figure denotes the position of the stack-top.

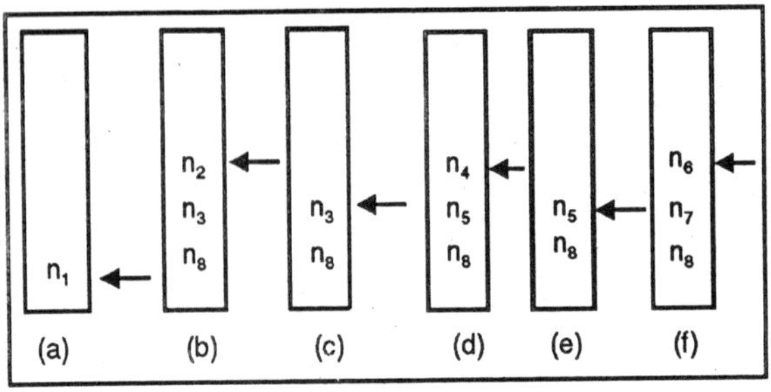

Fig. B: A Snapshot of the Stack at the First Few Iterations

Space Complexity

Maximum memory in depth first search is required, when we reach the largest depth at the first time. Assuming that each node has a branching factor b, when a node at depth d is examined, the number of nodes saved in memory are all the unexpanded nodes up to depth d plus the node being examined.

Since at each level there are (b-1) unexpanded nodes, the total number of memory required = d (b -1) +1. Thus the space complexity of depth first search is a linear function of b, unlike breadth first search, where it is an exponential function of b. This, in fact, is the most useful aspect of the depth first search.

Time Complexity

If we find the goal at the leftmost position at depth d, then the number. of nodes examined = (d +1). On the other hand, if we find the goal at the extreme right at depth d, then the number of nodes examined include all the nodes in the tree, which is,

$$1+b+b^2+b^3+...+b^d=\left(b^{d+1}-1\right)/(b-1)$$

So, the total number of nodes examined in an average case

$$=(d+1)/2+\left(b^{d+1}-1\right)/2(b-1)$$

$$\cong b\left(b^d+d\right)/2(b-1)$$

This is the average case time complexity of the depth first search algorithm. Since for large depth d, the depth first search requires quite a large runtime, an alternative way to solve the problem is by controlling the depth of the search tree. Such an algorithm, where the user mentions the initial depth cut-off at each iteration, is called an Iterative Deepening Depth First Search or simply an Iterative deepening search.

Iterative Deepening Search

When the initial depth cut-off is one, it generates only the root node and examines it. If the root node is not the goal, then depth cut-off is set to two and the tree up to depth 2 is generated using typical depth first search. Similarly, when the depth cut-off is set to m, the tree is constructed up to depth m by depth first search. One may thus wonder that in an iterative deepening search, one has to regenerate all the nodes excluding the fringe nodes at the current depth cut-off. Since the number of nodes generated by depth first search up to depth h is,

$$\left(b^{b+1}-1\right)/(b-1)$$

the total number of nodes expanded in failing searches by an iterative deepening search will be

$$\{1/(b-1)\}\sum_{h=0}^{(d-1)}\left(b^{b+1}-1\right)$$

$$\cong b\left(b^{d}-d\right)/(b-1)^{2}$$

The last pass in the algorithm results in a successful node at depth d, the average time complexity of which by typical depth first search is given by,

$$b\left(b^{d}+d\right)/2(b-1)$$

Thus the total average time complexity is given by,

$$b\left(b^{d}-d\right)/(b-1)^{2}+b\left(b^{d}+d\right)/2(b-1)$$

$$\cong(b+1)b^{d+1}/2(b-1)^{2}$$

Consequently, the ratio of average time complexity of the iterative deepening search to depth first search is given by,

$$\{(b+1)b^{d+1}/2(b-1)^{2}\}:\{b^{d+1}/2(b-1)\}$$

$$=(b+1):(b-1)$$

The iterative deepening search thus does not take much extra time, when compared to the typical depth first search. The unnecessary expansion of the entire tree by depth first search, thus, can be avoided by iterative deepening. A formal algorithm of iterative deepening is presented below.

Begin

- Set current depth cutoff =1;
- Put the initial node into a stack, pointed to by stack-top;
- While the stack is not empty and the depth is within the given depth cut-off do

Begin

- Pop stack to get the stack-top element;
- If stack-top element = goal, return it and stop
- Else push the children of the stack-top in any order
- Into the stack; End.
  - End While;
- Increment the depth cut-off by 1 and repeat Through step 2;

End

The breadth first, depth first and the iterative deepening search can be equally used for Generate and Test type algorithms. However, while the breadth first search requires an exponential amount of memory, the depth first search calls for memory proportional to the largest depth of the tree. The iterative deepening, on the other hand, has the advantage of searching in a depth first manner in an environment of controlled depth of the tree.

Hill Climbing

The 'generate and test' type of search algorithms presented above only expands the search space and examines the existence of the goal in that space. An alternative approach to solve the search problems is to employ a function f(x) that would give an estimate of the measure of distance of the goal from node x. After f(x) is evaluated at the possible initial nodes x, the nodes are sorted in ascending order of their functional values and pushed into a stack in the ascending order of their 'f' values. So, the stack-top element has the least f value. It is now popped out and compared with the goal. If the stack-top element is not the goal, then it is expanded and f is measured for each of its children. They are now sorted according to their ascending order of the functional values and then pushed into the stack. If the stack-top element is the goal, the algorithm exits; otherwise the process is continued until the stack becomes empty. Pushing the sorted nodes into the stack adds a depth first flavour to the present algorithm.

Procedure

Begin

- Identify possible starting states and measure the distance (f) of their closeness with the goal node; Push them in a stack according to the ascending order of their f ;
- Repeat
  - Pop stack to get the stack-top element;
  - If the stack-top element is the goal, announce it and exit
  - Else push its children into the stack in the ascending order of their f values;
- Until the stack is empty;

End

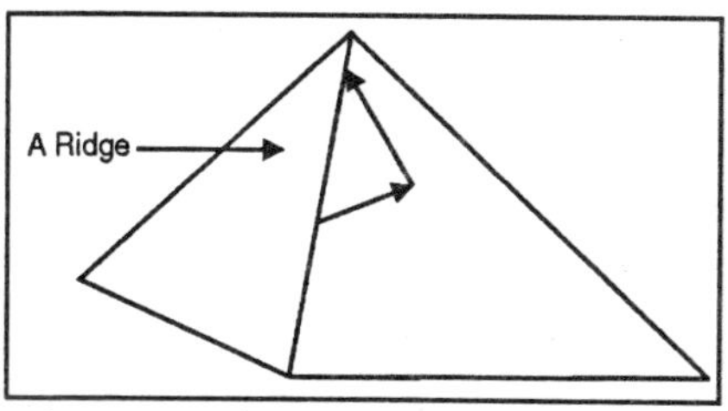

Moving along a ridge in two steps (by two successive operators) in hill climbing. The hill climbing algorithm too is not free from shortcomings. One common problem is trapping at local maxima at a foothill. When trapped at local maxima, the measure of f at all possible next legal states yield less promising values than the current state. A second drawback of the hill climbing is reaching a plateau. Once a state on a plateau is reached, all legal next states will also lie on this surface, making the search ineffective. A new algorithm, called simulated annealing, discussed below could easily solve the first two problems.

Besides the above, another problem that too gives us trouble is the traversal along the ridge. A ridge on many occasions leads to a local maxima. However, moving along the ridge is not possible by a single step due to non-availability of appropriate operators. A multiple step of movement is required to solve this problem.

Simulated Annealing

Annealing' is a process of metal casting, where the metal is first melted at a high temperature beyond its melting point and then is allowed to cool down, until it returns to the solid form. Thus in the physical process of annealing, the hot material gradually loses energy and finally at one point of time reaches a state of minimum energy.

A common observation reveals that most physical processes have transitions from higher to lower energy states, but there still remains a small probability that it may cross the valley of energy states [2] and move up to a energy state, higher than the energy state of the valley. The concept can be verified with a rolling ball. For instance, consider a rolling ball that falls from a higher (potential) energy state to a valley and then moves up to a little higher energy state.

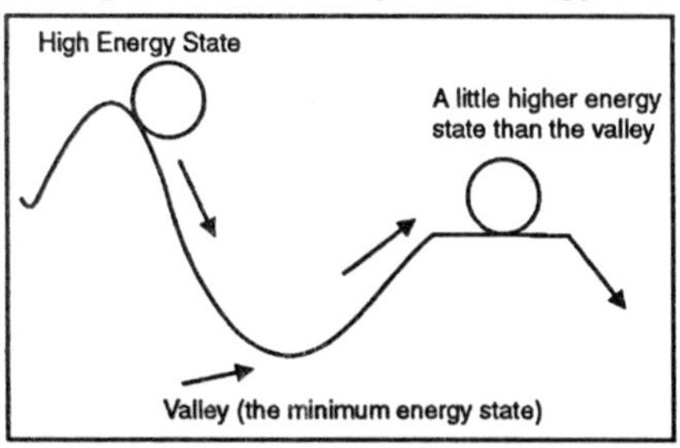

A rolling ball passes through a valley to a higher energy state. Transition to a higher energy state, however, is very small and is given by,

$$p = \exp(-\Delta E / KT)$$

where p is the probability of transition from a lower to a higher energy state, ΔE denotes a positive change in energy, K is the Boltzman constant and T is the temperature at the current thermal state.

For small ΔE, p is higher than the value of p, for large ΔE. This follows intuitively, as w.r.t the example of ball movement, the probability of transition to a slightly higher state is more than the probability of transition to a very high state.

An obvious question naturally arises: how to realise annealing in search? Readers, at this stage, would remember that the need for simulated annealing is to identify the direction of search, when the function f yields no better next states than the current state. Under this circumstance, ΔE is computed for all possible legal next states and p' is also evaluated for each such next state by the following formula:

$$p' = \exp(-\Delta E / KT)$$

A random number in the closed interval of [0,1] is then computed and p' is compared with the value of the random number. If p' is more, then it is selected for the next transition. The parametre T, also called temperature, is gradually decreased in the search programme. The logic behind this is that as T decreases, p' too decreases, thereby allowing the algorithm to terminate at a stable state.

The algorithm for simulated annealing is formally presented below.

Procedure Simulated Annealing

- Begin
  - Identify possible starting states and measure the distance (f) of their closeness with the goal; Push them in a stack according to the ascending order of their f ;
- Repeat
  - Pop stack to get stack-top element;
  - If the stack-top element is the goal, announce it and exit;
  - Else do

- Begin
  - Generate children of the stack-top element N and compute f for each of them;
  - If measure of f for at least one child of N is improving
  - Then push those children into stack in ascending order of their f;
  - If none of the children of N is better in f
  - Then do
- Begin

Select any one of them randomly, compute its p' and test whether p' exceeds a randomly generated number in the interval [0,1]; If yes, select that state as the next state; If no, generate another alternative legal next state and test in this way until one move can be selected; Replace stack-top element by the selected move (state):

- Reduce T slightly; If the reduced value is negative, set it to zero;
- End;
- End.
- Until the stack is empty;
- End.

The algorithm is similar to hill climbing, if there always exists at least one better next state than the state, pointed to by the stack-top. If it fails, then the last begin-end bracketed part of the algorithm is invoked. This part corresponds to simulated annealing. It examines each legal next state one by one, whether the probability of occurrence of the state is higher than the random value in [0,1]. If the answer is yes, the state is selected, else the next possible state is examined. Hopefully, at least one state will be found whose probability of occurrence is larger than the randomly generated probability.

Another important point that we did not include in the algorithm is the process of computation of ΔE. It is computed by taking the difference of the value of f of the next state and that of the current (stack-top) state. The third point to note is that T should be decreased once a new state with less promising value is selected. T is always kept non-negative. When T becomes zero, p' will be zero and thus the probability of transition to any other state will be zero.

HEURISTIC SEARCH

This section is devoted to solve the search problem by a new technique, called heuristic search. The term 'heuristics' stands for ' thumb rules', *i.e.*, rules which work successfully in many cases but its success is not guaranteed. In fact, we would expand nodes by judiciously selecting the more promising nodes, where these nodes are identified by measuring their strength compared to their competitive counterparts with the help of specialized intuitive functions, called heuristic functions.

Heuristic search is generally employed for two distinct types of problems:

1. Forward reasoning and
2. Backward reasoning.

We have already discussed that in a forward reasoning problem we move towards the goal state from a pre-defined starting state, while in a backward reasoning problem, we move towards the starting state from the given goal. The former class of search algorithms, when realised with heuristic functions, is generally called heuristic Search for OR-graphs or the Best First search Algorithms.

It may be noted that the best first search is a class of algorithms, and depending on the variation of the performance measuring function it is differently named. One typical member of this class is the algorithm A. On the other hand, the heuristic backward reasoning algorithms are generally called AND-OR graph search algorithms and one ideal member of this class of algorithms is the AO algorithm. We will start this section with the best first search algorithm.

Heuristic Search for OR Graphs

Most of the forward reasoning problems can be represented by an OR-graph, where a node in the graph denotes a problem state and an arc represents an application of a rule to a current state to cause transition of states. When a number of rules are applicable to a current state, we could select a better state among the children as the next state. We remember that in hill climbing, we ordered the promising initial states in a sequence and examined the state occupying the beginning of the list. If it was a goal, the algorithm was terminated. But, if it was not the goal, it was replaced by its offsprings in any order at the beginning of the list.

The hill climbing algorithm thus is not free from depth first flavour. In the best first search algorithm to be devised shortly, we start with a promising state and generate all its offsprings. The performance (fitness) of each of the nodes is then examined and the most promising node, based on its fitness, is selected for expansion. The most promising node is then expanded and the fitness of all the newborn children is measured. Now, instead of selecting only from the generated children, all the nodes having no children are examined and the most promising of these fringe nodes is selected for expansion. Thus unlike hill climbing, the best first search provides a scope of corrections, in case a wrong step has been selected earlier. This is the prime advantage of the best first search algorithm over hill climbing. The best first search algorithm is formally presented below.

Procedure Best-First-Search

- Begin
  - Identify possible starting states and measure the distance (f) of their closeness with the goal; Put them in a list L;
  - While L is not empty do
- Begin
- Identify the node n from L that has the minimum f; If there exist more than one node with minimum f, select any one of them (say, n) arbitrarily;
- If n is the goal Then return n along with the path from the starting node, and exit; Else remove n from L and add all the children of n to the list L, with their labeled paths from the starting node;
- End.

- End While

- End

As already pointed out, the best first search algorithm is a generic algorithm and requires many more extra features for its efficient realisation. For instance, how we can define f is not explicitly mentioned in the algorithm. Further, what happens if an offspring of the current node is not a fringe node. The A algorithm to be discussed shortly is a complete realisation of the best first algorithm that takes into account these issues in detail. The following definitions, however, are required for presenting the A* algorithm.

These are in order:

- *Definition*: A node is called open if the node has been generated and the h' (x) has been applied over it but it has not been expanded yet.
- *Definition*: A node is called closed if it has been expanded for generating offsprings. In order to measure the goodness of a node in A* algorithm, we require two cost functions: i) heuristic cost and ii) generation cost. The heuristic cost measures the distance of the current node x with respect to the goal and is denoted by h(x). The cost of generating a node x, denoted by g(x), on the other hand measures the distance of node x with respect to the starting node in the graph. The total cost function at node x, denoted by f(x), is the sum of g(x) plus h(x).

The generation cost g(x) can be measured easily as we generate node x through a few state transitions. For instance, if node x was generated from the starting node through m state transitions, the cost g(x) will be proportional to m (or simply m). But how does one evaluate the h(x)? It may be recollected that h(x) is the cost yet to be spent to reach the goal from the current node x. Obviously, any cost we assign as h(x) is through prediction. The predicted cost for h(x) is generally denoted by h'(x). Consequently, the predicted total cost is denoted by f'(x), where,

$$f'(x) = g(x) + h'(x).$$

Now, we shall present the A* algorithm formally.

Procedure A*

- Begin
  - Put a new node n to the set of open nodes (hereafter open); Measure its f'(n) = g(n) + h' (n); Presume the set of closed nodes to be a null set initially;
  - While open is not empty do
- Begin
  - If n is the goal, stop and return n and the path of n from the beginning node to n through back pointers;
  - Else do
- Begin
  - Remove n from open and put it under closed;
  - Generate the children of n;
  - If all of them are new *i.e.,* do not exist in the graph before generating them Then add them to open and label their f' and the path from the root node through back pointers;

If one or more children of n already existed as open nodes in the graph before their generation. Then those children must have multiple parents; Under this circumstance compute their f' through current path and compare it through their old paths, and keep them connected only through the shortest path from the starting node and label the back pointer from the children of n to their parent, if such pointers do not exist; If one or more children of n already existed as closed nodes before generation of them, then they too must have multiple parents; Under this circumstance, find the shortest path from the starting node, *i.e.,* the path through which f' of n is minimum; If the current path is selected, then the nodes in the sub-tree rooted at the corresponding child of n should have revised f' as the g' for many of the nodes in that sub-tree changed; Label the back pointer from the children of n to their parent, if such pointers do not exist;

```
End
End
End While;
End.
```

LOGIC PROGRAMMING

PROLOG PROGRAMMING

Let us, for instance, consider the problem of a 'classroom scene' interpretation.We assume that the scene has been passed through various stages of low and medium level image processing and the objects in the scene thus have been recognized and labeled by a computing machine.

The data (clauses) received from the scene and the knowledge used to analyse it are presented in both English and Predicate Logic below.

Database:

```
Object (board)
Writes-on (john, board, classhour)
Sits-on (mita, bench, classhour)
Sits-on (rita, bench, classhour)
Person (john)
Person (rita)
Person (mita)
The above are called clauses in PROLOG.
```

Logic Programmes-A Formal Definition

We are now in a position to formally define Logic Programmes. We first define a Horn clause, the constituents of a logic programme

Definition

A clause consists of two parts: the head and the body. One side of the clause to which the arrowhead (if-then operator) points to is called the head and the other side of it is called the body. A Horn clause contains at most one literal (proposition/predicate) at the head of the clause.

Example

The following are two examples of Horn clauses:

- $P(X), Q(Y) \rightarrow W(X,Y)$
- $R(X, Y), Q(Y) \rightarrow ?$

In (i) W (X, Y) is the head and P (X), Q (Y) is the body. In (ii) R(X, Y), Q(Y) is the body and the head comprises of a null clause (sub-clause). In fact (ii) represents a query, asking whether R (X, Y), Q (Y) is true, or what are the set of instantiations for X and Y, which makes R (X, Y)^Q (Y) true.

A Logic Programme is a programme, comprising of Horn clauses.

The following example illustrates a logic programme:

Example: Consider the following two sentences in Predicate Logic with one head clause in each sentence.

Father (X, Y) ← Child (Y, X), Male (X).

Son (Y, X) ← Child (Y, X), Male (Y).

The above two clauses being horn clauses are constituents of a Logic Programme. Let us now assume that along with the above knowledge, we have the following three data clauses:

Child (ram, dasaratha).

Male (ram).

Male (dasaratha).

Suppose that the above set of clauses is properly structured in PROLOG and the programme is then compiled and executed. If we now submit the following queries (goals), the system responds correctly as follows.

- Goal: Father (X, Y)
  Response: Father (dasaratha, ram).
- Goal: Son (Y, X)
  Response: Son (ram, dasaratha).

But how does the system respond to our queries? Before that let us learn a little bit of syntax of PROLOG programmes. We take up the scene interpretation problem as an example to learn the syntax of PROLOG programming.

Scene Interpretation Programme

```
/* PROLOG PROGRAMME FOR SCENE INTERPRETATION
*/
Domains
Time, X, Y, Z, W, board, classhour, bench =
symbol
```

```
Predicates
Teacher (X)
Writes-on (X, board, Time)
Equal (Time, classhour)
Person (X) Person (Y) Person (Z) Person (W)
Sits-on (Y, bench, Time) Sits-on (Z, bench,
Time)
Student (Y)
Student (Z)
Object (W)
Clauses
Object (board). 1
Writes-on (john, board, classhour). 2
Male (dasaratha).
Sits-on (mita, bench, classhour). 3
Sits-on (rita, bench, classhour). 4
Person (john). 5
Person (mita). 6
Person (rita). 7
Equal (Time, classhour):- 8
Object (board),
Writes-on (X, board, Time),
Teacher (X).
Equal (Time, classhour):- 9
Person (Y),
Sits-on (Y, bench, classhour),
Person (X),
Writes-on (X, board, Time).
Teacher (X):- 10
Person (X),
Writes-on (X, board, classhour).
Student (Y):- 11
Person (Y),
Sits-on (Y, bench, Time),
Equal (Time, classhour).
```

This is all about the programme. Readers may note that we mentioned no procedure to solve the problem of scene interpretation; rather we stated the facts only in the programme. Here lies the significance of a logic programme.

Now, suppose, the user makes a query:

Goal: Teacher (X)?

System prompts: Teacher (john).

Further, if the user asks:

Goal: Equal (Time, classhour) ?

System prompts: Yes.

BACKTRACKING

To explain how the system answers these queries, we have to learn a very useful phenomenon, called backtracking. Let us now concentrate on the query: Teacher (X), Since

```
Teacher (X)
    Person (X),
    Writes-on (X, board, classhour).
```

To satisfy the Goal: Teacher (X), one has to satisfy the sub-goals: Person (X), Writes-on (X, board, classhour). Now, PROLOG searches a sub-goal Person() for the predicate Person (X). At clause 5, it finds a match and X is instantiated to john. PROLOG puts a marker at clause 5.

Now, it continues searching Writes-on (john, board, classhour) in the remaining clauses. But it fails to find so, since Writes-on is at 2nd position in the list of clauses. So, it has to trace back above the marker place and then ultimately it finds Writes-on (john, board, classhour). Since the sub-goals are succeeded, the goal also succeeds, yielding a solution.

For answering the query Equal (Time, classhour), a number of backtracking is required. We omit this for space constraints and ask the reader to study it herself. The next important issue that we will learn is SLD (Select Linear Definite clauses) resolution.

MACHINE LEARNING

CHARACTERISTICS

Learning is an inherent characteristic of the human beings. By virtue of this, people, while executing similar tasks, acquire the ability to improve their performance. This chapter provides an overview of the principle of learning that can be adhered to machines to improve their performance. Such learning is usually referred to as 'machine learning'.

Machine learning can be broadly classified into three categories:

1. Supervised learning,
2. Unsupervised learning and
3. Reinforcement learning.

Supervised learning requires a trainer, who supplies the input-output training instances. The learning system adapts its parametres by some algorithms to generate the desired output patterns from a given input pattern. In absence of trainers, the desired output for a given input instance is not known, and consequently the learner has to adapt its parametres autonomously.

Such type of learning is termed 'unsupervised learning'. The third type called the reinforcement learning bridges a gap between supervised and unsupervised categories. In reinforcement learning, the learner does not explicitly know the input-output instances, but it receives some form of feedback from its environment.

The feedback signals help the learner to decide whether its action on the environment is rewarding or punishable. The learner thus adapts its parametres based on the states (rewarding/punishable) of its actions. Among the supervised learning techniques, the most common are inductive and analogical learning. The inductive learning technique, presented in the chapter, includes decision tree and version space based learning.

Analogical learning is briefly introduced through illustrative examples. The principle of unsupervised learning is illustrated here with a clustering problem. The section on reinforcement learning includes Q learning and temporal difference learning.

A fourth category of learning, which has emerged recently from the disciplines of knowledge engineering, is called 'inductive logic programming'. The principles of inductive logic programming have also been briefly introduced in this chapter. The chapter ends with a brief discussion on the 'computational theory of learning'. With the background of this theory, one can measure the performance of the learning behaviour of a machine from the training instances and their count.

SUPERVISED LEARNING

As already mentioned, in supervised learning a trainer submits the inputoutput exemplary patterns and the learner has to adjust the parametres of the system autonomously, so that it can yield the correct output pattern when excited with one of the given input patterns. We shall cover two important types of supervised learning in this section. These are i) inductive learning and ii) analogical learning.

Inductive Learning

In supervised learning we have a set of {xi, f (xi)} for $1 \le i \le n$, and our aim is to determine 'f' by some adaptive algorithm. The inductive learning is a special class of the supervised learning techniques, where given a set of {xi, f(xi)} pairs, we determine a hypothesis h(xi) such that h(xi)≈f(xi),? i. A natural question that may be raised is how to compare the hypothesis h that approximates f.

For instance, there could be more than one h(xi) where all of which are approximately close to f(xi). Let there be two hypothesis h1 and h2, where h1(xi) ≈ f(xi) and h2(xi) = f(xi). We may select one of the two hypotheses by a preference criterion, called bias. When {xi, f(xi)}, $1 \le i \le n$ are numerical quantities we may employ the neural learning techniques presented in the next chapter.

Readers may wonder: could we find 'f' by curve fitting as well. Should we then call curve fitting a learning technique? The answer to this, of course, is in the negative. The learning algorithm for such numerical sets {xi, f(xi)} must be able to adapt the parametres of the learner.

The more will be the training instance, the larger will be the number of adaptations. But what happens when xi and f(xi) are non-numerical? For instance, suppose given the truth table of the following training instances.

Table. Truth: Training Instances

Input Instances	Output Instances
a_1, $a_1 \rightarrow b_1$	b_1
a_2, $a_2 \rightarrow b_2$	b_2
.	
.	
a_n, $a_n \rightarrow b_n$	b_n

Here we may denote bi = f (ai, ai→bi) for all i=1 to n. From these training instances we infer a generalized hypothesis h as follows.

Analogical Learning

In inductive learning we observed that there exist many positive and negative instances of a problem and the learner has to form a concept that supports most of the positive and no negative instances. This demonstrates that a number of training instances are required to form a concept in inductive learning. Unlike this, analogical learning can be accomplished from a single example. For instance, given the following training instance, one has to determine the plural form of bacilus.

Obviously, one can answer that the plural form of bacillus is bacilli. But how do we do so? From common sense reasoning, it follows that the result is because of the similarity of bacillus with fungus. The analogical learning system thus learns that to get the plural form of words ending with 'us' is to replace it with 'i'.

The main steps in analogical learning are now formalized below:

- *Identifying Analogy:* Identify the similarity between an experienced problem instance and a new problem.
- *Determining the Mapping Function:* Relevant parts of the experienced problem are selected and the mapping is determined.
- *Apply Mapping Function:* Apply the mapping function to transform the new problem from the given domain to the target domain.
- *Validation:* The newly constructed solution is

validated for its applicability through its trial processes like theorem or simulation.

- *Learning:* If the validation is found to work well, the new knowledge is encoded and saved for future usage.

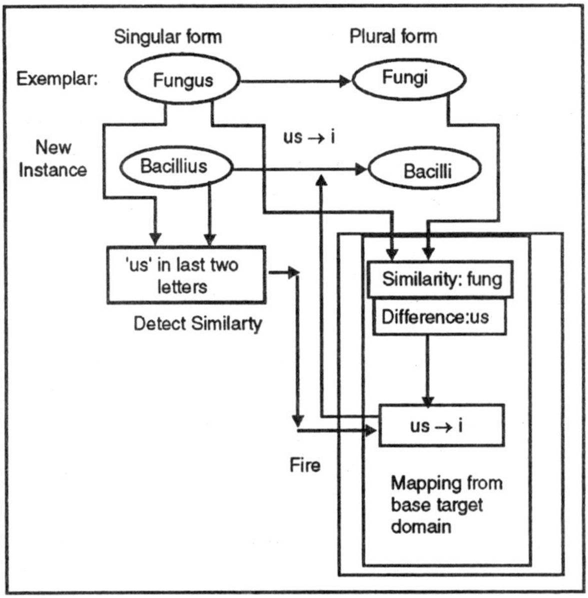

Analogical reasoning has been successfully realised in many systems. Winston's analogical system was designed to demonstrate that the relationship between acts and actors in one story can explain the same in another story. Carbonell's transformational analogy system employs a new approach to problem solving. It solves new problems by modifying existing solutions to problems until they may be applied to new problem instances.

NEURAL NETWORKS

ROBOT CONTROL

An important area of application of neural networks is in the field of robotics. Usually, these networks are designed to direct a manipulator, which is the most important form of the industrial robot, to grasp objects, based on sensor data. Another applications include the steering and path-planning of autonomous robot vehicles.

In robotics, the major task involves making movements dependent on sensor data. There are four, related, problems to be distinguished.

Forward kinematics

Kinematics is the science of motion which treats motion without regard to the forces which cause it. Within this science one studies the position, velocity, acceleration, and all higher order derivatives of the position variables. A very basic problem in the study of mechanical manipulation is that of forward kinematics.

This is the static geometrical problem of computing the position and orientation of the end-efector ('hand') of the manipulator. Specifi- cally, given a set of joint angles, the forward kinematic problem is to compute the position and orientation of the tool frame relative to the base frame.

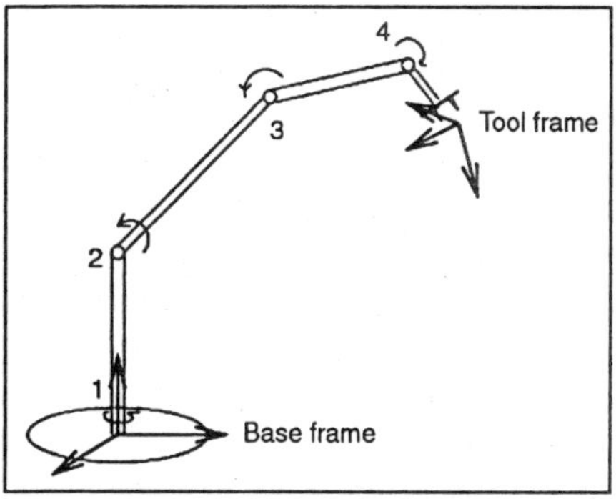

Fig. An Exemplar Robot Manipulator

Inverse kinematics

This problem is posed as follows: given the position and orientation of the end-efector of the manipulator, calculate all possible sets of joint angles which could be used to attain this given position and orientation. This is a fundamental problem in the practical use of manipulators. The inverse kinematic problem is not as simple as the forward one. Because the kinematic equations are nonlinear, their solution is not always easy or even possible in a closed form. Also, the questions of existence of a solution, and of multiple solutions, arise. Solving this problem is a least requirement for most robot control systems.

Dynamics

Dynamics is a field of study devoted to studying the forces required to cause motion. In order to accelerate a manipulator from rest, glide at a constant end-efector velocity, and finally decelerate to a stop, a complex set of torque functions must be applied by the joint actuators.

In dynamics not only the geometrical properties (kinematics) are used, but also the physical properties of the robot are taken into account. Take for instance the weight (inertia) of the robotarm, which determines the force required to change the motion of the arm. The dynamics introduces two extra problems to the kinematic problems.

- The robot arm has a 'memory'. Its responds to a control signal depends also on its history (*e.g.* previous positions, speed, acceleration).
- If a robot grabs an object then the dynamics change but the kinematics don't. This is because the weight of the object has to be added to the weight of the arm (that's why robot arms are so heavy, making the relative weight change very small).

Trajectory Generation

To move a manipulator from here to there in a smooth, controlled fashion each joint must be moved via a smooth function of time. Exactly how to compute these motion functions is the problem of trajectory generation.

In the first section of this chapter we will discuss the problems associated with the positioning of the end-efector (in efect, representing the inverse kinematics in combination with sensory transformation).

END-EFECTOR POSITIONING

The final goal in robot manipulator control is often the positioning of the hand or end-effector in order to be able to, *e.g.*, pick up an object. With the accurate robot arm that are manufactured, this task is often relatively simple, involving the following steps:

- Determine the target coordinates relative to the base of the robot. Typically, when this position is not always the same, this is done with a number of fixed cameras or other sensors which observe the work scene, from the image frame determine the position of the object in that frame, and perform a pre-determined coordinate transformation;
- With a precise model of the robot (supplied by the manufacturer), calculate the joint angles to reach the target (*i.e.*, the inverse kinematics). This is a relatively simple problem;
- Move the arm (dynamics control) and close the gripper.

Involvement of neural networks. So if these parts are relatively simple to solve with a high accuracy, why involve neural networks?

The reason is the applicability of robots. When 'traditional' methods are used to control a robot arm, accurate models of the sensors and manipulators (in some cases with unknown parametres which have to be estimated from the system's behaviour; yet still with accurate models as starting point) are required and the system must be calibrated.

Also, systems which suffer from wear-and-tear (and which mechanical systems don't?) need frequent recalibration or parametre determination. Finally, the development of more complex (adaptive!) control methods allows the design and use of more exible (*i.e.*, less rigid) robot systems, both on the sensory and motory side.

Camera-robot Coordination

The system we focus on in this section is a work oor observed by a fixed cameras, and a robot arm. The visual system must identify the target as well as determine the visual position of the end-effector. The target position Xtarget together with the visual position of the hand Xhand are input to the neural controller N(.).

This controller then generates a joint position θ for the robot:

$$\theta = N(Xtarget, Xhand)$$

We can compare the neurally generated θ with the optimal $\theta 0$ generated by a fictitious perfect controller R(.):

$$\theta 0 = R(Xtarget, Xhand):$$

The task of learning is to make the N generate an output 'close enough' to $\theta 0$ There are two problems associated with teaching N(.):

- Generating learning samples which are in accordance with eq. $\theta 0 = R(Xtarget, Xhand)$. This is not trivial, since in useful applications R(.) is an unknown function. Instead, a form of self-supervised or unsupervised learning is required. Some examples to solve this problem are given below;
- Constructing the mapping N(.)from the available learning samples. When the (usually randomly drawn) learning samples are available, a neural network uses these samples to represent the whole input space over which the robot is active. This is evidently a form of interpolation, but has the problem that the input space is of a high dimensionality, and the samples are randomly distributed.

Approach 1: Feed-forward Networks

When using a feed-forward system for controlling the manipulator, a self-supervised learning system must be used. One such a system has been reported by Psaltis, Sideris and Yamamura.

Here, the network, which is constrained to two-dimensional positioning of the robot arm, learns by experimentation. Three methods are proposed:

Indirect learning.In indirect learning, a Cartesian target point x in world coordinates is generated, *e.g.*, by a two cameras looking at an object. This target point is fed into the network, which generates an angle vector θ. The manipulator moves to position θ, and the cameras determine the new position x' of the end-effector in world coordinates. This x' again is input to the network, resulting in θ'. The network is then trained on the error $\varepsilon 1 = \theta - \theta'$

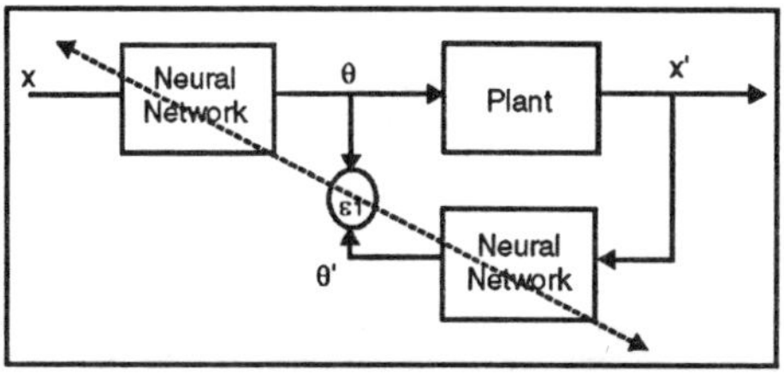

Indirect learning system for robotics. In each cycle, the network is used in two different places: first in the forward step, then for feeding back the error.

However, minimisation of ε1 does not guarantee minimisation of the overall error ε = x-x'. For example, the network often settles at a 'solution' that maps all x's to a single θ (*i.e.*, the mapping).

General Learning

The method is basically very much like supervised learning, but here the plant input θ must be provided by the user. Thus the network can directly minimise $|\theta - \theta'|$. The success of this method depends on the interpolation capabilities of the network. Correct choice of θ may pose a problem.

Specialised Learning

Keep in mind that the goal of the training of the network is to minimise the error at the output of the plant: ε=x - x'. We can also train the neural network by 'backpropagating' this error trough the plant (compare this with the back propagation of the error).

This method requires knowledge of the Jacobian matrix of the plant. A Jacobian matrix of a multidimensional function F is a matrix of partial derivatives of F, *i.e.*, the multidimensional form of the derivative. For example, if we have Y = F(X), *i.e.*,

$$y_1 = f_1(x_1, x_2, \ldots, x_n),$$
$$y_2 = f_2(x_1, x_2, \ldots, x_n),$$
$$\vdots$$
$$y_m = f_m(x_1, x_2, \ldots, x_n)$$

then,

$$\delta y_1 = \frac{\delta f_1}{\delta x_1}\delta x_1 + \frac{\delta f_1}{\delta x_2}\delta x_2 + \ldots + \frac{\delta f_1}{\delta x_n}\delta x_n,$$
$$\delta y_2 = \frac{\delta f_2}{\delta x_1}\delta x_1 + \frac{\delta f_2}{\delta x_2}\delta x_2 + \ldots + \frac{\delta f_2}{\delta x_n}\delta x_n,$$
$$\vdots$$
$$\delta y_m = \frac{\delta f_m}{\delta x_1}\delta x_1 + \frac{\delta f_m}{\delta x_2}\delta x_2 + \ldots + \frac{\delta f_m}{\delta x_n}\delta x_n$$

or,

$$\delta Y = \frac{\delta F}{\delta X}\delta X$$

also written as,

$$\delta Y = J(X)\delta X$$

where J is the Jacobian matrix of F. So, the Jacobian matrix can be used to calculate the change in the function when its parametres change.

Now, in this case we have,

$$J_{ij} = \left[\frac{\delta Pi}{\delta \theta j}\right]$$

where $Pi(\theta)$ the ith element of the plant output for input θ. The learning rule applied here regards the plant as an additional and unmodiable layer in the neural network. The total error $\varepsilon = x - x'$ is propagated back through the plant by calculating the δ as in eq.

$$\delta_j = F'(s_j)\sum_i \delta_i \frac{\delta Pi(\theta)}{\delta \theta_j}$$

$$\delta_i = x_i - x_{i,}$$

where i iterates over the outputs of the plant. When the plant is an unknown function,
where,

$$\frac{\delta Pi(\theta)}{\delta \theta_j}$$

can be approximated by

$$\frac{\delta Pi(\theta)}{\delta \theta_j} \approx \frac{Pi\left(\theta + h\theta_j e_j\right) - Pi(\theta)}{h}$$

where ej is used to change the scalar θj into a vector.

This approximate derivative can be measured by slightly changing the input to the plant and measuring the changes in the output.Again a two-layer feed-forward network is trained with back-propagation.

However, instead of calculating a desired output vector the input vector which should have invoked the current output vector is reconstructed, and back-propagation is applied to this new input vector and the existing output vector.

The configuration used consists of a monocular manipulator which has to grasp objects. Due to the fact that the camera is situated in the hand of the robot, the task is to move the hand such that the object is in the centre of the image and has some predetermined size (in a later article, a biologically inspired system is proposed in which the visual flow-field is used to account for the monocularity of the system, such that the dimensions of the object need not to be known anymore to the system).

One step towards the target consists of the following operations:

- Measure the distance from the current position to the target position in camera domain, x.
- Use this distance, together with the current state ? of the robot, as input for the neural network. The network then generates a joint displacement vector Δθ.
- Send Δθ to the manipulator.

- Again measure the distance from the current position to the target position in camera domain, x'.
- Calculate the move made by the manipulator in visual domain, $x -_{t}^{t+1} Rx'$ where ${}_{t}^{t+1}R$
- The rotation matrix of the second camera image with respect to the First camera image;
- Teach the learning pair $\left(x -_{t}^{t+1} Rx', \theta; \Delta\theta\right)$ to the neural network.

This system has shown to learn correct behaviour in only tens of iterations, and to be very adaptive to changes in the sensor or manipulator. By using a feed-forward network, the available learning samples are approximated by a single, smooth function consisting of a summation of sigmoid functions. As mentioned in section 4, a feed-forward network with one layer of sigmoid units is capable of representing practically any function. But how are the optimal weights determined in finite time to obtain this optimal representation? Experiments have shown that, although a reasonable representation can be obtained in a short period of time, an accurate representation of the function that governs the learning samples is often not feasible or extremely dificult.

The reason for this is the global character of the approximation obtained with a feed-forward network with sigmoid units: every weight in the network has a global effect on the final approximation that is obtained. Building local representations is the obvious way out: every part of the network is responsible for a small subspace of the total input space. Thus accuracy is obtained locally. This is typically obtained with a Kohonen neural network.

Approach 2: Topology Conserving Maps

The system described consists of a robot manipulator with three degrees of freedom (orientation of the end-effector is not included) which has to grab objects in 3D-space. The system is observed by two fixed cameras which output their (x; y) coordinates of the object and the end effector

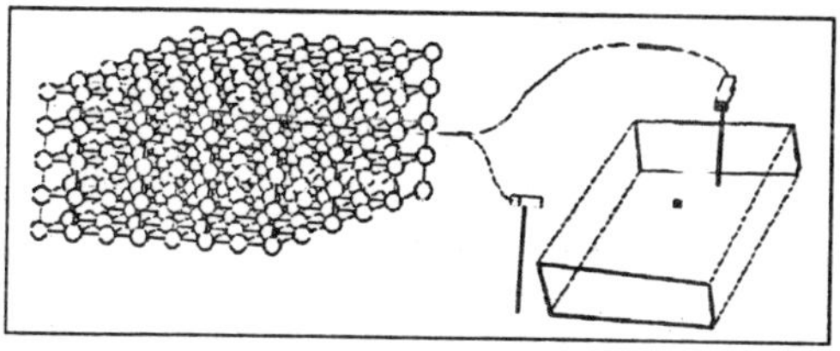

A Kohonen network merging the output of two cameras. Each run consists of two movements. In the gross move, the observed location of the object x (a four-component vector) is input to the network.

As with the Kohonen neural network, the neuron k with highest activation value is selected as winner, because its weight vector Wk is nearest to x. The neurons, which are arranged in a 3-dimensional lattice, correspond in a 1-1 fashion with subregions of the 3D workspace of the robot, *i.e.*, the neuronal lattice is a discrete representation of the workspace.

With each neuron a vector θ and Jacobian matrix A are associated. During gross move θk is fed to the robot which makes its move, resulting in retinal coordinates X g of the end-effector. To correct for the discretisation of the working space, an additional move is made which is dependent of the distance between the neuron and the object in space wk - x; this small displacement in Cartesian space is translated to an angle change using the Jacobian Ak:

$$\theta^{\text{final}} = \theta_k + A_k(x - w_k)$$

which is a first-order Taylor expansion of θ^{final}. The final retinal coordinates of the end-effector after this fine move are in xf. Learning proceeds as follows: when an improved estimate (θ,A) has been found, the following adaptations are made for all neurons j:

$$w_j^{\text{new}} = w_j^{\text{old}} + \gamma(t) g_{jk}(t)\left(x - w_j^{\text{old}}\right),$$

$$(\theta, A)_j^{\text{new}} = (\theta, A)_j^{\text{old}} + \gamma(t) g'_{jk}(t)\left((\theta, A)_j^{*} - (\theta, A)_j^{\text{old}}\right.$$

If gjk(t) = g'jk(t) = δjk, this is similar to perceptron learning. Here, as with the Kohonen learning rule, a distance function is used such that gjk(t) and g'jk(t) are Gaussians depending on the distance between neurons j and k with a maximum at j = k. An improved estimate $(\theta,A)^*$ is obtained as follows.

$$\theta^* = \theta_k + A_k(x - x_f),$$

$$A^* = A_k + A_k\left(x - w_k - x_f + x_g\right)\times\frac{\left(x_f - x_g\right)^T}{\| x_f - x_g\|^2}$$

$$= A_k + \left(\Delta\theta - A_k\Delta x\right)\frac{\Delta x^T}{\| \Delta x\|^2}$$

SPEECH RECOGNITION

Speech is a natural mode of communication for people. We learn all the relevant skills during early childhood, without instruction, and we continue to rely on speech communication throughout our lives. It comes so naturally to us that we don't realise how complex a phenomenon speech is. The human vocal tract and articulators are biological organs with nonlinear properties, whose operation is not just under conscious control but also affected by factors ranging from gender to upbringing to emotional state.

As a result, vocalizations can vary widely in terms of their accent, pronunciation, articulation, roughness, nasality, pitch, volume, and speed; moreover, during transmission, our irregular speech patterns can be further distorted by background noise and echoes, as well as electrical characteristics (if telephones or other electronic equipment are used). All these sources of variability make speech recognition, even more than speech generation, a very complex problem.

What makes people so good at recognizing speech? Intriguingly, the human brain is known to be wired differently than a conventional computer; in fact it operates under a radically different computational paradigm. While conventional computers use a very fast and complex central processor with explicit programme instructions and locally addressable memory, by contrast the human brain uses a massively parallel collection of slow and simple processing elements (neurons), densely connected by weights (synapses) whose strengths are modified with experience, directly supporting the integration of multiple constraints, and providing a distributed form of associative memory. The brain's impressive superiority at a wide range of cognitive skills, including speech recognition, has motivated research into its novel computational paradigm since the 1940's, on the assumption that brainlike models may ultimately lead to brainlike performance on many complex tasks.

This fascinating research area is now known as connectionism, or the study of artificial neural networks. What is the current state of the art in speech recognition? This is a complex question, because a system's accuracy depends on the conditions under which it is evaluated: under sufficiently narrow conditions almost any system can attain human-like accuracy, but it's much harder to achieve good accuracy under general conditions. The conditions of evaluation - and hence the accuracy of any system - can vary along the following dimensions:

Vocabulary Size and Confusability

As a general rule, it is easy to discriminate among a small set of words, but error rates naturally increase as the vocabulary size grows. For example, the 10 digits 'zero' to 'nine' can be recognized essentially perfectly, but vocabulary sizes of 200, 5000, or 100000 may have error rates of 3%, 7%, or 45%.

On the other hand, even a small vocabulary can be hard to recognize if it contains confusable words. For example, the 26 letters of the English alphabet (treated as 26 'words') are very difficult to discriminate because they contain so many confusable words (most notoriously, the E-set: 'B, C, D, E, G, P, T, V, Z'); an 8% error rate is considered good for this vocabulary

Speaker Dependence vs. Independence

By definition, a speaker dependent system is intended for use by a single speaker, but a speaker independent system is intended for use by any speaker. Speaker independence is difficult to achieve because a system's parametres become tuned to the speaker(s) that it was trained on, and these parametres tend to be highly speaker-specific.

Isolated, Discontinuous, or Continuous Speech

Isolated speech means single words; discontinuous speech means full sentences in which words are artificially separated by silence; and continuous speech means naturally spoken sentences. Isolated and discontinuous speech recognition is relatively easy because word boundaries are detectable and the words tend to be cleanly pronounced.

Task and Language Constraints

Even with a fixed vocabulary, performance will vary with the nature of constraints on the word sequences that are allowed during recognition. Some constraints may be task-dependent (for example, an airlinequerying application may dismiss the hypothesis 'The apple is red'); other constraints may be semantic (rejecting 'The apple is angry'), or syntactic (rejecting 'Red is apple the').

Constraints are often represented by a grammar, which ideally filters out unreasonable sentences so that the speech recognizer evaluates only plausible sentences. Grammars are usually rated by their perplexity, a number that indicates the grammar's average branching factor (*i.e.*, the number of words that can follow any given word). The difficulty of a task is more reliably measured by its perplexity than by its vocabulary size.

Read vs. Spontaneous Speech

Systems can be evaluated on speech that is either read from prepared scripts, or speech that is uttered spontaneously. Spontaneous speech is vastly more difficult, because it tends to be peppered with disfluencies like 'uh' and 'um', false starts, incomplete sentences, stuttering, coughing, and laughter; and moreover, the vocabulary is essentially unlimited, so the system must be able to deal intelligently with unknown words (*e.g.*, detecting and flagging their presence, and adding them to the vocabulary, which may require some interaction with the user).

Adverse Conditions

A system's performance can also be degraded by a range of adverse conditions. These include environmental noise (*e.g.*, noise in a car or a factory); acoustical distortions (*e.g*, echoes, room acoustics); different microphones (*e.g.*, close-speaking, omnidirectional, or telephone); limited frequency bandwidth (in telephone transmission); and altered speaking manner (shouting, whining, speaking quickly, etc.).

In order to evaluate and compare different systems under well-defined conditions, a number of standardized databases have been created with particular characteristics. For example, one database that has been widely used is the DARPA Resource Management database - a large vocabulary (1000 words), speaker-independent, continuous speech database, consisting of 4000 training sentences in the domain of naval resource management, read from a script and recorded under benign environmental conditions; testing is usually performed using a grammar with a perplexity of 60. Under these controlled conditions, state-of-the-art performance is about 97% word recognition accuracy (or less for simpler systems).

FUNDAMENTALS OF SPEECH RECOGNITION

Speech recognition is a multileveled pattern recognition task, in which acoustical signals are examined and structured into a hierarchy of subword units (*e.g.*, phonemes), words, phrases, and sentences. Each level may provide additional temporal constraints, *e.g.*, known word pronunciations or legal word sequences, which can compensate for errors or uncertainties at lower levels. This hierarchy of constraints can best be exploited by combining decisions probabilistically at all lower levels, and making discrete decisions only at the highest level.

The elements are as follows:

- *Raw speech:* Speech is typically sampled at a high

frequency, *e.g.*, 16 KHz over a microphone or 8 KHz over a telephone. This yields a sequence of amplitude values over time.

- *Signal analysis*: Raw speech should be initially transformed and compressed, in order to simplify subsequent processing. Many signal analysis techniques are available which can extract useful features and compress the data by a factor of ten without losing any important information. Among the most popular:
  - Fourier analysis (FFT) yields discrete frequencies over time, which can be interpreted visually. Frequencies are often distributed using a Mel scale, which is linear in the low range but logarithmic in the high range, corresponding to physiological characteristics of the human ear.
  - Perceptual Linear Prediction (PLP) is also physiologically motivated, but yields coefficients that cannot be interpreted visually.
  - Linear Predictive Coding (LPC) yields coefficients of a linear equation that approximate the recent history of the raw speech values.
  - Cepstral analysis calculates the inverse Fourier transform of the logarithm of the power spectrum of the signal.

In practice, it makes little difference which technique is used1. Afterwards, procedures such as Linear Discriminant Analysis (LDA) may optionally be applied to further reduce the dimensionality of any representation, and to decorrelate the coefficients.

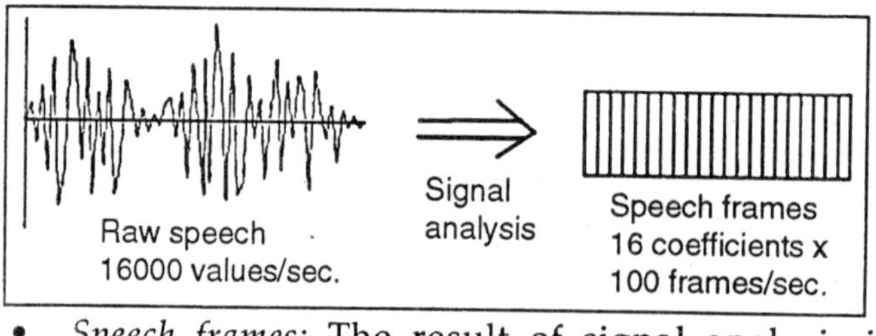

- *Speech frames:* The result of signal analysis is a

sequence of speech frames, typically at 10 msec intervals, with about 16 coefficients per frame. These frames may be augmented by their own first and/or second derivatives, providing explicit information about speech dynamics; this typically leads to improved performance. The speech frames are used for acoustic analysis.

- *Acoustic models*: In order to analyse the speech frames for their acoustic content, we need a set of acoustic models. There are many kinds of acoustic models, varying in their representation, granularity, context dependence, and other properties.

It shows two popular representations for acoustic models. The simplest is a template, which is just a stored sample of the unit of speech to be modeled, *e.g.*, a recording of a word. An unknown word can be recognized by simply comparing it against all known templates, and finding the closest match. Templates have two major drawbacks:–

- They cannot model acoustic variabilities, except in a coarse way by assigning multiple templates to each word; and
- In practice they are limited to whole-word models, because it's hard to record or segment a sample shorter than a word - so templates are useful only in small systems which can afford the luxury of using whole-word models.

A more flexible representation, used in larger systems, is based on trained acoustic models, or states. In this approach, every word is modeled by a sequence of trainable states, and each state indicates the sounds that are likely to be heard in that segment of the word, using a probability distribution over the acoustic space. Probability distributions can be modeled parametrically, by assuming that they have a simple shape (*e.g.*, a Gaussian distribution) and then trying to find the parametres that describe it; or non-parametrically, by representing the distribution directly (*e.g.*, with a histogram over a quantization of the acoustic space, or, as we shall see, with a neural network).

TIME WARPING

In this we motivate and explain the Dynamic Time Warping algorithm, one of the oldest and most important algorithms in speech recognition. The simplest way to recognize an isolated word sample is to compare it against a number of stored word templates and determine which is the 'best match'.

This goal is complicated by a number of factors. First, different samples of a given word will have somewhat different durations. This problem can be eliminated by simply normalizing the templates and the unknown speech so that they all have an equal duration. However, another problem is that the rate of speech may not be constant throughout the word; in other words, the optimal alignment between a template and the speech sample may be nonlinear. Dynamic Time Warping (DTW) is an efficient method for finding this optimal nonlinear alignment.

DTW is an instance of the general class of algorithms known as dynamic programming. Its time and space complexity is merely linear in the duration of the speech sample and the vocabulary size. The algorithm makes a single pass through a matrix of frame scores while computing locally optimized segments of the global alignment path.

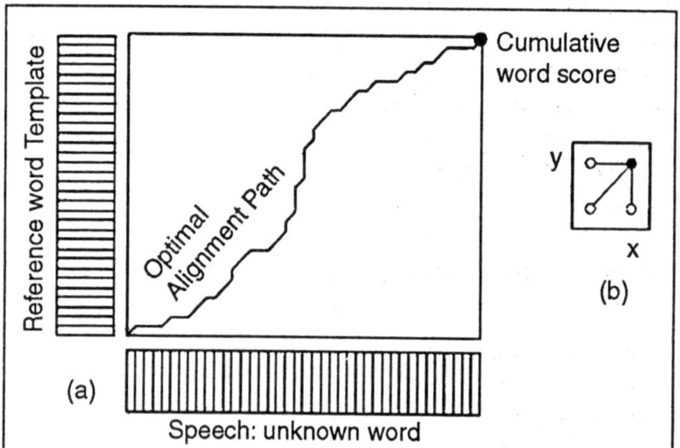

If D(x,y) is the Euclidean distance between frame x of the speech sample and frame y of the reference template, and if C(x,y) is the cumulative score along an optimal alignment path that leads to (x,y), then

$$C(x, y) = MIN(C(x-1,y), C(x-1,y-1), C(x, y-1)) + D(x, y)$$

The resulting alignment path may be visualized as a low valley of Euclidean distance scores, meandering through the hilly landscape of the matrix, beginning at (0, 0) and ending at the final point (X, Y).

By keeping track of backpointers, the full alignment path can be recovered by tracing backwards from (X, Y). An optimal alignment path is computed for each reference word template, and the one with the lowest cumulative score is considered to be the best match for the unknown speech sample.

There are many variations on the DTW algorithm. For example, it is common to vary the local path constraints, *e.g.*, by introducing transitions with slope 1/2 or 2, or weighting the transitions in various ways, or applying other kinds of slope constraints. While the reference word models are usually templates, they may be state-based models (as shown previously in Figure). When using states, vertical transitions are often disallowed (since there are fewer states than frames), and often the goal is to maximize the cumulative score, rather than to minimize it.

A particularly important variation of DTW is an extension from isolated to continuous speech. This extension is called the One Stage DTW algorithm. Here the goal is to find the optimal alignment between the speech sample and the best sequence of reference words. The complexity of the extended algorithm is still linear in the length of the sample and the vocabulary size. The only modification to the basic DTW algorithm is that at the beginning of each reference word model (*i.e.*, its first frame or state), the diagonal path is allowed to point back to the end of all reference word models in the preceding frame.

Local backpointers must specify the reference word model of the preceding point, so that the optimal word sequence can be recovered by tracing backwards from the final point of the word W with the best final score. Grammars can be imposed on continuous speech recognition by restricting the allowed transitions at word boundaries.

NEURAL NETWORK APPROACHES

Because speech recognition is basically a pattern recognition problem, and because neural networks are good at pattern recognition, many early researchers naturally tried applying neural networks to speech recognition. The earliest attempts involved highly simplified tasks, *e.g.*, classifying speech segments as voiced/unvoiced, or nasal/fricative/plosive.

Success in these experiments encouraged researchers to move on to phoneme classification; this task became a proving ground for neural networks as they quickly achieved world-class results. There are two basic approaches to speech classification using neural networks: static and dynamic, as illustrated in Figure.

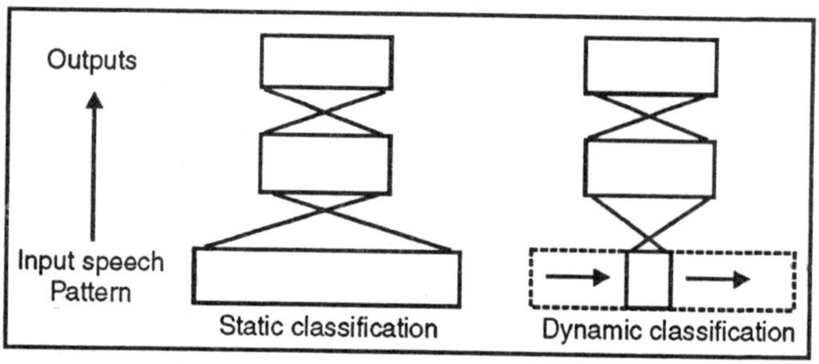

Fig. Static and Dynamic Approaches to Classification

In static classification, the neural network sees all of the input speech at once, and makes a single decision. By contrast, in dynamic classification, the neural network sees only a small window of the speech, and this window slides over the input speech while the network makes a series of local decisions, which have to be integrated into a global decision at a later time. Static classification works well for phoneme recognition, but it scales poorly to the level of words or sentences; dynamic classification scales better. Either approach may make use of recurrent connections, although recurrence is more often found in the dynamic approach.

Phoneme Classification

Phoneme classification can be performed with high accuracy by using either static or dynamic approaches. Here we review some typical experiments using each approach.

Static Approaches

A simple but elegant experiment was performed by Huang and Lippmann, demonstrating that neural networks can form complex decision surfaces from speech data. They applied a multilayer perceptron with only 2 inputs, 50 hidden units, and 10 outputs, to Peterson and Barney's collection of vowels produced by men, women, and children, using the first two formants of the vowels as the input speech representation. After 50,000 iterations of training, the network produced the decision regions.

These decision regions are nearly optimal, resembling the decision regions that would be drawn by hand, and they yield classification accuracy comparable to that of more conventional algorithms, such as k-nearest neighbour and Gaussian classification. In a more complex experiment, Elman and Zipser trained a network to classify the vowels/a,i,u/and the consonants/b,d,g/as they occur in the utterances ba,bi,bu; da,di,du; and ga,gi,gu.

Their network input consisted of 16 spectral coefficients over 20 frames (covering an entire 64 msec utterance, centered by hand over the consonant's voicing onset); this was fed into a hidden layer with between 2 and 6 units, leading to 3 outputs for either vowel or consonant classification. This network achieved error rates of roughly 0.5% for vowels and 5.0% for consonants.

An analysis of the hidden units showed that they tend to be feature detectors, discriminating between important classes of sounds, such as consonants versus vowels. Among the most difficult of classification tasks is the so-called E-set, *i.e.*, discriminating between the rhyming English letters 'B, C, D, E, G, P, T, V, Z'. Burr applied a static network to this task, with very good results. His network used an input window of 20 spectral frames, automatically extracted from the whole utterance using energy information. These inputs led directly to 9 outputs representing the E-set letters. The network was trained and tested using 180 tokens from a single speaker. When the early portion of the utterance was oversampled, effectively highlighting the disambiguating features, recognition accuracy was nearly perfect.

Dynamic Approaches

In a seminal paper, Waibel *et al* demonstrated excellent results for phoneme classification using a Time Delay Neural Network (TDNN), shown in Figure.

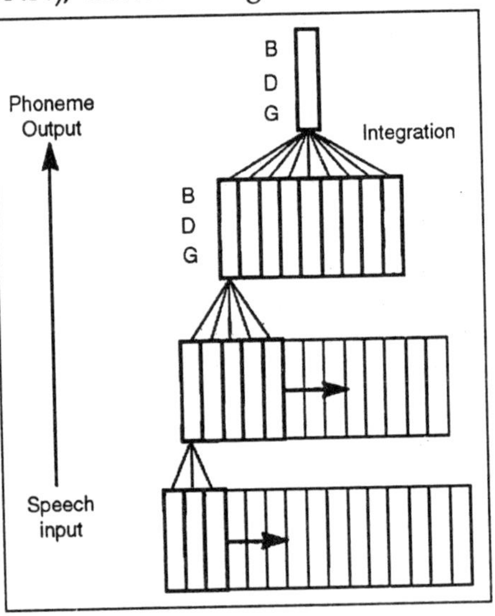

This architecture has only 3 and 5 delays in the input and hidden layer, respectively, and the final output is computed by integrating over 9 frames of phoneme activations in the second hidden layer.

The TDNN's design is attractive for several reasons: its compact structure economizes on weights and forces the network to develop general feature detectors; its hierarchy of delays optimizes these feature detectors by increasing their scope at each layer; and its temporal integration at the output layer makes the network shift invariant (*i.e.*, insensitive to the exact positioning of the speech). The TDNN achieved an error rate of 1.5%, compared to 6.5% achieved by a simple HMM-based recognizer.

NEURAL NETWORKS

It is nowadays a common notion that vast amounts of capital are traded through the Stock Markets all around the world. National economies are strongly linked and heavily influenced of the performance of their Stock Markets. Moreover, recently the Markets have become a more accessible investment tool, not only for strategic investors but for common people as well.

Consequently they are not only related to macroeconomic parametres, but they influence everyday life in a more direct way. Therefore they constitute a mechanism which has important and direct social impacts. The characteristic that all Stock Markets have in common is the uncertainty, which is related with their short and long-term future state. This feature is undesirable for the investor but it is also unavoidable whenever the Stock Market is selected as the investment tool. The best that one can do is to try to reduce this uncertainty. Stock Market Prediction (or Forecasting) is one of the instruments in this process.

The Stock Market prediction task divides researchers and academics into two groups those who believe that we can devise mechanisms to predict the market and those who believe that the market is efficient and whenever new information comes up the market absorbs it by correcting itself, thus there is no space for prediction (EMH). Furthermore they believe that the Stock Market follows a Random Walk, which implies that the best prediction you can have about tomorrow's value is today's value.

In literature a number of different methods have been applied in order to predict Stock Market returns. These methods can be grouped in four major categories: i) Technical Analysis Methods, ii) Fundamental Analysis Methods, iii) Traditional Time Series Forecasting and iv) Machine Learning Methods. Technical analysts, known as chartists, attempt to predict the market by tracing patterns that come from the study of charts which describe historic data of the market. Fundamental analysts study the intrinsic value of an stock and they invest on it if they estimate that its current value is lower that its intrinsic value. In Traditional Time Series forecasting an attempt to create linear prediction models to trace patterns in historic data takes place.

These linear models are divided in two categories: the univariate and the multivariate regression models, depending on whether they use one of more variables to approximate the Stock Market time series. Finally a number of methods have been developed under the common label Machine Learning these methods use a set of samples and try to trace patterns in it (linear or non-linear) in order to approximate the underlying function that generated the data.

INVESTMENTS

Investment Theories:An investment theory suggests what parametres one should take into account before placing his (or her) capital on the market. Traditionally the investment community accepts two major theories: the Firm Foundation and the Castles in the Air. Reference to these theories allows us to understand how the market is shaped, or in other words how the investors think and react. It is this sequence of 'thought and reaction' by the investors that defines the capital allocation and thus the level of the market.

There is no doubt that the majority of the people related to stock markets is trying to achieve profit. Profit comes by investing in stocks that have a good future (short or long term future). Thus what they are trying to accomplish one way or the other is to predict 16 the future of the market. But what determines this future? The way that people invest their money is the answer; and people invest money based on the information they hold. Therefore we have the following schema:

Information→Investor→Market Level

The factors that are under discussion on this schema are: the content of the 'Information' component and the way that the 'Investor' reacts when having this info.

On the other hand, according to the Castles in the Air theory the investors are triggered by information that is related to other investors' behaviour. So for this theory the only concern that the investor should have is to buy today with the price of 20 and sell tomorrow with the price of 30, no matter what the intrinsic value of the firm he (or she) invests on is.

Prediction Methods:The prediction of the market is without doubt an interesting task. In the literature there are a number of methods applied to accomplish this task. These methods use various approaches, ranging from highly informal ways (*e.g.* the study of a chart with the fluctuation of the market) to more formal ways (*e.g.* linear or non-linear regressions).

We have categorized these techniques as follows:

- Technical Analysis Methods
- Fundamental Analysis Methods
- Traditional Time Series Prediction Methods
- Machine Learning Methods

The criterion to this categorization is the type of tools and the type of data that each method is using in order to predict the market. What is common to these techniques is that they are used to predict and thus benefit from the market's future behaviour.

Technical Analysis

'Technical analysis is the method of predicting the appropriate time to buy or sell a stock used by those believing in the castles-in-the-air view of stock pricing'. The idea behind technical analysis is that share prices move in trends dictated by the constantly changing attributes of investors in response to different forces.

Using technical data such as price, volume, highest and lowest prices per trading period the technical analyst uses charts to predict future stock movements. Price charts are used to detect trends, these trends are assumed to be based on supply and demand issues which often have cyclical or noticeable patterns. From the study of these charts trading rules are extracted and used in the market environment. The technical analysts are known and as 'chartists'. Most chartists believe that the market is only 10 per cent logical and 90 per cent psychological. The chartist's belief is that a careful study of what the other investors are doing will shed light on what the crowed is likely to do in the future.

This is a very popular approach used to predict the market, which has been heavily criticized. The major point of criticism is that the extraction of trading rules from the study of charts is highly subjective therefore different analysts might extract different trading rules by studying the same charts. Although it is possible to use this methodology to predict the market on daily basis we will not follow this approach on this study due to its subjective character.

Fundamental Analysis

'Fundamental analysis is the technique of applying the tenets of the firm foundation theory to the selection of individual stocks". The analysts that use this method of prediction use fundamental data in order to have a clear picture of the firm (industry or market) they will choose to invest on. They are aiming to compute the 'real' value of the asset that they will invest in and they determine this value by studying variables such as the growth, the dividend payout, the interest rates, the risk of investment, the sales level, the tax rates an so on.

Their objective is to calculate the intrinsic value of an asset (*e.g.* of a stock). Since they do so they apply a simple trading rule. If the intrinsic 21 value of the asset is higher than the value it holds in the market, invest in it. If not, consider it a bad investment and avoid it. The fundamental analysts believe that the market is defined 90 per cent by logical and 10 per cent by physiological factors.

This type of analysis is not possible to fit in the objectives of our study. The reason for this is that the data it uses in order to determine the intrinsic value of an asset does not change on daily basis. Therefore fundamental analysis is helpful for predicting the market only in a long-term basis.

Traditional Time Series Prediction

The Traditional Time Series Prediction analyses historic data and attempts to approximate future values of a time series as a linear combination of these historic data. In econometrics there are two basic types of time series forecasting: univariate (simple regression) and multivariate (multivariate regression).

These types of regression models are the most common tools used in econometrics to predict time series. The way they are applied in practice is that firstly a set of factors that influence (or more specific is assumed that influence) the series under prediction is formed. These factors are the explanatory variables xi of the prediction model. Then a mapping between their values xit and the values of the time series yt (y is the to-be explained variable) is done, so that pairs {xit, yt} are formed.

These pairs are used to define the importance of each explanatory variable in the formulation of the to-be explained variable. In other words the linear combination of xi that approximates in an optimum way y is defined. Univariate models are based on one explanatory variable (I=1) while multivariate models use more than one variable (I>1). Regression models have been used to predict stock market time series. A good example of the use of multivariate regression is the work of Pesaran and Timmermann (1994).

They attempted prediction of the excess returns time series of S&P 500 and the Dow Jones on monthly, quarterly and annually basis. The data they used was from Jan 1954 until Dec 1990. Initially they used the subset from Jan 1954 until Dec 1959 to adjust the coefficients of the explanatory variables of their models, and then applied the models to predict the returns for the next year, quarter and month respectively.

Machine Learning Methods

Several methods for inductive learning have been developed under the common label 'Machine Learning'. All these methods use a set of samples to generate an approximation of the underling function that generated the data. The aim is to draw conclusions from these samples in such way that when unseen data are presented to a model it is possible to infer the to-be explained variable from these data.

The methods we discuss here are: The Nearest Neighbour and the Neural Networks Techniques. Both of these methods have been applied to market prediction; particularly for Neural Networks there is a rich literature related to the forecast of the market on daily basis.

PREDICTION USING NEURAL NETWORKS

The experiment consisted of three phases. In the first phase a genetic algorithm (GA) searched the space of NNs with different structures and resulted a generation with the fittest of all networks searched based on a metric which was either: TheilA or TheilB or TheilC or MAE. The GA search was repeated three times for each metric. Then the best three networks were selected from each repetition of the GA search and for each one of the metrics.

The output of the first phase was a set of thirtysix network structures. In the second phase for each one of the thirty-six resulting network structures we applied the following procedure. We trained (on Training1 set) and validated (on Validation1 set) the network. Then we used the indicated number of epochs from the validation procedure and based on it we retrained the network on the Training1 plus the Validation1 set. Finally we tested the performance of the network on unseen data.

This procedure was repeated 50 times for each network structure for random initializations of its weights. From the nine networks for each performance statistic, we selected the most stable in terms of standard deviation of their performance.

Thus the output of the second phase was a set of four network structures. During the third phase for each one of these four networks we applied the following procedure 50 times. We trained each network on the first half of the

Training Set and we used the remaining half for validation. Then, using the indicated epochs by the validation procedure, we retrained the network on the complete Training Set. Finally we tested the network on the Test Set calculating all four metrics.

The performance for each network on each metric was measured again in terms of standard deviation and mean of its performance over 50 times that it was trained, validated and tested.

4

Network Training Models

CONCEPT AND THEORY

ARTIFICIAL NEURAL NETWORK

An artificial neural network is a system based on the operation of biological neural networks, in other words, is an emulation of biological neural system. Why would be necessary the implementation of artificial neural networks?

Although computing these days is truly advanced, there are certain tasks that a programme made for a common microprocessor is unable to perform; even so a software implementation of a neural network can be made with their advantages and disadvantages.

Qualities

- A neural network can perform tasks that a linear programme can not.
- When an element of the neural network fails, it can continue without any problem by their parallel nature.
- A neural network learns and does not need to be reprogrammed.
- It can be implemented in any application.
- It can be implemented without any problem.

Drawbacks

- The neural network needs training to operate.

- The architecture of a neural network is different from the architecture of microprocessors therefore needs to be emulated.
- Requires high processing time for large neural networks.

Another aspect of the artificial neural networks is that there are different architectures, which consequently requires different types of algorithms, but despite to be an apparently complex system, a neural network is relatively simple.Artificial neural networks (ANN) are among the newest signal-processing technologies in the engineer's toolbox.

The field is highly interdisciplinary, but our approach will restrict the view to the engineering perspective. In engineering, neural networks serve two important functions: as pattern classifiers and as nonlinear adaptive filters.

We will provide a brief overview of the theory, learning rules, and applications of the most important neural network models. Definitions and Style of Computation An Artificial Neural Network is an adaptive, most often nonlinear system that learns to perform a function (an input/output map) from data. Adaptive means that the system parametres are changed during operation, normally called the training phase.

After the training phase the Artificial Neural Network parametres are fixed and the system is deployed to solve the problem at hand (the testing phase). The Artificial Neural Network is built with a systematic step-by-step procedure to optimize a performance criterion or to follow some implicit internal constraint, which is commonly referred to as the learning rule.

The input/output training data are fundamental in neural network technology, because they convey the necessary information to 'discover' the optimal operating point. The nonlinear nature of the neural network processing elements (PEs) provides the system with lots of flexibility to achieve practically any desired input/output map, *i.e.*, some Artificial Neural Networks are universal mappers. There is a style in neural computation that is worth describing.

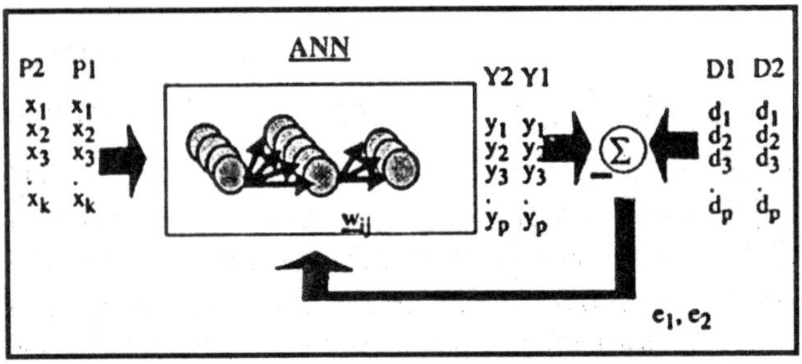

An input is presented to the neural network and a corresponding desired or target response set at the output (when this is the case the training is called supervised). An error is composed from the difference between the desired response and the system output.

This error information is fed back to the system and adjusts the system parametres in a systematic fashion (the learning rule). The process is repeated until the performance is acceptable. It is clear from this description that the performance hinges heavily on the data.

If one does not have data that cover a significant portion of the operating conditions or if they are noisy, then neural network technology is probably not the right solution. On the other hand, if there is plenty of data and the problem is poorly understood to derive an approximate model, then neural network technology is a good choice.

This operating procedure should be contrasted with the traditional engineering design, made of exhaustive subsystem specifications and intercommunication protocols. In artificial neural networks, the designer chooses the network topology, the performance function, the learning rule, and the criterion to stop the training phase, but the system automatically adjusts the parametres.

So, it is difficult to bring a priori information into the design, and when the system does not work properly it is also hard to incrementally refine the solution. But ANN-based solutions are extremely efficient in terms of development time and resources, and in many difficult problems artificial neural networks provide performance that is difficult to match with other technologies. Denker 10 years ago said that 'artificial neural networks are the second best way to implement a solution' motivated by the simplicity of their design and because of their universality, only shadowed by the traditional design obtained by studying the physics of the problem.

At present, artificial neural networks are emerging as the technology of choice for many applications, such as pattern recognition, prediction, system identification, and control.

BIOLOGICAL MODEL

Artificial neural networks emerged after the introduction of simplified neurons by McCulloch and Pitts in 1943. These neurons were presented as models of biological neurons and as conceptual components for circuits that could perform computational tasks. The basic model of the neuron is founded upon the functionality of a biological neuron. 'Neurons are the basic signaling units of the nervous system' and 'each neuron is a discrete cell whose several processes arise from its cell body'.

The neuron has four main regions to its structure. The cell body, or soma, has two offshoots from it, the dendrites, and the axon, which end in presynaptic terminals. The cell body is the heart of the cell, containing the nucleus and maintaining protein synthesis. A neuron may have many dendrites, which branch out in a treelike structure, and receive signals from other neurons.

A neuron usually only has one axon which grows out from a part of the cell body called the axon hillock. The axon conducts electric signals generated at the axon hillock down its length. These electric signals are called action potentials. The other end of the axon may split into several branches, which end in a presynaptic terminal. Action potentials are the electric signals that neurons use to convey information to the brain. All these signals are identical. Therefore, the brain determines what type of information is being received based on the path that the signal took. The brain analyses the patterns of signals being sent and from that information it can interpret the type of information being received. Myelin is the fatty tissue that surrounds and insulates the axon. Often short axons do not need this insulation. There are uninsulated parts of the axon. These areas are called Nodes of Ranvier. At these nodes, the signal traveling down the axon is regenerated. This ensures that the signal traveling down the axon travels fast and remains constant (*i.e.* very short propagation delay and no weakening of the signal). The synapse is the area of contact between two neurons. The neurons do not actually physically touch. They are separated by the synaptic cleft, and electric signals are sent through chemical 13 interaction. The neuron sending the signal is called the presynaptic cell and the neuron receiving the signal is called the postsynaptic cell.

The signals are generated by the membrane potential, which is based on the differences in concentration of sodium and potassium ions inside and outside the cell membrane. Neurons can be classified by their number of processes (or appendages), or by their function. If they are classified by the number of processes, they fall into three categories. Unipolar neurons have a single process (dendrites and axon are located on the same stem), and are most common in invertebrates. In bipolar neurons, the dendrite and axon are the neuron's two separate processes. Bipolar neurons have a subclass called pseudo-bipolar neurons, which are used to send sensory information to the spinal cord. Finally, multipolar neurons are most common in mammals. Examples of these neurons are spinal motor neurons, pyramidal cells and Purkinje cells (in the cerebellum). If classified by function, neurons again fall into three separate categories. The first group is sensory, or afferent, neurons, which provide information for perception and motor coordination.

The second group provides information (or instructions) to muscles and glands and is therefore called motor neurons. The last group, interneuronal, contains all other neurons and has two subclasses. One group called relay or projection interneurons have long axons and connect different parts of the brain. The other group called local interneurons are only used in local circuits.

MATHEMATICAL MODEL

When creating a functional model of the biological neuron, there are three basic components of importance. First, the synapses of the neuron are modeled as weights. The strength of the connection between an input and a neuron is noted by the value of the weight. Negative weight values reflect inhibitory connections, while positive values designate excitatory connections. The next two components model the actual activity within the neuron cell. An adder sums up all the inputs modified by their respective weights. This activity is referred to as linear combination. Finally, an activation function controls the amplitude of the output of the neuron. An acceptable range of output is usually between 0 and 1, or -1 and 1.Mathematically, this process is described in the figure

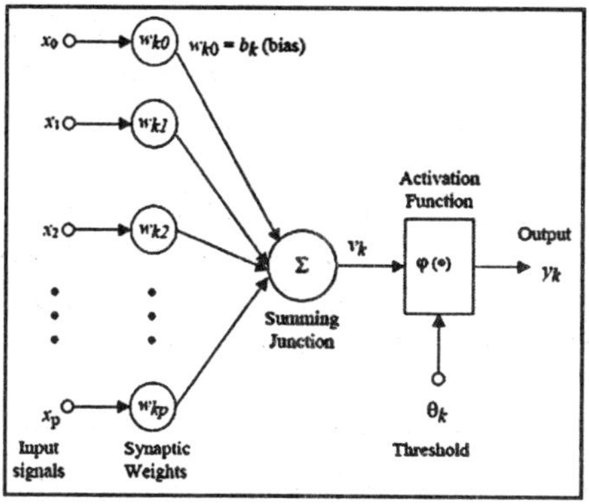

From this model the interval activity of the neuron can be shown to be:

$$v_k = \sum_{j=1}^{p} w_{kj} x_j$$

The output of the neuron, yk, would therefore be the outcome of some activation function on the value of vk.

Activation Functions

As mentioned previously, the activation function acts as a squashing function, such that the output of a neuron in a neural network is between certain values. In general, there are three types of activation functions, denoted.

First, there is the Threshold Function which takes on a value of 0 if the summed input is less than a certain threshold value (v), and the value 1 if the summed input is greater than or equal to the threshold value.

$$\varphi(v) = \begin{cases} 1 \text{ if } v \geq 0 \\ 0 \text{ if } v < 0 \end{cases}$$

Secondly, there is the Piecewise-Linear function. This function again can take on the values of 0 or 1, but can also take on values between that depending on the amplification factor in a certain region of linear operation.

$$\varphi(v) = \begin{cases} 1 & v \geq 1/2 \\ v & -1/2 > v > 1/2 \\ 0 & v \leq -1/2 \end{cases}$$

Thirdly, there is the sigmoid function. This function can range between 0 and 1, but it is also sometimes useful to use the -1 to 1 range. An example of the sigmoid function is the hyperbolic tangent function.

$$\varphi(v) = \tan h\left(\frac{v}{2}\right) = \frac{1-\exp(-v)}{1+\exp(-v)}$$

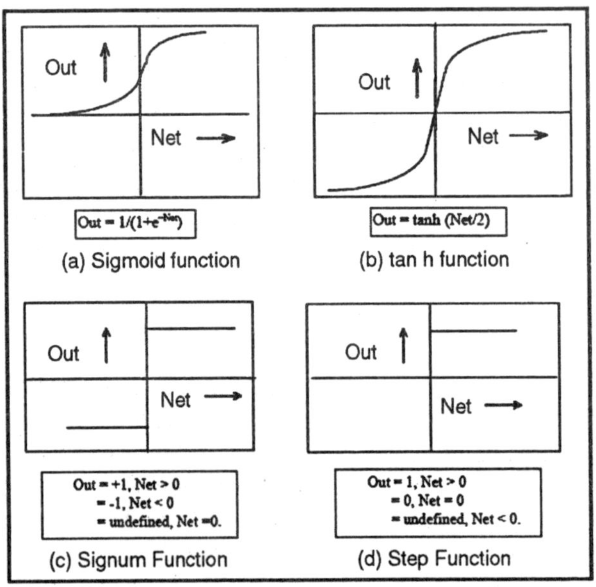

(a) Sigmoid function (b) tan h function (c) Signum Function (d) Step Function

The artifcial neural networks are all variations on the parallel distributed processing (PDP) idea, The architecture of each neural network is based on very similar building blocks which perform the processing. In this chapter we first discuss these processing units and discuss diferent neural network topologies. Learning strategies as a basis for an adaptive system

DISTRIBUTED REPRESENTATION

An artifcial neural network consists of a pool of simple processing units which communicate by sending signals to each other over a large number of weighted connections. A set of major aspects of a parallel distributed model can be distinguished :

- A set of processing units ('neurons,' 'cells');
- A state of activation yk for every unit, which equivalent to the output of the unit;
- Connections between the units. Generally each connection is defined by a weight wjk which determines the effect which the signal of unit j has on unit k;
- A propagation rule, which determines the effective input sk of a unit from its external inputs;
- An activation function Fk, which determines the new level of activation based on the efective input sk(t) and the current activation yk(t) (*i.e.*, the update);
- An external input (aka bias, offset) øk for each unit;
- A method for information gathering (the learning rule);
- An environment within which the system must operate, providing input signals and|if necessary|error signals.

Processing Units

Each unit performs a relatively simple job: receive input from neighbours or external sources and use this to compute an output signal which is propagated to other units. Apart from this processing, a second task is the adjustment of the weights. The system is inherently parallel in the sense that many units can carry out their computations at the same time. Within neural systems it is useful to distinguish three types of units: input units (indicated by an index i) which receive data from outside the neural network, output units (indicated by an index o) which send data out of the neural network, and hidden units (indicated by an index h) whose input and output signals remain within the neural network.

During operation, units can be updated either synchronously or asynchronously. With synchronous updating, all units update their activation simultaneously; with asynchronous updating, each unit has a (usually fixed) probability of updating its activation at a time t, and usually only one unit will be able to do this at a time. In some cases the latter model has some advantages.

TOPOLOGIES

In the previous section we discussed the properties of the basic processing unit in an artificial neural network. This section focuses on the pattern of connections between the units and the propagation of data. As for this pattern of connections, the main distinction we can make is between:

FEED-FORWARD NEURAL NETWORKS

Where the data ow from input to output units is strictly feedforward. The data processing can extend over multiple (layers of) units, but no feedback connections are present, that is, connections extending from outputs of units to inputs of units in the same layer or previous layers.

RECURRENT NEURAL NETWORKS

That do contain feedback connections. Contrary to feed-forward networks, the dynamical properties of the network are important. In some cases, the activation values of the units undergo a relaxation process such that the neural network will evolve to a stable state in which these activations do not change anymore. In other applications, the change of the activation values of the output neurons are significant, such that the dynamical behaviour constitutes the output of the neural network.Classical examples of feed-forward neural networks are the Perceptron and Adaline. Examples of recurrent networks have been presented.

TRAINING OF ARTIFCIAL NEURAL NETWORKS

A neural network has to be configured such that the application of a set of inputs produces (either 'direct' or via a relaxation process) the desired set of outputs. Various methods to set the strengths of the connections exist. One way is to set the weights explicitly, using a priori knowledge. Another way is to'train' the neural network by feeding it teaching patterns and letting it change its weights according to some learning rule We can categorise the learn.ing situations in two distinct sorts.

These are:

- Supervised learning or Associative learning in which the network is trained by providing it with input and matching output patterns. These input-output pairs can be provided by an external teacher, or by the system which contains the neural network
- Unsupervised learning or Self-organisation in which an (output) unit is trained to respond to clusters of pattern within the input. In this paradigm the system is supposed to discover statistically salient features of the input population. Unlike the supervised learning paradigm, there is no a priori set of categories into which the patterns are to be classified; rather the system must develop its own representation of the input stimuli.
- Reinforcement Learning This type of learning may be considered as an intermediate form of the above two types of learning. Here the learning machine does some action on the environment and gets a feedback response from the environment. The learning system grades its action good (rewarding) or bad (punishable) based on the environmental response and accordingly adjusts its parametres.

Generally, parametre adjustment is continued until an equilibrium state occurs, following which there will be no more changes in its parametres. The selforganizing neural learning may be categorized under this type of learning.

Patterns of Connectivity of Neural Networks

Both learning paradigms supervised learning and unsupervised learning result in an adjustment of the weights of the connections between units, according to some modification rule. The basic idea is that if two units j and k are active simultaneously, their interconnection must be strengthened. If j receives input from k, the simplest version of Hebbian learning prescribes to modify the weight wjk with

$$\Delta w_{jk} = \gamma y_j y_k$$

where γ is a positive constant of proportionality representing the learning rate. Another common rule uses not the actual activation of unit k but the difference between the actual and desired activation for adjusting the weights:

$\Delta w_{jk} = \gamma y_j (d_k - y_k)$ in which dk is the desired activation provided by a teacher. This is often called the Widrow-Hoff rule or the delta rule, and will be discussed in the next chapter. Many variants (often very exotic ones) have been published the last few years.

ADAPTIVE RESONANCE THEORY

FEATURES

One of the nice features of human memory is its ability to learn many new things without necessarily forgetting things learned in the past. A frequently cited example is the ability to recognize your parents even if you have not seen them for some time and have learned many new faces in the interim. It would be highly desirable if we could impart this same capability to an Artificial Neural Networks. Most neural networks will tend to forget old information if we attempt to add new information incrementally. When developing an artificial neural network to perform a particular pattern-classification operation, we typically proceed by gathering a set of exemplars, or training patterns, then using these exemplars to train the system. During the training, information is encoded in the system by the adjustment of weight values. Once the training is deemed to be adequate, the system is ready to be put into production, and no additional weight modification is permitted. This operational scenario is acceptable provided the problem domain has well-defined boundaries and is stable.

Under such conditions, it is usually possible to define an adequate set of training inputs for whatever problem is being solved. Unfortunately, in many realistic situations, the environment is neither bounded nor stable. Consider a simple example. Suppose you intend to train a backpropagation to recognize the silhouettes of a certain class of aircraft.

The appropriate images can be collected and used to train the network, which is potentially a time-consuming task depending on the size of the network required. After the network has learned successfully to recognize all of the aircraft, the training period is ended and no further modification of the weights is allowed. If, at some future time, another aircraft in the same class becomes operational, you may wish to add its silhouette to the store of knowledge in your neural network.

To do this, you would have to retrain the network with the new pattern plus all of the previous patterns. Training on only the new silhouette could result in the network learning that pattern quite well, but forgetting previously learned patterns. Although retraining may not take as long as the initial training, it still could require a significant investment.

ART OF ADAPTATIVE RESONANCE THEORY

Grossberg introduced a model for explaining biological phenomena.

The model has three crucial properties:

1. A normalisation of the total network activity. Biological systems are usually very adaptive to large

changes in their environment. For example, the human eye can adapt itself to large variations in light intensities;

2. Contrast enhancement of input patterns. The awareness of subtle dierences in input patterns can mean a lot in terms of survival. Distinguishing a hiding panther from a resting one makes all the diference in the world. The mechanism used here is contrast enhancement;
3. Short-term memory (STM) storage of the contrast-enhanced pattern. Before the input pattern can be decoded, it must be stored in the short-term memory. The long-term memory (LTM) implements an arousal mechanism (*i.e.*, the classi cation), whereas the STM is used to cause gradual changes in the LTM.

The system consists of two layers, F1 and F2, which are connected to each other via the LTM

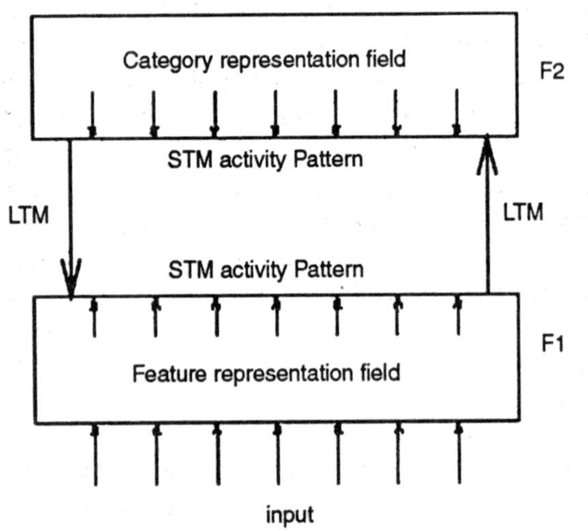

The ART architecture

The input pattern is received at F1, whereas classication takes place in F2. As mentioned before, the input is not directly classified. First a characterisation takes place by means of extracting features, giving rise to activation in the feature representation field. The expectations, residing in the LTM connections, translate the input pattern to a categorisation in the category representation field. The classication is compared to the expectation of the network, which resides in the LTM weights from F2 to F1. If there is a match, the expectations are strengthened, otherwise the classification is rejected.

ART1: The Simplified Neural Network Model

The ART1 simplified model consists of two layers of binary neurons (with values 1 and 0), called F1 (the comparison layer) and F2 (the recognition layer)

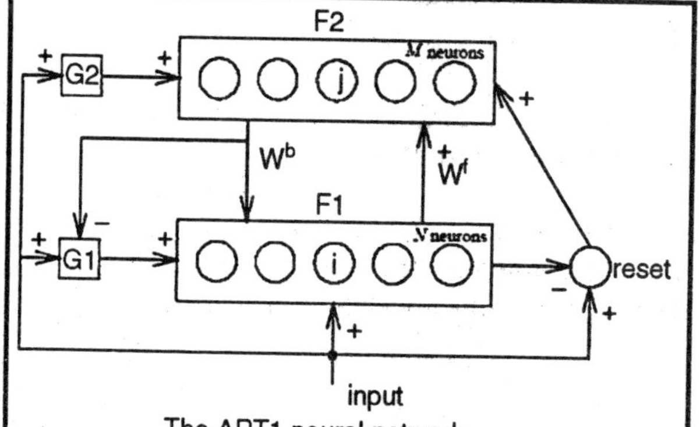

The ART1 neural network

Each neuron in F1 is connected to all neurons in F2 via the continuous-valued forward long term memory (LTM) Wf, and vice versa via the binary-valued backward LTM Wb. The other modules are gain 1 and 2 (G1 and G2), and a reset module. Each neuron in the comparison layer receives three inputs: a component of the input pattern, a component of the feedback pattern, and a gain G1.

A neuron outputs a 1 if and only if at least three of these inputs are high: the 'two-thirds rule.' The neurons in the recognition layer each compute the inner product of their incoming (continuous-valued) weights and the pattern sent over these connections. The winning neuron then inhibits all the other neurons via lateral inhibition. Gain 2 is the logical 'or' of all the elements in the input pattern x. Gain 1 equals gain 2, except when the feedback pattern from F2 contains any 1;. then it is forced to zero. Finally, the reset signal is sent to the active neuron in F2 if the input vector x and the output of F1 dier by more than some vigilance level.

Operation

The network starts by clamping the input at F1. Because the output of F2 is zero, G1 and G2 are both on and the output of F1 matches its input.The pattern is sent to F2, and in F2 one neuron becomes active. This signal is then sent back over the backward LTM, which reproduces a binary pattern at F1. Gain 1 is inhibited, and only the neurons in F1 which receive a 'one' from both x and F2 remain active. If there is a substantial mismatch between the two patterns, the reset signal will inhibit the neuron in F2 and the process is repeated.

- Initialisation

$$w^b_{ji}(0) = 1$$

$$w^f_{ij}(0) = \frac{1}{1+N}$$

where N is the number of neurons in F1, M the number of neurons in F2,0i<N, and 0≤j<M. Also, choose the vigilance threshold $\rho, 0 \le \rho \le 1$;

- Apply the new input pattern x:
- Compute the activation values y0 of the neurons in F2

$$Y_i' = \sum_{j=1}^{N} w^f_{ij}(t)x_{i;}$$

- Select the winning neuron k (0≤k<M)
- Vigilance test: if

$$\frac{w^b_k(t)\cdot x}{x\cdot x} > \rho$$

where.denotes inner product, go to step 7, else go to step 6. Note that $w^b_k \cdot x$ essentially is the inner product, $x^* \cdot x$ which will be large if x* and x near to each other;

- Neuron k is disabled from further activity. Go to step 3;
- Set for all l, $0 \le l < N$:

$$w^{b}_{kl}(t+1) = w^{b}_{kl}(t)x_{l},$$

$$w^{f}_{lk}(t+1) = \frac{w^{b}_{kl}(t)x_{l}}{1/2 + \sum_{i=1}^{N} w^{b}_{kl}(t)x_{i}}$$

- Re-enable all neurons in F2 and go to step 2

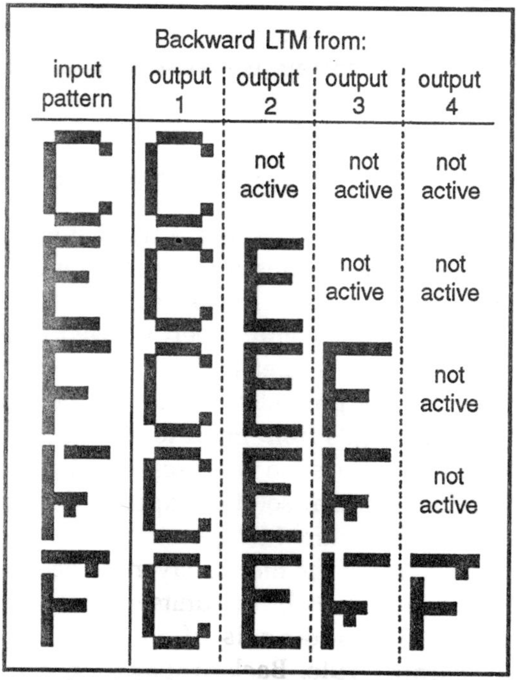

An example of the behaviour of the Carpenter Grossberg network for letter patterns. The binary input patterns on the left were applied sequentially. On the right the stored patterns (*i.e.,* the weights of Wb for the first four output units) are shown.

ART1: The Original Model

In later work, Carpenter and Grossberg present several neural network models to incorporate parts of the complete theory. We will only discuss the first model, ART1. The network incorporates a follow-the-leader clustering algorithm. This algorithm tries to fit each new input pattern in an existing class. If no matching class can be found, *i.e.*, the distance between the new pattern and all existing classes exceeds some threshold, a new class is created containing the new pattern. The novelty in this approach is that the network is able to adapt to new incoming patterns, while the previous memory is not corrupted.

In most neural networks, such as the backpropagation network, all patterns must be taught sequentially; the teaching of a new pattern might corrupt the weights for all previously learned patterns. By changing the structure of the network rather than the weights, ART1 overcomes this problem.

BACKPROPAGATION NEURAL NETWORK

A single-layer network has severe restrictions: the class of tasks that can be accomplished is very limited. In this chapter we will focus on feed-forward networks with layers of processing units. Minsky and Papert showed in 1969 that a two layer feed-forward network can overcome many restrictions, but did not present a solution to the problem of how to adjust the weights from input to hidden units.

An answer to this question was presented by Rumelhart, Hinton and Williams similar solutions appeared to have been published earlier. The central idea behind this solution is that the errors for the units of the hidden layer are determined by back-propagating the errors of the units of the output layer. For this reason the method is often called the back-propagation learning rule. Back-propagation can also be considered as a generalisation of the delta rule for non-linear activation functions1 and multilayer networks.

MULTI-LAYER FEED-FORWARD NETWORKS

A feed-forward network has a layered structure. Each layer consists of units which receive their input from units from a layer directly below and send their output to units in a layer directly above the unit. There are no connections within a layer. The Ni inputs are fed into the first layer of Nh;1 hidden units. The input units are merely 'fan-out' units; no processing takes place in these units. The activation of a hidden unit is a function Fi of the weighted inputs plus a bias, as given in in eq.

$$y_k(t+1) = F_k\left(S_k(t)\right) = F_k\left(\sum_j w_{jk}(t)y_j(t) + \theta_k(t)\right),$$

The output of the hidden units is distributed over the next layer of Nh;2 hidden units, until the last layer of hidden units, of which the outputs are fed into a layer of No output units.

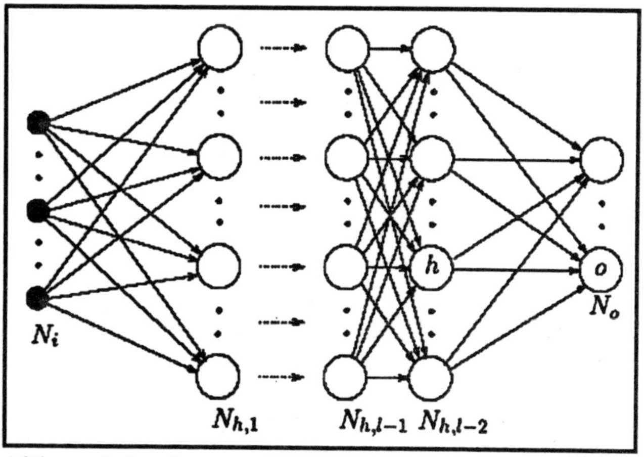

Although backpropagation can be applied to networks with any number of layers, just as for networks with binary units it has been shown that only one layer of hidden units suces to approximate any function with finitely many discontinuities to arbitrary precision, provided the activation functions of the hidden units are non-linear. In most applications a feed-forward network with a single layer of hidden units is used with a sigmoid activation function for the units.

DELTA RULE

Since we are now using units with nonlinear activation functions, we have to generalise the delta rule:

The activation is a differentiable function of the total input, given by

$$y_k^p = F\left(S_k^p\right)$$

in which

$$\left(S_k^p\right) = \sum_j w_{jk} y_j^p + \theta_k$$

to get the correct generalisation of the delta rule as presented in the previous chapter, we must set

$$\Delta_p w_{jk} = -\gamma \frac{\delta E^p}{\delta w_{jk}}$$

The error measure Ep is defined as the total quadratic error for pattern p at the output units:

$$E^p = \frac{1}{2} \sum_{0=1}^{N_0} \left(d_0^p - y_0^p\right),$$

where dpo is the desired output for unit o when pattern p is clamped. We further set

$$E = \sum_p E^p$$

as the summed squared error. We can write

$$\frac{\delta E^p}{\delta w_{jk}} = \frac{\delta E^p}{\delta S_k^p} \frac{\delta S_k^p}{\delta w_{jk}}$$

By equation

$$S_k^p = \sum_j w_{jk} y_j^p + \theta_k$$

we see that the second factor is

$$\frac{\delta S_k^p}{\delta w_{jk}} = y_j^p$$

When we define

$$\delta_k^p = -\frac{\delta E^p}{\delta S_k^p}$$

we will get an update rule which is equivalent to the delta rule as described in the previous chapter, resulting in a gradient descent on the error surface if we make the weight changes according to:

$$\Delta_p w_{jk} = \gamma \delta_k^p y_j^p$$

The trick is to figure out what δp k should be for each unit k in the network. The interesting result, which we now derive, is that there is a simple recursive computation of these δ's which can be implemented by propagating error signals backward through the network.

To compute δp k we apply the chain rule to write this partial derivative as the product of two factors, one factor reflecting the change in error as a function of the output of the unit and one re ecting the change in the output as a function of changes in the input. Thus, we have

$$\delta_k^p = -\frac{\delta E^p}{\delta s_k^p} = -\frac{\delta E^p}{\delta y_k^p}\frac{\delta y_k^p}{\delta s_k^p}$$

Let us compute the second factor.

By equation,

$$y_k^p = F\left(S_k^p\right)$$

we see that,

$$\frac{\delta y_k^p}{\delta s_k^p} = F'\left(s_k^p\right)$$

which is the same result as we obtained with the standard delta rule. Substituting this and equation

$$\delta_k^p = -\frac{\delta E^p}{\delta s_k^p} = -\frac{\delta E^p}{\delta y_k^p}\frac{\delta y_k^p}{\delta s_k^p}$$

in equation, we get $\delta_0^p = (d_0^p - y_0^p)F_0'(s_0^p)$ for any output unit o. Secondly, if k is not an output unit but a hidden unit k = h, we do not readily know the contribution of the unit to the output error of the network.

However, the error measure can be written as a function of the net inputs from hidden to output layer; Ep = Ep(sp 1,sp 2,....... sp j.....) and we use the chain rule to write substituting this in equation yields. Equations and give a recursive procedure for computing the δ's for all units in the network, which are then used to compute the weight changes according to equation. This procedure constitutes the generalised delta rule for a feed-forward network of non-linear units.

UNDERSTANDING BACKPROPAGATION

The equations derived in the previous section may be mathematically correct, but what do they actually mean? Is there a way of understanding back-propagation other than reciting the necessary equations? In fact, the whole back-propagation process is intuitively very clear.

When a learning pattern is clamped, the activation values are propagated to the output units, and the actual network output is compared with the desired output values, we usually end up with an error in each of the output units. Let's call this error eo for a particular output unit o. We have to bring eo to zero.

The simplest method to do this is the greedy method: we strive to change the connections in the neural network in such a way that, next time around, the error eo will be zero for this particular pattern. We know from the delta rule that, in order to reduce an error, we have to adapt its incoming weights according to.

$$\Delta w_{ho} = (d_0 - y_0) y_h$$

That's step one. But it alone is not enough: when we only apply this rule, the weights from input to hidden units are never changed, and we do not have the full representational power of the feed-forward network as promised by the universal approximation theorem. In order to adapt the weights from input to hidden units, we again want to apply the delta rule. This is solved by the chain rule which does the following: distribute the error of an output unit o to all the hidden units that is it connected to, weighted by this connection.

Differently put, a hidden unit h receives a delta from each output unit o equal to the delta of that output unit weighted with (=multiplied by)the weight of the connection between those units.

WORKING WITH BACK-PROPAGATION

The application of the generalised delta rule thus involves two phases: During the first phase the input x is presented and propagated forward through the network to compute the output values yp o for each output unit. This output is compared with its desired value do, resulting in an error signal δp o for each output unit. The second phase involves a backward pass through the network during which the error signal is passed to each unit in the network and appropriate weight changes are calculated.Weight adjustments with sigmoid activation function.

The weight of a connection is adjusted by an amount proportional to the product of an error signal on the unit k receiving the input and the output of the unit j sending this signal along the connection.If the unit is an output unit, the error signal is given by Take as the activation function F the 'sigmoid' function as definedIn this case the derivative is equal to such that the error signal for an output unit can be written as the error signal for a hidden unit is determined recursively in terms of error signals of the units to which it directly connects and the weights of those connections. For the sigmoid activation function:

$$\delta_h^p = F'\left(s_h^p\right)\sum_{0=1}^{N_0} \delta_0^p w_{ho} = y_h^p\left(1 - y_h^p\right)\sum_{0=1}^{N_0} \delta_0^p w_{ho}$$

Learning Rate and Momentum

The learning procedure requires that the change in weight is proportional to $\delta E^p / \delta w$ True gradient descent requires that in nitesimal steps are taken. The constant of proportionality is the learning rate. For practical purposes we choose a learning rate that is as large as possible without leading to oscillation. One way to avoid oscillation at large, is to make the change in weight dependent of the past weight change by adding a momentum term. Where indexes the presentation number and F is a constant which determines the efect of the previous weight change. Although, theoretically, the back-propagation algorithm performs gradient descent on the total error only if the weights are adjusted after the full set of learning patterns has been presented, more often than not the learning rule is applied to each pattern separately, *i.e.*, a pattern p is applied, Ep is calculated, and the weights are adapted (p = 1, 2,..... P). There exists empirical indication that this results in faster convergence. Care has to be taken, however, with the order in which the patterns are taught. For example, when using the same sequence over and over again the network may become focused on the few patterns. This problem can be overcome by using a permuted training method.

KOHONEN NEURAL NETWORK

The cerebral cortex is arguably the most fascinating structure in all of human physiology. Although vastly complex on a microscopic level, the cortex reveals a consistently uniform structure on a macroscopic scale, from one brain to another. Centres for such diverse activities as thought, speech, vision, hearing, and motor functions lie in specific areas of the cortex, and these areas are located consistently relative to one another. Moreover, individual areas exhibit a logical ordering of their functionality.

An example is the so-called tonotopic map of the auditory regions, where neighbouring neurons respond to similar sound frequencies in an orderly sequence from high pitch to low pitch. Another example is the somatotopic map of motor nerves. Regions such as the tonotopic map and the somatotopic map can be referred to as ordered feature maps. The purpose of this chapter is to investigate a mechanism by which these ordered feature maps might develop naturally.

It appears likely that our genetic makeup predestines our neural development to a large extent. Whether the mechanisms that we shall describe here play a major or a minor role in the organization of neural tissue is not an issue for us. It was, however, an interest in discovering how such an organization might be learned that led Kohonen. The cortex is essentially a large (approximately 1-metre-square, in adult humans) thin (2-to-4-millimetre thick) sheet consisting of six layers of neurons of varying type and density. It is folded into its familiar shape to maximize packing density in the cranium. Since we are not so much concerned with the details of anatomy here, we shall consider an adequate model of the cortex to be a two-dimensional sheet of processing elements. As a simplified definition, we can say that, in a topology-preserving map, units located physically next to each other will respond to classes of input vectors that are likewise next to each other.

Although it is easy to visualize units next to each other in a two-dimensional array, it is not so easy to determine which classes of vectors are next to each other in a high-dimensional space. Large-dimensional input vectors are, in a sense, projected down on the twodimensional map in a way that maintains the natural order of the input vectors.

This dimensional reduction could allow us to visualize easily important relationships among the data that otherwise might go unnoticed. In the next section, we shall formalize some of the definitions presented in this section, and shall look at the mathematics of the topology-preserving map. Henceforth, we shall refer to the topology-preserving map as a self-organizing map (SOM).

The Kohonen network can be seen as an extension to the competitive learning network, although this is chronologically incorrect. Also, the Kohonen network has a diferent set of applications.In the Kohonen network, the output units in S are ordered in some fashion, often in a twodimensional grid or array, although this is application-dependent. The ordering, which is chosen by the user1, determines which output neurons are neighbours.

Now, when learning patterns are presented to the network, the weights to the output units are thus adapted such that the order present in the input space $\Re N$ is preserved in the output, *i.e.,* the neurons in S. This means that learning patterns which are near to each other in the input space (where 'near' is determined by the distance measure used in finding the winning unit) must be mapped on output units which are also near to each other, *i.e.,* the same or neighbouring units. Thus, if inputs are uniformly distributed in ℜN and the order must be preserved, the dimensionality of S must be at least ℜN. The mapping, which represents a discretisation of the input space, is said to be topology preserving.

However, if the inputs are restricted to a subspace of ℜN, a Kohonen network can be used of lower dimensionality. For example: data on a twodimensional manifold in a high dimensional input space can be mapped onto a two-dimensional Kohonen network, which can for example be used for visualisation of the data. Usually, the learning patterns are random samples from ?N. At time t, a sample x(t) is generated and presented to the network. Using the same formulas as in section 6.1, the winning unit k is determined. Next, the weights to this winning unit as well as its neighbours are adapted using the learning rule

$$w_0(t+1) = w_0(t) + \gamma g(0,k)(x(t) - w_0(t)) \ \forall_0 \in S$$

Here, g(o,k) is a decreasing function of the grid-distance between units o and k, such that g(k,k) = 1. For example, for g() a Gaussian function can be used, such that (in one dimension!) g(o,k) = exp -(-(o - k)2).Due to this collective learning scheme, input signals.

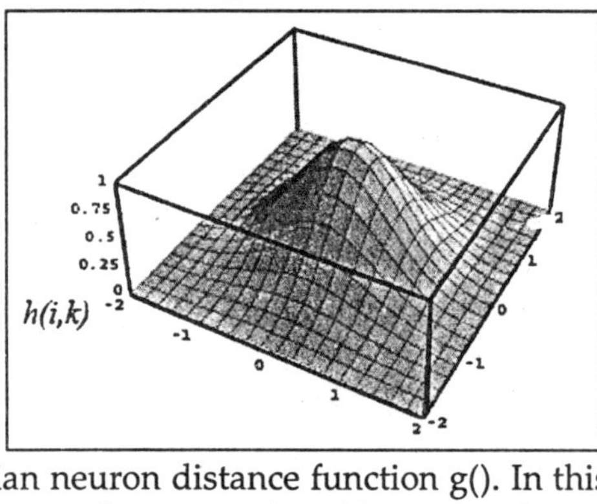

Gaussian neuron distance function g(). In this case, g() is shown for a two-dimensional grid because it looks nice. which are near to each other will be mapped on neighbouring neurons. A topology-conserving map converging. The weight vectors of a network with two inputs and 8x8 output neurons arranged in a planar grid are shown. A line in each figure connects weight wi(o1,o2) with weights wi(o1+1,o2) and wi(i1,i2+1). The left most gure shows the initial weights; the rightmost when the map is almost completely formed. If the intrinsic dimensionality of S is less than N, the neurons in the network are 'folded' in the input space, such as depicted in figure.

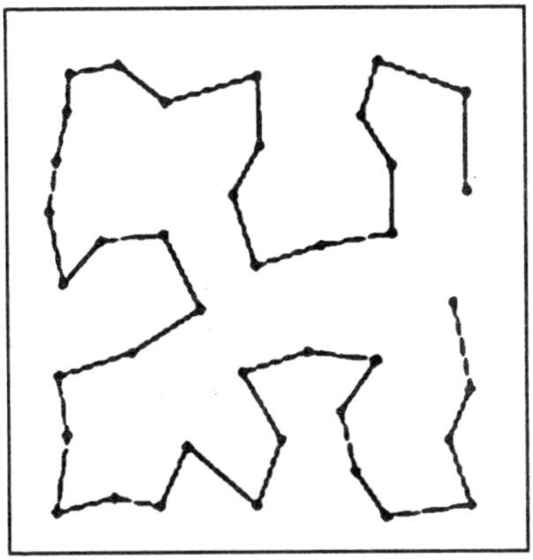

The topology-conserving quality of this network has many counterparts in biological brains. The brain is organised in many places so that aspects of the sensory environment are represented in the form of two-dimensional maps. For example, in the visual system, there are several topographic mappings of visual space onto the surface of the visual cortex. There are organised mappings of the body surface onto the cortex in both motor and somatosensory areas, and tonotopic mappings of frequency in the auditory cortex.

The use of topographic representations, where some important aspect of a sensory modality is related to the physical locations of the cells on a surface, is so common that it obviously serves an important information processing function.It does not come as a surprise, therefore, that already many applications have been devised of the Kohonen topology-conserving maps. Kohonen himself has successfully used the network for phoneme-recognition (Kohonen, Makisara, and Saramaki, 1984). Also, the network has been used to merge sensory data from dierent kinds of sensors, such as auditory and visual, 'looking' at the same scene. To explain the plausibility of a similar structure in biological networks, Kohonen remarks that the lateral inhibition between the neurons could be obtained via e erent connections between those neurons. In one dimension, those connection strengths form a 'Mexican hat'

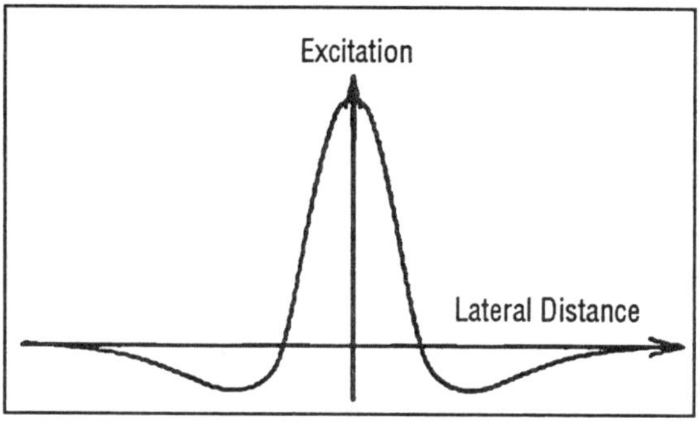

Mexican hat. Lateral interaction around the winning neuron as a function of distance: excitation to nearby neurons, inhibition to farther of neurons.

SOM LEARNING ALGORITHM

During the training period, each unit with a positive activity within the neighbourhood of the winning unit participates in the learning process.We can describe the learning process by the equations:

$$wi = (t)(x - wi,)U(Yi)$$

where w, is the weight vector of the ith unit and x is the input vector. The function U(yi) is zero unless yi > 0 in which case U(yi) = 1, ensuring that only those units with positive activity participate in the learning process. The factor ?(t) is written as a function of time to anticipate our desire to change it as learning progresses.To demonstrate the formation of an ordered feature map, we shall use an example in which units are trained to recognize their relative positions in two-dimensional space.

Each processing element is identified by its coordinates, (u,v), in two-dimensional space. Weight vectors for this example are also two dimensional and are initially assigned to the processing elements randomly. As with other competitive structures, a winning processing element is determined for each input vector based on the similarity between the input vector and the weight vector. For an input vector x, the winning unit can be determined by,

$$||xwc||=\min\{||x-wi||\}$$

where the index c refers to the winning unit. To keep subscripts to a minimum, we identify each unit in the two-dimensional array by a single subscript. Instead of updating the weights of the winning unit only, we define a physical neighbourhood around the unit, and all units within this neighbourhood participate in the weight-update process. As learning proceeds, the size of the neighbourhood is diminished until it encompasses only a single unit.If c is the winning unit, and N,. is the list of unit indices that make up the neighbourhood, then the weight-update equations are

$$w_i(t+1)=\begin{cases} w_i(t)+\alpha(t)(x-w_i(t))i \in N \\ 0 \qquad \text{otherwise} \end{cases}$$

Each weight vector participating in the update process rotates slightly towards the input vector, x. Once training has progressed sufficiently, the weight vector on each unit will converge to a value that is representative of the coordinates of the points near the physical location of the unit.

HOPFIELD NEURAL NETWORK

One of the earliest recurrent neural networks reported in literature was the auto-associator independently described by Anderson and Kohonen in 1977. It consists of a pool of neurons with connections between each unit i and j, i 6= j.

The auto-associator network. All neurons are both input and output neurons, *i.e.*, a pattern is clamped, the network iterates to a stable state, and the output of the network consists of the new activation values of the neurons.All connections are weighted. In 1982, Hopfield brings together several earlier ideas concerning these networks and presents a complete mathematical analysis based on Ising spin models. It is therefore that this network, which we will describe in this chapter, is generally referred to as the Hopfield network. The Hopfield network consists of a set of N interconnected neurons which update their activation values asynchronously and independently of other neurons. All neurons are both input and output neurons.

The activation values are binary. Originally, Hopfield chose activation values of 1 and 0, but using values +1 and -1 presents some advantages discussed below. We will therefore adhere to the latter convention. The state of the system is given by the activation values1 y = (yk). The net input sk(t+1) of a neuron k at cycle t+1 is a weighted sum

$$s_k(t+1) = \sum_{j \neq k} y_j(t) w_{jk} + \theta_k$$

A simple threshold function is applied to the net input to obtain the new activation value yi(t + 1) at time t + 1:

$$y_k(t+1) = \begin{cases} +1 & \text{if } s_k(t+1) > U_k \\ -1 & \text{if } s_k(t+1) < U_k \\ y_k(t) & \text{otherwise} \end{cases}$$

Hopfield Network as Associative Memory

A primary application of the Hopfield network is an associative memory. In this case, the weights of the connections between the neurons have to be thus set that the states of the system corresponding with the patterns which are to be stored in the network are stable. These states can be seen as 'dips' in energy space. When the network is cued with a noisy or incomplete test pattern, it will render the incorrect or missing data by iterating to a stable state which is in some sense 'near' to the cued pattern.

$$w_{jk} = \begin{cases} \sum_{p=1}^{P} x_j^p x_k^p & \text{if } j \neq k \\ 0 & \end{cases}$$

i.e., if xp j and xp k are equal, wjk is increased, otherwise decreased by one (note that, in the original Hebb rule, weights only increase). It appears, however, that the network gets saturated very quickly, and that about 0:15N memories can be stored before recall errors become severe. There are two problems associated with storing too many patterns:

- The stored patterns become unstable;
- Spurious stable states appear (*i.e.*, stable states which do not correspond with stored patterns).

The first of these two problems can be solved by an algorithm proposed by Bruce *et al.*

Algorithm 1 Given a starting weight matrix for each pattern xp to be stored and each element xp k in xp de ne a correction εk such that

$$\epsilon_k = \begin{cases} 0 & \text{if } y_k \text{ is stable and } x^p \text{ is clamped;} \\ 1 & \text{otherwise} \end{cases}$$

Now modify wjk by $\Delta w_{jk} = y_j y_k (\epsilon_j + \epsilon_k)$ if $j \neq k$ Repeat this procedure until all patterns are stable.

It appears that, in practice, this algorithm usually converges. There exist cases, however, where the algorithm remains oscillatory.

NEOCOGNITRON NEURAL NETWORK

Artificial neural network architectures such as backpropagation tend to have general applicability. We can use a single network type in many different applications by changing the network's size, parametres, and training sets. In contrast, the developers of the neocognitron set out to tailor architecture for a specific application: recognition of handwritten characters.

Such a system has a great deal of practical application, although, judging from the introductions to some of their papers, Fukushima and his coworkers appear to be more interested in developing a model of the brain.To that end, their design was based on the seminal work performed by Hubel and Weisel elucidating some of the functional architecture of the visual cortex. We could not begin to provide a complete accounting of what is knownabout the anatomy and physiology of the mammalian visual system. Nevertheless, we shall present a brief and highly simplified description of some of that system's features as an aid to understanding thejbasis of the neocognitron design.Some nerve fibres from each eye cross over into the opposite hemisphere of the brain, where they meet nerve fibres from the other eye at the LGN. From the LGN, neurons project back to area 17. From area 17, neurons project into other cortical areas, other areas deep in the brain, and also back to the LGN.

Figure shows the main pathways for neurons leading from the retina back to the area of the brain known as the viiual, or striate, cortex. This area is also known as area 17. The optic nerve ii made up of axons from nerve cells called retinal ganglia. The ganglia receive stimulation indirectly from the light-receptive rods and cones through several intervening neurons.

Hubel and Weisel used an amazing technique to discern the function of the various nerve cells in the visual system. They used microelectrodes to record the response of individual neurons in the cortex while stimulating the retina with light. By applying a variety of patterns and shapes, they were able to determine the particular stimulus to which a neuron was most sensitive. The retinal ganglia and the cells of the lateral geniculate nucleus (LGN) appear to have circular receptive fields.

They respond most strongly to circular spots of light of a particular size on a particular part of the retina. The part of the retina responsible for stimulating a particular ganglion cell is called the receptive field of the ganglion. Some of these receptive fields give an excitatory response to a centrally located spot of light, and an inhibitory response to a larger, more diffuse spot of light.

These fields have an on-centre off-surround response characteristic. Other receptive fields have the opposite characteristic, with an inhibitory response to the centrally located spot-an off-centre on-surround response characteristic. The visual cortex itself is composed of six layers of neurons.

Most of the neurons from the LGN terminate on cells in layer IV. These cells have circularly symmetric receptive fields like the retinal ganglia and the cells of the LGN. Further along the pathway, the response characteristic of the cells begins to increase in complexity.

Cells in layer IV project to a group of cells directly above called simple cells. Simple cells respond to line segments having a particular orientation. Simple cells project to cells called complex cells. Complex cells respond to lines having the same orientation as their corresponding simple cells, although complex cells appear to integrate their response over a wider receptive field. In other words, complex cells are less sensitive to the position of the line on the retina than are the simple cells. Some complex cells are sensitive to line segments of a particular orientation that are moving in a particular direction.

Cells in different layers of area 17 project to different locations of the brain. For example, cells in layers II and III project to cells in areas 18 and 19. These areas contain cells called hypercomplex cells.Hypercomplex cells respond to lines that form angles or corners and that move in various directions across the receptive field.

The picture that emerges from these studies is that of a hierarchy of cells with increasingly complex response characteristics. It is not difficult to extrapolate this idea of a hierarchy into one where further data abstraction takes place at higher and higher levels. The neocognitron design adopts this hierarchical structure in a layered architecture, as illustrated schematically in Figure.

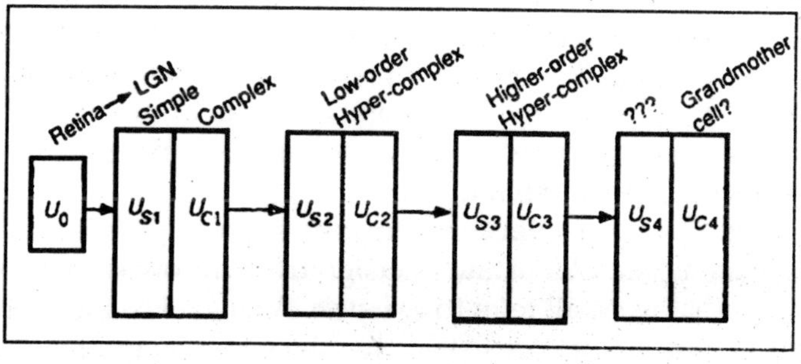

Figure: The neocognitron hierarchical structure is shown. Each box represents a level in the neocognitron comprising a simplecell layer, usi, and a complex-cell layer, Ua, where i is the layer number. U0 represents signals originating on the retina. There is also a suggested mapping to the hierarchical structure of the brain. The network concludes with single cells that respond to complex visual stimuli. These final cells are often called grandmother cells after the notion that there may be some cell in your brain that responds to complex visual stimuli, such as a picture of your grandmother.

We remind you that the description of the visual system that we have presented here is highly simplified. There is a great deal of detail that we have omitted. The visual system does not adhere to a strict hierarchical structure as presented here. Moreover, we do not subscribe to the notion that grandmother cells *per se* exist in the brain. We know from experience that strict adherence to biology often leads to a failed attempt to design a system to perform the same function as the biological prototype: Flight is probably the most significant example. Nevertheless, we do promote the use of neurobiological results if they prove to be appropriate. The neocognitron is an excellent example of how neurobiological results can be used to develop a new network architecture.

NEOCOGNITRON ARCHITECTURE

The neocognitron design evolved from an earlier model called the cognitron, and there are several versions of the neocognitron itself. The one that we shall describe has nine layers of PEs (Processing elements), including the retina layer. The system was designed to recognize the numerals 0 through 9, regardless of where they are placed in the field of view of the retina. Moreover, the network has a high degree of tolerance to distortion of the character and is fairly insensitive to the size of the character.

This first architecture contains only feedforward connections. The PEs of the neocognitron are organized into modules that we shall refer to as levels. A single level is shown in Figure. Each level consists of two layers: a layer of simple cells, or S-cells, followed by a layer of complex cells, or C-cells. Each layer, in turn, is divided into a number of planes, each of which consists of a rectangular array of PEs. On a given level, the S-layer and the C-layer may or may not have the same number of planes. All planes on a given layer will have the same number of PEs; however, the number of PEs on the S-planes can be different from the number of PEs on the C-planes at the same level.

Moreover, the number of PEs per plane can vary from level to level. There are also PEs called Vs-cells and Vc-cells that are not shown in the figure. These elements play an important role in the processing, but we can describe the functionality of the system without reference to them. We construct a complete network by combining an input layer, which we shall call the retina, with a number of levels in a hierarchical fashion, as shown in Figure.

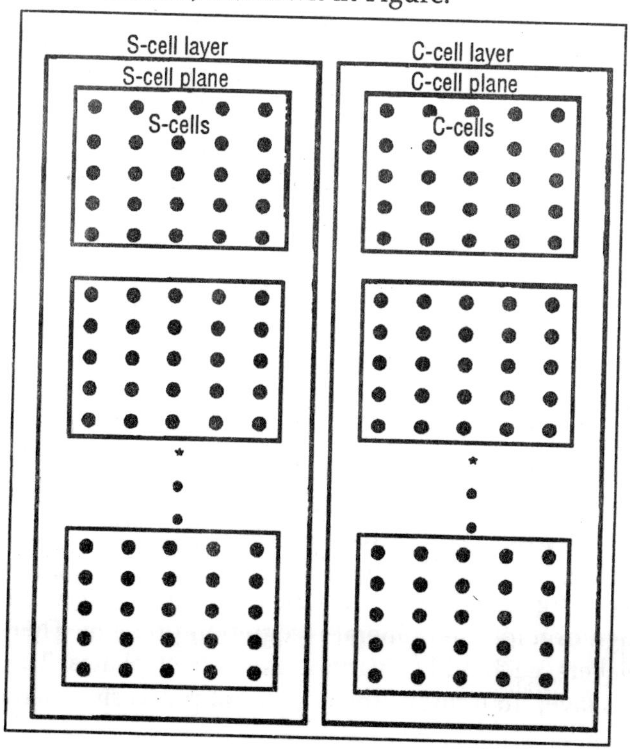

Figure: A single level of a neocognitron is shown. Each level consists of two layers, and each layer consists of a number of planes. The planes contain the PEs in a rectangular array. Data pass from the S-layer to the C-layer through connections that are not shown here. In neocognitrons having feedback, there also will be connections from the C-layer to the S-layer.

That figure shows the number of planes on each layer for the particular implementation that we shall describe here. We call attention to the fact that there is nothing, in principle, that dictates a limit to the size of the network in terms of the number of levels. The interconnection strategy is unlike that of networks that are fully interconnected between layers, such as the backpropagation network.

Figure shows a schematic illustration of the way units are connected in the neocognitron.

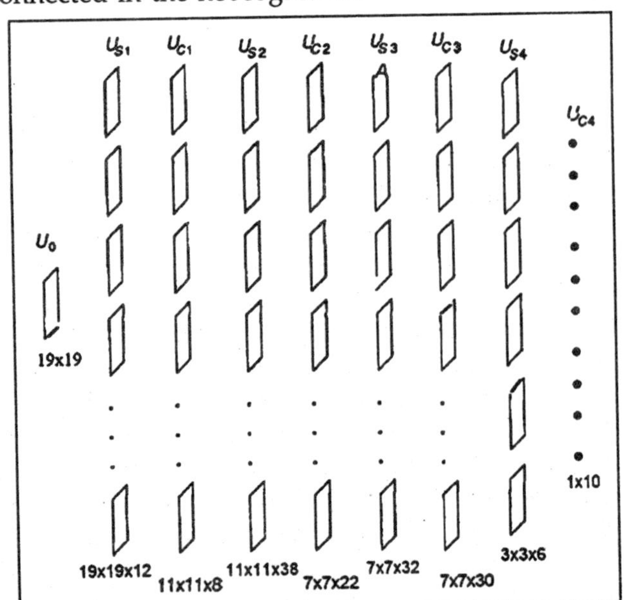

The figure shows the basic organization of the neocognitron for the numeral-recognition problem. There are nine layers, each with a varying number of planes. The size of each layer, in terms of the number of processing elements, is given below each layer. For example, layer Uc2 has 22 planes of 7 x 7 processing elements arranged in a square matrix. The layer of C-cells on the final level is made up of 10 planes, each of which has a single element. Each element corresponds to one of the numerals from 0 to 9. The identification of the pattern appearing on the retina is made according to which C-cell on the final level has the strongest response. As we look deeper into the network, the S-cells respond to features at higher levels of abstraction; for example, corners with intersecting lines at various angles and orientations.

The C-cells integrate the responses of groups of Scells. Because each S-cell is looking for the same feature in a different location, the C-cells' response is less sensitive to the exact location of the feature on the input layer.

This behaviour is what gives the neocognitron its ability to identify characters regardless of their exact position in the field of the retina. By the time we have reached the final layer of C-cells, the effective receptive field of each cell is the entire retina. Figure 10.6 shows the character identification process schematically.

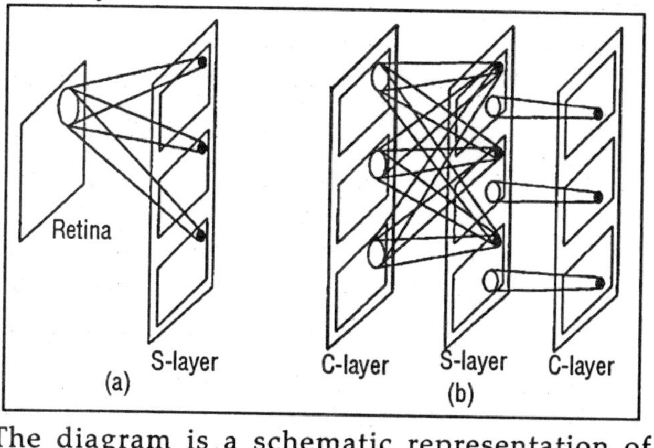

The diagram is a schematic representation of the interconnection strategy of the neocognitron. (a) On the first level, each S unit receives input connections from a small region of the retina. Units in corresponding positions on all planes receive input connections from the same region of the retina. The region from which an S-cell receives input connections defines the receptive field of the cell, (b) On intermediate levels, each unit on an s-plane receives input connections from corresponding locations on all C-planes in the previous level. C-eells have connections from a region of S-cells on the S level preceding it. If the number of C-planes is the same as that of S-planes at that level, then each C-cell has connections from S-cells on a single s-plane. If there are fewer C-planes than S-planes, some C-cells may receive connections from more than one S-plane.

Each cell in a plane on the first S-layer receives inputs from a single input layer-namely, the retina. On subsequent layers, each S-cell plane receives inputs from each of the C-cell planes immediately preceding it. The situation is slightly different for the C-cell planes. Typically, each cell on a C-cell plane examines a small region of S-cells on a single S-cell plane. For example, the first C-cell plane on layer 2 would have connections to only a region of S-cells on the first S-cell plane of the previous layer.

Reference back to Figure reveals that there is not necessarily a one-to-one correspondence between C-cell planes and S-cell planes at each layer in the system. This discrepancy occurs because the system designers found it advantageous to combine the inputs from some S-planes to a single C-plane if the features that the S-planes were detecting were similar. This tuning process is evident in several areas of the network architecture and processing equations.

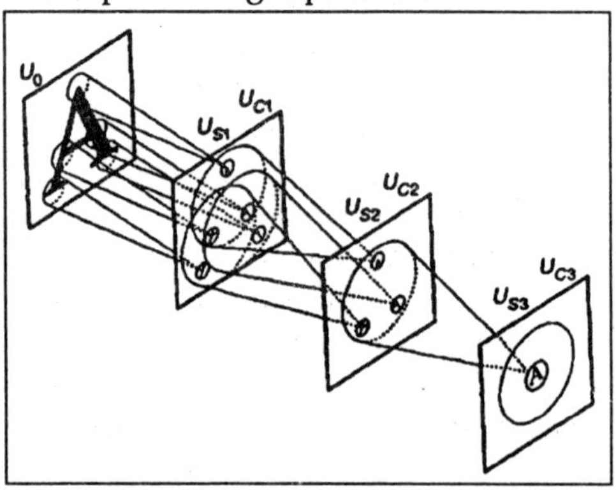

The figure illustrates how the neocognitron performs its character-recognition function. The neocognitron decomposes the input pattern into elemental parts consisting of line segments at various angles of rotation. The system then integrates these elements into higher-order structures at each successive level in the network.

Cells in each level integrate the responses of cells in the previous level over a finite area. This behaviour gives the neocognitron its ability to identify characters regardless of their exact position or size in the field of view of the retina. Source: Reprinted with permission from Kunihiko Fukushima, 'A neural network for visual pattern recognition.

The weights on connections to S-cells are determined by a training process. Unlike in many other network architectures (such as backpropagation), where each unit has a different weight vector, all S-cells on a single plane share the same weight vector. Sharing weights in this manner means that all S-cells on a given plane respond to the identical feature in their receptive fields, as we indicated. Moreover, we need to train only one S-cell on each plane, then to distribute the resulting weights to the other cells.

The weights on connections to C-cells are not modifiable in the sense that they are not determined by a training process. All C-cell weights are usually determined by being tailored to the specific network architecture. As with Splanes, all cells on a single C-plane share the same weights. Moreover, in some implementations, all C-planes on a given layer share the same weights.

NEOCOGNITRON DATA PROCESSING

In this section we shall discuss the various processing algorithms of the neocognitron cells. First we shall look at the S-cell data processing including the method used to train the network. Then, we shall describe processing on the C-layer.

S-Cell Processing

We shall first concentrate on the cells in a single plane of \Js\, as indicated in Figure:

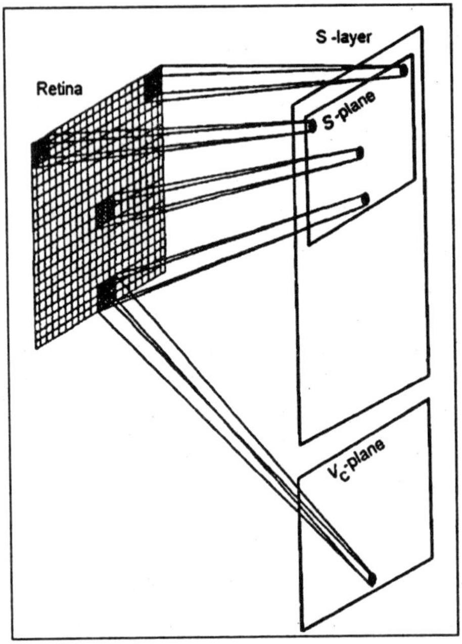

The retina, layer U0, is a 19-by-19-pixel array, surrounded by inactive pixels to account for edge effects as described in the text. One of the S-planes is shown, along with an indication of the regions of the retina scanned by the individual cells. Associated with each S-layer in the system is a plane of vrcells. These cells receive input connections from the same receptive field as do the S-cells in corresponding locations in the plane.

The processing done by these Vc-cells is described in the text. We shall assume that the retina, layer Uo, is an array of 19 by 19 pixels. Therefore, each Usi plane will have an array of 19 by 19 cells. Each plane scans the entire retina for a particular feature.

As indicated in the figure, each cell on a plane is looking for the identical feature but in a different location on the retina. Each S-cell receives input connections from an array of 3 by 3 pixels on the retina. The receptive field of each S-cell corresponds to the 3 by 3 array centered on the pixel that corresponds to the cell's location on the plane. When building or simulating this network, we must make allowances for edge effects. If we surround the active retina with inactive pixels (outputs always set to zero), then we can automatically account for cells whose fields of view are centered on edge pixels. Neighbouring S-cells scan the retina array displaced by one pixel from each otlier.

In this manner, the entire image is scanned from left to right and top to bottom by the cells in each Splane. A single plane of Vc-cells is associated with the S-layer, as indicated in Figure H. The Vc-plane contains the same number of cells as does each Splane.

Vc-cells have the same receptive fields as the S-cells in corresponding locations in the plane. The output of a Vc-cell goes to a single S-cell in every plane in the layer. The S-cells that receive inputs from a particular Vc-cell are those that occupy a position in the plane corresponding to the position of the Vc-cell.

The output of the Vc-cell has an inhibitory effect on the S-cells. Figure shows the details of a single S-cell along with its corresponding inhibitory cell.

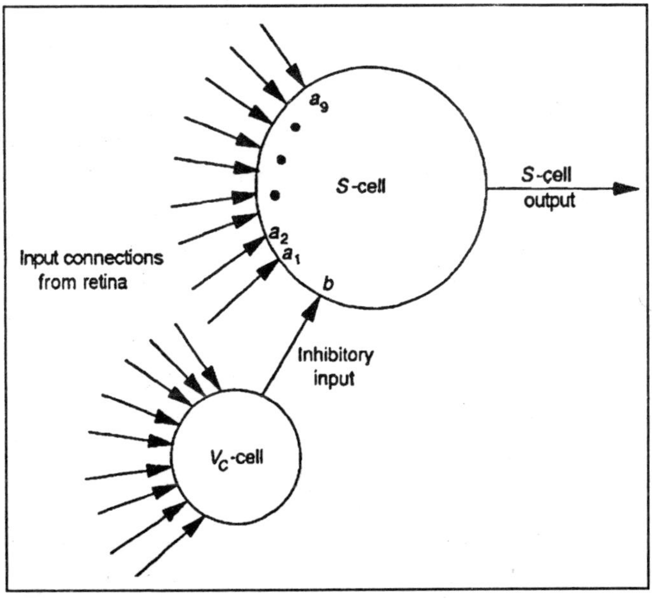

Figure: A single 5-cell and corresponding inhibitory cell on the Us\ layer are shown. Each unit receives the identical nine inputs from the retina layer. The weights, a,, on the S-ce\\ determine the feature for which the cell is sensitive. Both the a, weights on connections from the retina, and the weight, b, from the Vr-cells are modifiable and are determined during a training process, as described in the text.

Up to now, we have been discussing the first S-layer, in which cells receive input connections from a single plane (in this case the retina) in the previous layer. For what follows, we shall generalize our discussion to include the case of layers deeper in the network where an S-cell will receive input connections from all the planes on the previous C-layer. Let the index k refer to the kth plane on level 1.

We can label each cell on a plane with a two-dimensional vector, with n indicating its position on the plane; then, we let the vector v refer to the relative position of a cell in the previous layer lying in the receptive field of unit n. With these definitions, we can write the following equation for the output of any 5-cell. Where the function ϕ is a linear threshold function given by

$$\phi(x) = \begin{cases} x x \geq 0 \\ 0 x < 0 \end{cases}$$

Let's dissect these equations in some detail. The inner summation of first equation is the usual sum-of-products calculation of inputs, UCi-1(ki-1,n+v), and weights, ai(ki-1, v. ki). The sum extends over all units in the previous Clayer that lie within the receptive field of unit n. Those units are designated by the vector n + v.

Because we shall assume that all weights and cell output values are nonnegative, the sum-of-products calculation yields a measure of how closely the input pattern matches the weight vector on a unit.

We have labeled the receptive field Ai, indicating that the geometry of the receptive field is the same for all units on a particular layer. The outer summation of the equation extends over all of the ki-1planes of the previous C-layer. In the case of Us1, there would be no need for this outer summation. The product, bi(ki). Vc,(n), in the denominator of Equation, represents the inhibitory contribution of the Vc-cell. Thc paramctrc ri, where 0<ri<∞, determines the cell's selectivity for a specific pattern.

The factor ri/(1 + ri) goes from zero to one as ri goes from zero to infinity. Thus, for small values of r;, the denominator of Equation could be relatively small compared to the numerator even if the input pattern did not exactly match the weight vector.

This situation could result in a positive argument to the ϕ function. If ri were large, then the match between the input pattern and the weights in the numerator of the equation would have to be more exact to overcome the inhibitory effects of the Vc-cell input.

Notice also that this same ri parametre appears as a multiplicative factor of the 0 function. If ri is small, and cell selectivity is small, this factor ensures that the output from the cell itself cannot become very large. We can view the function of r; in another way. We rewrite the argument of the function in the equation as

$$\frac{e-[rl/(1+rl)]h}{1+[rl/(1+rl)]h}$$

where e is the net excitatory term and h is the net inhibitory term. According to function,

$$\phi(x)=\begin{cases} x x \geq 0 \\ 0 x < 0 \end{cases}$$

the S-cell output will be nonzero only if,

$$e-\frac{rl}{1+rl}h>0$$

or,

$$\frac{e}{h}>\frac{rl}{1+rl}$$

Thus, the quantity ri determines the minimum relative strength of excitation versus inhibition that will result in a nonzero output of the unit. As r; increases, ri/(l + ri) ? 1. Therefore, a larger ri requires a larger excitation relative to inhibition for a nonzero output. Notice that neither of the weight expressions, ai(ki-1,v,ki), or bi(ki) depend explicitly on the position, n, of the cell. Remember that all cells on a plane share the same weights, even the bi(ki) weights, which we did not discuss previously.

We must now specify the output from the inhibitory nodes. The Vc-cell at position n has an output value of where ci(v) is the weight on the connection from a cell at position v of the Vc -cell's receptive field. These weights are not subject to training. They can take the form of any normalized function that decreases monotonically as the magnitude of v increases.

TRAINING WEIGHTS ON THE S-LAYERS

In principle, training proceeds as it does for many networks. First, an input pattern is presented at the input layer and the data are propagated through the network. Then, weights are allowed to make incremental adjustments according to the specified algorithm. After weight updates have occurred, a new pattern is presented at the input layer, and the process is repeated with all patterns in the training set until the network is classifying the input patterns properly.In the neocognitron, sharing of weights on a given plane means that only a single cell on each plane needs to participate in the learning process. Once its weights have been updated, a copy of the new weight vector can be distributed to the other cells on the same plane. To understand how this works, we can think of the 5-planes on a given layer as being stacked vertically on top of one another, aligned so that cells at corresponding locations are directly on top of one another. We can now imagine many overlapping columns running perpendicular to this stack. These columns define groups of S-cells, where all of the members in a group have receptive fields in approximately the same location of the input layer.

Unsupervised Training

With this model in mind, we now apply an input pattern

and examine the response of the S'-cells in each column. To ensure that each 5-cell provides a distinct response, we can initializc thc a; weights to small, positive random values. The bi weights on the inhibitory connections can be initialized to zero. We first note the plane and position of the S-cell whose response is the strongest in each column.

Then we examine the individual planes so that, if one plane contains two or more of these S-cells, we disregard all but the cell responding the strongest. In this manner, we will locate the S-cell on each plane whose response is the strongest, subject to the condition that each of those cells is in a different column.

Those S-cells become the prototypes, or representatives, of all the cells on their respective planes. Likewise, the strongest responding Vf-cell is chosen as the representative for the other cells on the Vc-plane.

Once the representatives are chosen, weight updates are made according to the following equations:

$$\Delta a_l\left(K_{l-1,}v,\hat{K}_l\right) = q_l c_{l-1}(v) UC_{l-1}\left(K_{l-1,}\hat{n}+v\right)$$

$$\Delta b_l\left(\hat{K}_l\right) = q_l V_{C_{l-1}}(\hat{n})$$

where qi is the learning rate parametre, ci-1(v), is the monotonically decreasing function as described in the previous section, and the location of the representative for plane ki is A. Notice that the largest increases in the weights occur on those connections that have the largest input signal, Uci-1(ki-1, n + v).

Because the 5-cell whose weights are being modified was the one with the largest output, this learning algorithm implements a form of Hebbian learning. Notice also that weights can only increase, and that there is no upper bound on the weight value. Once the cells on a given plane begin to respond to a certain feature, they tend to respond less to other features. After a short time, each plane will have developed a strong response to a particular feature. Moreover, as we look deeper into the network, planes will be responding to more complex features.

Other Learning Methods

The designers of the original neocognitron knew to what features they wanted each level, and each plane on a level, to respond. Under these circumstances, a set of training vectors can be developed for each layer, and the layers can be trained independently. It is also possible to select the representative cell for each plane in advance. Care must be taken, however, to ensure that the input pattern is presented in the proper location with respect to the representative's receptive field. Here again, some foreknowledge of the desired features is required.

PERCEPTRON AND ADALINE NEURAL NETWORK

This part describes single layer neural networks, including some of the classical approaches to the neural computing and learning problem. In the first part of this chapter we discuss the representational power of the single layer networks and their learning algorithms and will give some examples of using the networks. In the second part we will discuss the representational limitations of single layer networks. Two 'classical' models will be described in the first part of the chapter: the Perceptron, proposed by Rosenblatt in the late 50's and the Adaline, presented in the early 60's by by Widrow and Hoff.

Networks with Threshold Activation Functions

A single layer feed-forward network consists of one or more output neurons o, each of which is connected with a weighting factor wio to all of the inputs i. In the simplest case the network has only two inputs and a single output, as sketched in figure:

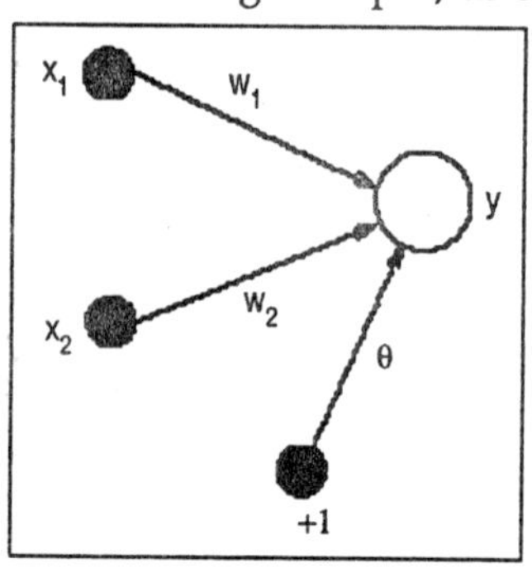

The input of the neuron is the weighted sum of the inputs plus the bias term. The output of the network is formed by the activation of the output neuron, which is some function of the input:

$$Y = F\left(\sum_{i-1}^{2} w_i x_i + \theta\right)$$

The activation function F can be linear so that we have a linear network, or nonlinear. In this section we consider the threshold (or Heaviside or sgn) function:

$$F(s) = \begin{cases} 1 & \text{if } s > 0 \\ -1 & \text{otherwise} \end{cases}$$

The output of the network thus is either +1 or -1 depending on the input. The network can now be used for a classication task: it can decide whether an input pattern belongs to one of two classes. If the total input is positive, the pattern will be assigned to class +1, if the total input is negative, the sample will be assigned to class -1. The separation between the two classes in this case is a straight line, given by the equation:

$$w_1 x_1 + w_2 x_2 + \theta = 0$$

We will describe two learning methods for these types of networks: the 'perceptron' learning rule and the 'delta' or 'LMS' rule. Both methods are iterative procedures that adjust the weights. A learning sample is presented to the network. For each weight the new value is computed by adding a correction to the old value. The threshold is updated in a same way:

$$w_i(t+1) = w_i(t) + \Delta w_i(t),$$
$$\theta(t+1) = \theta(t) + \Delta\theta(t)$$

Perceptron Learning Rule and Convergence Theorem

Suppose we have a set of learning samples consisting of an input vector x and a desired output d(x). For a classification task the d(x) is usually +1 or -1.The perceptron learning rule is very simple and can be stated as follows.

- Start with random weights for the connections;

- Select an input vector x from the set of training samples;
- If y≠d(x), modify all connections wi according to: wi = d(x)xi;
- Go back to 2.

Note that the procedure is very similar to the Hebb rule; the only dierence is that, when the network responds correctly, no connection weights are modied. Besides modifying the weights, we must also modify the threshold θ. This θ is considered as a connection w0 between the output neuron and a 'dummy' predicate unit which is always on: x0 = 1. Given the perceptron learning rule as stated above, this threshold is modified according to:

$$\Delta\theta = \begin{cases} 0 & \text{if the perceptron responds correctly;} \\ d(x) & \text{otherwise} \end{cases}$$

The Adaptive Linear Element (Adaline)

An important generalisation of the perceptron training algorithm was presented by Widrow and Hoff as the 'least mean square' learning procedure, also known as the delta rule. The main functional diference with the perceptron training rule is the way the output of the system is used in the learning rule. The perceptron learning rule uses the output of the threshold function for learning.The delta-rule uses the net output without further mapping into output values -1 or +1.The learning rule was applied to the 'adaptive linear element,' also named Adaline. In a simple physical implementation.

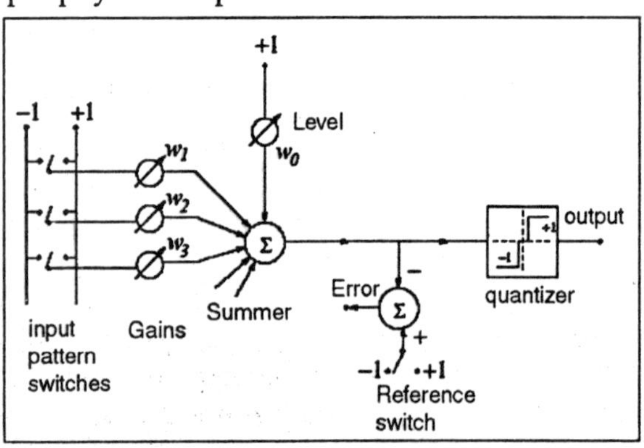

this device consists of a set of controllable resistors connected to a circuit which can sum up currents caused by the input voltage signals. Usually the central block, the summer, is also followed by a quantiser which outputs either +1 of -1,depending on the polarity of the sum.

Although the adaptive process is here exemplified in a case when there is only one output, it may be clear that a system with many parallel outputs is directly implementable by multiple.

Units of the Above Kind

If the input conductances are denoted by wi, i = 0; 1;::: ; n, and the input and output signals by xi and y, respectively, then the output of the central block is defined to be:

$$y = \sum_{i=1}^{n} w_i x_i + \theta,$$

where y = w0. The purpose of this device is to yield a given value y = dp at its output when the set of values xp i, i = 1,2....., n, is applied at the inputs. The problem is to determine the coeficients wi, i = 0, 1......., n, in such a way that the input-output response is correct for a large number of arbitrarily chosen signal sets.

If an exact mapping is not possible, the average error must be minimised, for instance, in the sense of least squares. An adaptive operation means that there exists a mechanism by which the wi can be adjusted, usually iteratively, to attain the correct values.

Networks with Linear Activation Functions

For a single layer network with an output unit with a linear activation function the output is simply given by:

$$y = \sum_{i=1}^{n} w_i x_i + \theta,$$

Such a simple network is able to represent a linear relationship between the value of the output unit and the value of the input units. By thresholding the output value, a classifier can be constructed, but here we focus on the linear relationship and use the network for a function approximation task. In high dimensional input spaces the network represents a (hyper)plane and it will be clear that also multiple output units may be defined.

Suppose we want to train the network such that a hyperplane is fitted as well as possible to a set of training samples consisting of input values xp and desired (or target) output values dp. For every given input sample, the output of the network difers from the target value dp by whereYp is the actual output for this pattern. The delta-rule now uses a cost- or error-function based on these dierences to adjust the weights.

The error function, as indicated by the name least mean square, is the summed squared error. That is, the total error E is dened to be

$$E = \sum_{p} E^{p} = \frac{1}{2}\sum_{p}\left(d^{p} - y^{p}\right)^{2},$$

where the index p ranges over the set of input patterns and Ep represents the error on pattern p. The LMS procedure finds the values of all the weights that minimise the error function by a method called gradient descent. The idea is to make a change in the weight proportional to the negative of the derivative of the error as measured on the current pattern with respect to each weight:

$$\Delta_{p} w_{j} = -\gamma \frac{\delta E^{p}}{\delta w_{j}}$$

where γ is a constant of proportionality. The derivative is

$$\frac{\delta E^{p}}{\delta w_{j}} = \frac{\delta E^{p}}{\delta y^{p}} \frac{\delta y^{p}}{\delta w_{j}}$$

Because of the linear units

$$\frac{\delta y^{p}}{\delta w_{j}} = x_{j}$$

$$\frac{\delta E^{p}}{\delta y^{p}} = -\left(d^{p} - y^{p}\right)$$

$$\Delta_p w_j = \gamma \delta^p x_j$$

where $\delta^p = d^p - y^p$ is the diference between the target output and the actual output for pattern p. The delta rule modes weight appropriately for target and actual outputs of either polarity and for both continuous and binary input and output units. These characteristics have opened up a wealth of new applications.

5

Mathematical Representation

CONCEPT OF CALCULUS

INFORMATION

A world may be assumed in which there is only one object a. In this case, both the universally quantified and the existentially quantified sentences (x)A(x) and (x)A(x) reduce to the simple sentence A(a), and all quantifiers can be eliminated.

It may easily be confirmed that, after the reduction, all theorems of the calculus become tautologies (*i.e.*, theorems in the propositional calculus). If F is any predicate, such a sentence as "Every x is F and not every x is F "-*i.e.*, (x)F(x)·(x)F(x)-is then reduced to "a is both A and not-A"-A(a)·A(a)-which is not a tautology; therefore, the original sentence is not a theorem; hence, no contradiction can be a theorem.

If F is simple, then F and A are the same. If F is complex and contains (y) or (z), etc., then A is the result obtained by iterating the transformation of eliminating (y), etc. In fact, it can be proved quite directly not only that the calculus is consistent but also that all its theorems are valid.

The discoveries that the calculus is complete and undecidable are much more profound than the discovery of its consistency. Its completeness was proved by Gödel; its undecidability was established with quite different methods. Given the general developments that occurred up to 1936, its undecidability also follows in another way from Theorem X of Gödel's paper of 1931. Completeness means that every valid sentence of the calculus is a theorem. It follows that if A is not a theorem, then A is not valid; and, therefore, A is satisfiable;*i.e.*, it has an interpretation, or a model. But to say that A is consistent means nothing other than that A is not a theorem. Hence, from the completeness, it follows that if A is consistent, then A is satisfiable.

Therefore, the semantic concepts of validity and satisfiability are seen to coincide with the syntactic concepts of derivability and consistency. First-order predicate calculus or first-order logic (FOL) is a theory in symbolic logic that permits the formulation of quantified statements such as "there is at least one X such that..." or "for any X, it is the case that...", where X is an element of a set called the domain of discourse.

A first-order theory is a theory that can be axiomatised as an extension of first-order logic by adding a recursive set of first-order sentences as axioms. First-order logic is distinguished from higher-order logic in that it does not allow statements such as "for every property, it is the case that..." or "there exists aset of objects such that..."Nevertheless, first-order logic is strong enough to formalize all of set theory and thereby virtually all of mathematics.

Its restriction to quantification over individuals makes it difficult to use for the purposes of topology, but it is the classical logical theory underlying mathematics. It is a stronger theory thansentential logic, but a weaker theory than arithmetic, set theory, or Second-order logic.

FIRST-ORDER LOGIC

Like any logical theory, the calculus of first-order logic consists of:

- A specification of how to construct syntactically correct statements (the well-formed formulas)
- A set of axioms, each axiom being a well-formed formula itself
- A set of inference rules which allow one to prove theorems from axioms or earlier proven theorems.

There are two types of axioms: the logical axioms which embody the general truths about proper reasoning involving quantified statements, and the axioms describing the subject matter at hand, for instance axioms describing sets in set theory or axioms describing numbers in arithmetic.

While the set of inference rules in first-order calculus is finite, the set of axioms may very well be and often is infinite. However we require that there is a general algorithm which can decide for a given well-formed formula whether it is an axiom or not. Furthermore, there should be an algorithm which can decide whether a given application of an inference rule is correct or not.

FORMULAS

The well-formed formulas contain:

- Variables such as x, y,... which are place holders for objects of the domain under consideration (these can be called "variable terms")
- Object constants such as 0, 1 or the empty set ø which stand for fixed individual objects in our domain (these can be called "constant terms"; it is also possible to use lower case letters such as a, b, c,..., w to represent such constants, as long as they are different from the letters used for the variable terms)
- Predicate constants such as (lessThan), (isIn), (equals) which stand for fixed relations between or properties of our objects. These are also calledfirst-order predicates to distinguish them from predicates that talk about predicates.
- Function constants such as, which stand for fixed functions taking objects as arguments and returning objects as values
- Logical connectives such as (and), (or), (conditional), (biconditional) (not), (thereExists or existential quantifier) and (forAll or universal quantifier). All of these except for the last two are also used in propositional logic.

Note that only, and are needed for a complete set of logical connectives. The object, predicate and function constants will typically depend on the particular domain we are talking about.

EXAMPLES

Instead of giving the lengthy definition of well-formed formulas, we will simply look at some examples from arithmetic together with their ordinary interpretation. Our domain here is the set of natural numbers: (*i.e.*: forAll x, thereExists y suchThat y isGreaterThan x)

For every number x there exists a bigger number y. That's true. There exists a number y which is bigger than every number x. That's not true. (*i.e.*: forAll x, (thereExists y suchThat 6*y=x) implies (thereExists y suchThat 3*y=x))

If a number x is divisible by 6, then it is also divisible by 3. True. (*i.e.*: thereExists x suchThat (not ThereExists y suchThat y < x)) There exists a number x such that there doesn't exist a smaller number y. True (take x=0).

Now one would have to write down 15 logical axioms and 2 inference rules to completely specify the first-order calculus. How can one be sure that those axioms and rules are enough?

This is the subject of Godel's completeness theorem: if you start out with some subject matter axioms and you look at a certain statement, then it is possible to prove that statement using only the subject matter axioms, the 15 logical axioms and the two inference rules if and only if the statement is true in every domain in which the subject matter axioms are true.

FIRST-ORDER LOGIC

The language describing the truth of mathematical formulas. Formulas describe properties of terms and have a truth value. The following are atomic formulas: True False p(t1,..tn) where t1,..,tn are terms and p is a predicate.

If F1, F2 and F3 are formulas and v is a variable then the following are compound formulas:

- F1 ^ F2 conjunction - true if both F1 and F2 are true,
- F1 V F2 disjunction - true if either or both are true,
- F1 => F2 implication - true if F1 is false or F2 is true,
- F1 is the antecedent, F2 is the consequent (sometimes written with a thin arrow),
- F1 <= F2 true if F1 is true or F2 is false,
- F1 == F2 true if F1 and F2 are both true or both false (normally written with a three line equivalence symbol)
- F1 negation - true if f1 is false (normally written as a dash '-' with a shorter vertical line hanging from its right hand end).

For all v. F universal quantification - true if F is true for all values of v (normally written with an inverted A). Exists v. F existential quantification - true if there exists some value of v for which F is true. (Normally written with a reversed E). The operators ^ V => <= == ~ are called connectives. "For all" and "Exists" are quantifiers whose scope is F.

A term is a mathematical expression involving numbers, operators, functions and variables. The "order" of a logic specifies what entities "For all" and "Exists" may quantify over. First-order logic can only quantify over sets of atomic propositions.

Second-order logic can quantify over functions on propositions, and higher-order logic can quantify over any type of entity. The sets over which quantifiers operate are usually implicit but can be deduced from well-formedness constraints.In first-order logic quantifiers always range over all the elements of the domain of discourse. By contrast, second-order logic allows one to quantify over subsets.

HORN CLAUSES

HORN CLAUSE LOGIC

There is an important special case where inference can be made substantially more focussed than in the case of general resolution. This is the case where all the clauses are Horn clauses.

Definition

A Horn clause is a clause with at most one positive literal. Any Horn clause therefore belongs to one of four categories:

A Rule

1 positive literal, at least 1 negative literal. A rule has the form "~P1 V ~P2 V... V ~Pk V Q". This is logically equivalent to "[P1^P2^... ^Pk] => Q"; thus, an if-then implication with any number of conditions but one conclusion.

Examples

"~man(X) V mortal(X)" (All men are mortal); "~parent(X,Y) V ~ancestor(Y,Z) V ancestor(X,Z)" (If X is a parent of Y and Y is an ancestor of Z then X is an ancestor of Z.) A fact or unit: 1 positive literal, 0 negative literals. Examples: "man(socrates)", "parent(elizabeth,charles)", "ancestor(X,X)" (Everyone is an ancestor of themselves (in the trivial sense).)

A negated goal : 0 positive literals, at least 1 negative literal. In virtually all implementations of Horn clause logic, the negated goal is the negation of the statement to be proved; the knowledge base consists entirely of facts and goals. The statement to be proven, therefore, called the goal, is therefore a single unit or the conjuction of units; an existentially quantified variable in the goal turns into a free variable in the negated goal. *E.g.* If the goal to be proven is "exists (X) male(X) ^ ancestor(elizabeth,X)" (show that there exists a male descendent of Elizabeth) the negated goal will be "~male(X) V ~ancestor(elizabeth,X)".

The null clause: 0 positive and 0 negative literals. Appears only as the end of a resolution proof. Now, if resolution is restricted to Horn clauses, some interesting properties appear. Some of these are evident; others I will just state and you can take on faith.

- If you resolve Horn clauses A and B to get clause C, then the positive literal of A will resolve against a negative literal in B, so the only positive literal left in C is the one from B (if any). Thus, the resolvent of two Horn clauses is a Horn clause.

- If you resolve a negated goal G against a fact or rule A to get clause C, the positive literal in A resolves against a negative literal in G. Thus C has no positive literal, and thus is either a negated goal or the null clause.
- Therefore suppose you are trying to prove Phi from Gamma, where ~Phi is a negated goal, and Gamma is a knowledge base of facts and rules. Suppose you use the set of support strategy, in which no resolution ever involves resolving two clauses from Gamma together.

Inductively, every resolution combines a negated goal with a fact or rule from Gamma and generates a new negated goal. Moreover, if you take a resolution proof, and trace your way back from the null clause at the end to ~Phi at the beginning, since every resolution involves combining one negated goal with one clause from Gamma, it is clear that the sequence of negated goals involved can be linearly ordered. That is, the final proof, ignoring dead ends has the form

```
~Phi resolves with C1 from Gamma, generating
negated goal P2
P2 resolves with C2 from Gamma, generating
negated goal P3
...
Pk resolves with C2 from Gamma, generating
the null clause.
```

- Therefore, the process of generating the null clause can be viewed as a state space search where:
  - A state is a negated goal.
  - A operator on negated goal P is to resolve it with a clause C from Gamma.
  - The start state is ~Phi
  - The goal state is the null clause.
- Moreover, it turns out that it doesn't really matter which literal in P you choose to resolve. All the

literals in P will have to be resolved away eventually, and the order doesn't really matter.

This takes a little work to prove or even to state precisely, but if you work through a few examples, it becomes reasonably evident.

BACKWARD CHAINING

Putting all the above together, we formulate the following non-deterministic algorithm for resolution in Horn theories. This is known as backward chaining.

```
bc(in P0 : negated goal;
GAMMA : set of facts and rules;)
{ if P0 = null then succeed;
pick a literal L in P0;
choose a clause C in GAMMA whose head resolves
with L;
 P := resolve(P0,GAMMA);
 bc(P,GAMMA)
}
```

If bc(~Phi,Gamma) succeeds, then Phi is a consequence of Gamma; if it fails, then Phi is not a consequence of Gamma. Moreover: Suppose that Phi contains existentially quantified variables. As remarked above, when ~Phi is Skolemized, these become free variables.

If you keep track of the successive bindings through the successful path of resolution, then the final bindings of these variables gives you a value for these variables; all proofs in Horn theories are constructive (assuming that function symbols in Gamma are constructive.) Thus the attempt to prove a statement like "exists(X,Y) p(X,Y)^q(X,Y)" can be interpreted as " Find X and Y such that p(X,Y) and q(X,Y)." The succcessive negated goals Pi can be viewed as negations of subgoals of Phi.

Thus, the operation of resolving ~P against C to get ~Q can be interpreted, "One way to prove P would be to prove Q and then use C to infer P". For instance, suppose P is "mortal(socrates)," C is "man(X) => mortal(X)" and Q is "man(socrates)." Then the step of resolving ~P against C to get ~Q can be viewed as, "One way to prove mortal(socrates) would to prove man(socrates) and then combine that with C." Propositional Horn theories can be decided in polynomial time.

First-order Horn theories are only semi-decidable, but in practice, resolution over Horn theories runs much more efficiently than resolution over general first-order theories, because of the much restricted search space used in the above algorithm. Backward chaining is complete for Horn clauses. If Phi is a consequence of Gamma, then there is a backward-chaining proof of Phi from Gamma.

PROLOG

The pure Prolog language is an implementation of the bc algorithm with the following specifications:

- The clauses in Gamma are ordered by the programmer, and the state space search above is carried out in depth-first search order.
- The negative literals in each clause are ordered by the programmer. When negative goal P is resolved with clause C, the negative literals in C are placed in order at the start of P.
- The "pick" operation picks the first literal in P. Thus, P is implemented as a LIFO stack.

A Prolog "programme" is a knowledge base Gamma. The programme is invoked by posing a query Phi. The value returned is the bindings of the variables in Phi, if the query succeeds, or failure. The interpreter returns one answer at a time; the user has the option to request it to continue and to return further answers. Actual Prolog differs from pure Prolog in three major respects.

- There are additional functionalities besides theorem proving, such as functions to assert statements, functions to do arithmetic, functions to do I/O.
- The "cut" operator allows the user to prune branches of the search tree.
- The unification routine is not quite correct, in that it does not check for circular bindings *e.g.* X -> Y, Y -> f(X).

Notation

The clause "~p V ~q V r" is written in Prolog in the form "r :- p,q."

Example

Let Gamma be the following knowledge base:

- Ancestor(X,X).
- Ancestor(X,Z):- parent(X,Y), ancestor(Y,Z).
- Parent(george,sam).
- Parent(george,andy).
- Parent(andy,mary).
- Male(george).
- Male(sam).
- Male(andy).
- Female(mary).

Let Phi be the query "exists(Q) ancestor(george,Q) ^ female(Q)." (*i.e.* find a female descendant of george.) Then the Skolemization of Phi is"~ancestor(george,Q) V ~female(Q)."

A Prolog search proceeds as follows: (The indentation indicates the subgoal structure. Note that the variables in clauses in Gamma are renamed each time.)

```
    G0: ~ancestor(george,Q) V ~female(Q). Resolve
with 1: Q=X1=george.
    G1: ~female
    Fail. Return to G0.
    G0: ancestor(george,Q) V ~female(Q).
    Resolve with 2: X2=george. Z2=Q.
    G2: parent(george,Y2) V ~ancestor(Y2,Q)
    V ~female(Q).

    Resolve with 3: Y2=sam.
    G3: ~ancestor(sam,Q) V ~female(Q).
    Resolve with 1: Q=X3=sam.
    G4: ~female(sam).
    Fail.
    Return to G3.
    G3: ~ancestor(sam,Q) V ~female(Q).
```

```
    Resolve with 2: X4=sam, Z4=Q
    G5: ~parent(sam,Y2) V ~ancestor(Y2,Q) V
~female(Q).
    Fail.
    Return to G3.
    G3: ~ancestor(sam,Q) V ~female(Q).
    Fail.
    Return to G2.
    G2: ~parent(george,Y2) V ~ancestor(Y2,Q) V
~female(Q).
    Resolve with 4: Y2=andy.
    G6: ~ancestor(andy,Q) V ~female(Q).
    Resolve with 1: X5=Q=andy
    G7 ~female(andy).
    Fail.
    Return to G6.
    G6: ~parent(andy,Y6) V ~ancestor(Y6,Q) V
~female(Q).
    Resolve with 5: Y6=mary.
    G8: ~ancestor(mary,Q) V ~female(mary).
    Resolve with 1: X7=Q=mary.
    G9 ~female(mary)
    Resolve with 9.
```

Null.

Return the binding Q=mary.

FORWARD CHAINING

An alternative mode of inference in Horn clauses is forward chaining. In forward chaining, one of the resolvents in every resolution is a fact. (Forward chaining is also known as "unit resolution.")

Forward chaining is generally thought of as taking place in a dynamic knowledge base, where facts are gradually added to the knowledge base Gamma. In that case, forward chaining can be implemented in the following routines.

```
    procedure add_fact(in F; in out GAMMA)
    /* adds fact F to knowledge base GAMMA and
forward chains */
```

```
if F is not in GAMMA then
{
GAMMA := GAMMA union {F};
for each rule R in GAMMA do
    {
let ~L be the first negative literal in R;
if L unifies with F then
then { resolve R with F to get C;
if C is a fact then add_fact(C,GAMMA)
else/* C is a rule */add_rule(C,GAMMA)
    }
}
}
end add_fact.
procedure add_rule(in R; in out GAMMA)
/* adds rule R to knowledge base GAMMA and
forward chains */
if R is not in GAMMA then
{
GAMMA := GAMMA union {R};
let ~L be the first negative literal in R;
for each fact F in GAMMA do
if L unifies with F
then { resolve R with F to get C;
if C is a fact then add_fact(C,GAMMA)
else/* C is a rule */add_rule(C,GAMMA)
 }
}
end add_fact.
procedure answer_query(in Q, GAMMA) return
boolean/* Success or failure */
{
QQ := {Q}/* A queue of queries
while QQ is non-empty do
{
 Q1 := pop(QQ);
 L1 := the first literal in Q1;
 for each fact F in GAMMA do
```

```
    if F unifies with L
    then
    {
    resolve F with Q1 to get Q2;
    if Q2=null then return(true)
    else add Q2 to QQ;
    }
  }
    return(false)
```

The forward chaining algorithm may not terminate if GAMMA contains recursive rules. Forward chaining is complete for Horn clauses; if Phi is a consequence of Gamma, then there is a forward chaining proof of Phi from Gamma. To be sure of finding it if Gamma contains recursive rules, you have to modify the above routines to use an exhaustive search technique, such as a breadth-first search.

CHANINGS

Forward chaining is often preferable in cases where there are many rules with the same conclusions. A well-known category of such rule systems are taxonomic hierarchies. *E.g.* the taxonomy of the animal kingdom includes such rules as:

animal(X):- sponge(X).
animal(X):- arthopod(X).
animal(X):- vertebrate(X).
...
vertebrate(X):- fish(X).
vertebrate(X):- mammal(X)
...
mammal(X):- carnivore(X)
...
carnivore(X):- dog(X).
carnivore(X):- cat(X).
...

Now, suppose we have such a knowledge base of rules, we add the fact "dog(fido)" and we query whether "animal(fido)". In forward chaining, we will successively add "carnivore(fido)", "mammal(fido)", "vertebrate(fido)", and "animal(fido)". The query will then succeed immediately.

The total work is proportional to the height of the hierarchy. By contast, if you use backward chaining, the query "~animal(fido)" will unify with the first rule above, and generate the subquery "~sponge(fido)", which will initiate a search for Fido through all the subdivisions of sponges, and so on. Ultimately, it searches the entire taxonomy of animals looking for Fido.

In some cases, it is desirable to combine forward and backward chaining. For example, suppose we augment the above animal with features of these various categories:

```
breathes(X):- animal(X).
...
backbone(X):- vertebrate(X).
has(X,brain):- vertebrate(X).
...
furry(X):- mammal(X).
warm_blooded(X):- mammal(X).
...
```

If all these rules are implemented as forward chaining, then as soon as we state that Fido is a dog, we have to add all his known properties to Gamma; that he breathes, is warm-blooded, has a liver and kidney, and so on. The solution is to mark these property rules as backward chaining and mark the hierarchy rules as forward chaining.

You then implement the knowledge base with both the forward chaining algorithm, restricted to rules marked as forward chaining, and backward chaining rules, restricted to rules marked as backward chaining. However, it is hard to guarantee that such a mixed inference system will be complete.

ROLE OF PROLOG

INTRODUCTION

It is particularly convenient for manipulation by computer and a successful programming languageProlog, from programming in logic, has been based on it. Predicate logic is closely linked to the theory of relations. Prolog is therefore suitable for use with relational databases and has given rise to the field of deductive databases. Prolog is also much used in artificial intelligence applications. Introduces the Prolog programming language. Here we will explain a bit of how Prolog works.

It is not intended to be a full description of how to become an expert Prolog programmer. For that, after reading this chapter, you should refer to another book, such as Programming in Prolog by Clocksin and Mellish, or if you are already very familiar with Prolog, you might look at The Craft of Prolog by Richard O'Keefe.

While this is an introduction to Prolog, even experts may find something of interest in this chapter, since I explain Prolog in a somewhat unusual way, that may give new insights to old Prolog programmers. Prolog's name is short for ``Programming in Logic" (or really for Programmation Logique?") As its name suggests, Prolog is firmly based on logic, and Prolog programmes can be understood as statements in a formal logic *i.e.*, a Prolog programme can be thought of as a set of statements in first-order logic, and the meaning of the programme is the set of true implications of those logical statements. This is the approach that is usually taken to describe Prolog programming to novices. However, the amazing thing about logic programming to me is not that it is logic, but that it is programming.

These Prolog programmes are not only statements in a logic but they are also statements in a programming language. This is referred to in the biz by saying that Prolog programmes have a procedural interpretation (*i.e.*, as programmes) as well as a declarative interpretation (*i.e.*, as statements in a logic.) The introduction to Prolog that I give here will emphasize its procedurality. This may be anathema to some Prolog purists.

A PROLOG SUBSET

Variable names begin with a capital letter. It simplifies matters to make a programme consist of zero or more rules followed by a single query; in other systems queries can be interspersed with the rules.

Note also that most Prologs use `:-' instead of `<=' and use `,' instead of `and' to separate atoms.

```
<Programme>::= [ <rules> ]
<query>
<rule>::= <atom>. |
<atom> <= <literals>.
<rules>::= <rule> [ <rules> ]
<query>::= ? <literals>.
<literal>::= <atom> | not <atom>
<literals>::= <literal> [ and <literals> ]
<atom>::= <ident> | <ident> (<terms>)
<term>::= <ident> | <numeral> |-- constants
<ident> (<terms>) |-- functions
<IDENT> -- variables
<terms>::= <term> [, <terms> ]
Prolog-S Syntax
```

PROGRAMMING TECHNIQUES

Family relationships can be used to illustrate Prolog's ability to define basic relations such as parenthood and derived relations such as grand-parent-hood. A child has two parents - a mother and a father. A parent is either a mother or a father. A grand-parent of a child is a parent of a parent of the child. These rules can easily be expressed in Prolog.

```
parents(william, diana, charles).
parents(henry, diana, charles).
parents(charles, elizabeth, philip).
parents(diana, frances, edward).
parent(C,M) <= parents(C,M,D).
parent(C,D) <= parents(C,M,D).
Grandparent(C,GP) <= parent(C,P) and
parent(P,GP).
grandparent(william, Who).
{\fB Grand-Parent Relation. \fP}
```

Note that a parent is either a mother or a father. This is expressed by two rules in Prolog. A mother is a parent and it is also true that a father is a parent.The query `? grandparent(william, Who)' asks if william has a grand-parent and if so who? William has four grand-parents and the simple Prolog interpreter described later finds them all:

```
grandparen(william, frances) yes
grandparen(william, edward) yes
grandparen(william, elizabeth) yes
grandparen(william, philip) yes
Solutions to ? grandparent
```

Duplicate Solutions

The definition of aunts and uncles is slightly more difficult than grand-parents. A sibling of a parent is an aunt or an uncle. Two sibling have the same parents. The spouse of an aunt or uncle is also an aunt or uncle. If naively coded in Prolog, this rule allows infinite loops - an aunt is married to an uncle is married to an aunt is married to.... A solution is to distinguish between the direct relation and the relation by marriage.

```
parents(william, diana, charles).
parents(henry, diana, charles).
parents(charles, elizabeth, philip).
parents(diana, frances, edward).
parents(anne, elizabeth, philip).
parents(andrew, elizabeth, philip).
parents(edwardW, elizabeth, philip).
married(diana, charles).
married(elizabeth, philip).
married(frances, edward).
married(anne, mark).
parent(C,M) <= parents(C,M,D).
parent(C,D) <= parents(C,M,D).
sibling(X,Y) <= parents(X,M,D)
and parents(Y,M,D). {NB. sibling(X, X)}
aORuDirect(C, A) <= parent(C,P) and
sibling(P,A).
aORuMarr(C, A) <= aORuDirect(C,X) and
married(X,A).
```

```
aORuMarr(C, A) <= aORuDirect(C,X) and
married(A,X).
aORu(C,A) <= aORuDirect(C,A).
aORu(C,A) <= aORuMarr(C,A).
aORu(william, A).
{\fB The Aunt/Uncle Relation. \fP}
```

When the programme is run it produces the following answers.

```
aORu(william, diana) yes
aORu(william, charles) yes
aORu(william, anne) yes
aORu(william, andrew) yes
aORu(william, edwardW) yes
aORu(william, charles) yes
aORu(william, mark) yes
aORu(william, diana) yes
```

Note that this includes the correct aunts and uncles - Andrew, Anne, Edward and Mark - but also includes Charles and Diana twice. The reason is that an individual is considered to be his or her own sibling (same parents). This makes Diana a direct aunt and Charles a direct uncle. Diana is married to Charles and therefore is also an aunt by marriage and Charles is similarly an uncle by marriage. The way to cure this problem is to state negative information; siblings must differ.

equal(X, X).

sibling(X, Y) <= parents(X, M, D) and parents(Y, M, D) and not equal(X, Y).

```
Use of Negative Information. ---
query:
sibling(X, Y).
part output:
 sibling(william, henry) yes
 sibling(henry, william) yes
 sibling(charles, anne) yes
 sibling(charles, andrew) yes
...
Siblings.
```

Negation (not) can be implemented using the negation by failure rule which attempts to prove `not equal(charles, charles' by proving `equal(charles, charles)'. The latter succeeds and so `not equal(charles, charles)' fails or is considered false. In general, `not p(...)' succeeds or is considered true if and only if `p(...)' fails. For example, `equal fails and so `not equal succeeds.

```
aORu(william, anne) yes
aORu(william, andrew) yes
aORu(william, edwardW) yes
aORu(william, mark) yes
 --- William's Genuine Aunts and Uncles.
```

Negation by failure is not guaranteed to behave correctly if there is an unbound variable in the negated atom. In particular, if the negated atom appeared immediately after the `<=' in the improved rule for sibling then the rule would not work correctly.

sibling (X, Y) <= not equal(X, Y) and parents(X, M, D) and parents(Y, M, D).

With this rule and assuming that X and Y are unbound, it is possible to satisfy `equal(X,Y)' by binding X to Y and therfore the `not equal(X,Y)' and the rule fail in Prolog. From the logic point of view, there are many ways for `not equal(X,Y)' to succeed, for example with X bound to `william' and Y bound to `plus(fred,7)'. Only when X and Y are bound to constant or ground terms is negation by failure guaranteed to work correctly. Note that some Prolog interpreters delay any negated atom that contains an unbound variable to cure this problem.

Catch-Alls

A symbolic differentiator can easily be written in Prolog. Most systems allow the use of infix operators but prefix operators plus, times and so on are sufficient and are used here.

```
diff(plus(A,B), X, plus(DA, DB))
<= diff(A, X, DA) and diff(B, X, DB).
diff(times(A,B), X, plus(times(A, DB),
```

```
times(DA, B)))
    <= diff(A, X, DA) and diff(B, X, DB).
    equal(X, X).
    diff(X, X, 1).
    diff(Y, X, 0) <= not equal(Y, X).
    ? diff(plus(times(x, x), times(3,x)), x, Dx).
    {\fB Symbolic Differentiator. \fP}
    The output includes the correct answer.
    diff(plus(times(x, x), times(3, x)), x,
    plus(plus(times(x, 1), times(1, x)),
plus(times(3, 1), times(0, x)))) yes
    equivalent infix: diff(x*x+3*x, x,
x*1+1*x+3*1+0*3)
    d/dx of x*x+3*x
```

This is correct although it could be usefully simplified to 2*x+3; it is straightforward to write a simplifier for polynomials in Prolog if the ability to do arithmetic is provided. The output also includes many incorrect answers not shown. The reason is that the rule diff(Y,X,0) catches too many cases. It should be more correctly stated as

diff(Y, X, 0) <= atomic(Y) and not equal(Y,X).

Correct dy/dx Rule.

This requires negation and also the predicate atomic.

atomic(x). atomic(y). atomic(3).

Atomic cannot in general be defined by the user but is usually part of a Prolog system. Integers and other constants are atomic. Note the conflict of terminology between an atom and an atomic term.

Running Forwards and Backwards

It is possible to do list processing in Prolog. The append predicate joins two lists together. The function c can stand for the list constructor. The result of appending nil and a list B is just B. The result of appending c(H,T) and B is c(H,TB) where TB is the result of appending T and B.

```
     c(H,T)+ B
     ------
   = c(H,T+B)
```

Appending to a non-null List

```
append(c(H,T), B, c(H,TB)) <= append(T, B,
TB).
append(nil, B, B).
? append(c(1, c(2, nil)), c(3, c(4, nil)),
X).
{\fB Append run Forwards. \fP}
```

The result of appending the lists c(1,c(2,nil)) and c(3,c(4,nil)) is c(1,c(2,c(3,c(4,nil)))). Note that most Prolog systems provide a nicer syntax for lists, eg. [1,2,3,4], append(c(1, c(2, nil)), c(3, c(4, nil)), c(1, c(2, c(3, c(4, nil))))) yes. Append two Lists.

A surprising feature of append is that it can be run backwards to take a list apart.

```
append(c(H,T), B, c(H,TB)) <= append(T, B,
TB).
append(nil, B, B).
append(X, Y, c(1, c(2, c(3, nil)))).
{\fB Append run Backwards. \fP}
```

There are four ways in which the list c(1,c(2,c(3,nil)))) can be made up of two other lists.

```
append(c(1, c(2, c(3, nil))), nil, c(1, c(2,
c(3, nil)))) yes
append(c(1, c(2, nil)), c(3, nil), c(1, c(2,
c(3, nil)))) yes
append(c(1, nil), c(2, c(3, nil)), c(1, c(2,
c(3, nil)))) yes
append(nil, c(1, c(2, c(3, nil))), c(1, c(2,
c(3, nil)))) yes
```

SEMANTIC NETS

INTRODUCTION TO SEMANTIC NETS

A semantic net "is a structure which is used to represent associations between objects. For each object of a given type, there is a corresponding collection of attributes which are applicable to it; some of these provide simple values, but others are found by following links in the net, which connect the object to other objects of various types". The following diagram illustrates a simple semantic net describing a mapObject (in this case, a point on a map of mineral occurrences). To see how this semantic net is stored in LegendBurster, click here. The following diagram illustrates a query expressed as a semantic net, and explains two important features of LegendBurster queries.

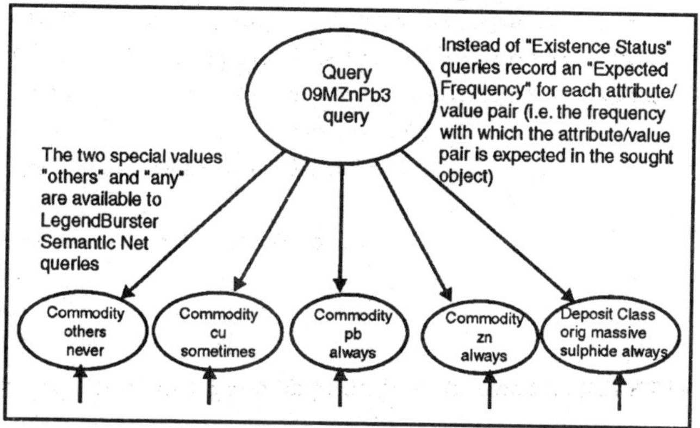

The major idea is that:

- The meaning of a concept comes from its relationship to other concepts, and that,
- The information is stored by interconnecting nodes with labelled arcs.

REPRESENTATION

The physical attributes of a person can be represented as in Fig.

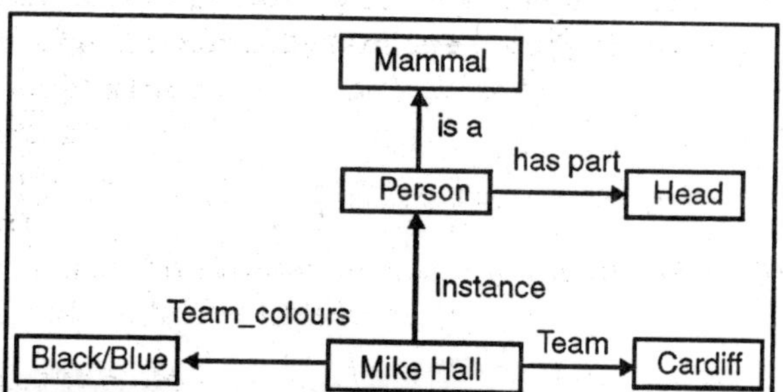

Fig. A Semantic Network

These values can also be represented in logic as: isa(person, mammal), instance team. We have already seen how conventional predicates such as lecturer(dave) can be written as instance (dave, lecturer) Recall that isa and instance represent inheritance and are popular in many knowledge representation schemes. But we have a problem: How we can have more than 2 place predicates in semantic nets?

E.g. Score Solution:

- Create new nodes to represent new objects either contained or alluded to in the knowledge, game and fixture in the current example.
- Relate information to nodes and fill up slots Fig.

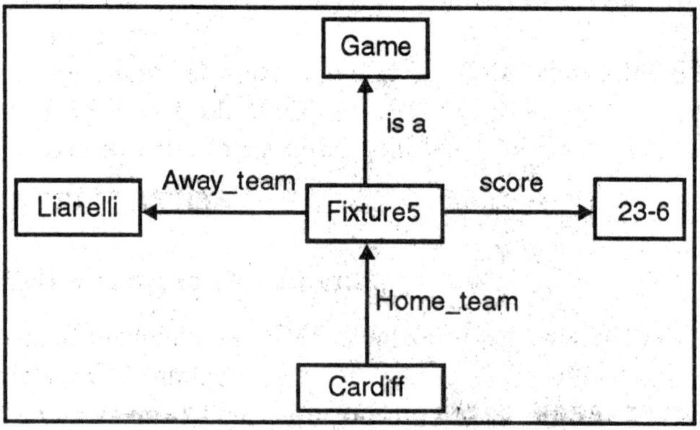

Fig. A Semantic Network for n-Place Predicate

As a more complex example consider the sentence: John gave Mary the book.

INFERENCE IN A SEMANTIC NET

Asic inference mechanism: follow links between nodes.

Two methods to do this:

Intersection search

The notion that spreading activation out of two nodes and finding their intersection finds relationships among objects. This is achieved by assigning a special tag to each visited node. Many advantages including entity-based organisation and fast parallel implementation. However very structured questions need highly structured networks.

Inheritance

The isa and instance representation provide a mechanism to implement this. Inheritance also provides a means of dealing with default reasoning. *E.g.* we could represent:

- Emus are birds.
- Typically birds fly and have wings.
- Emus run.

In the following Semantic net:

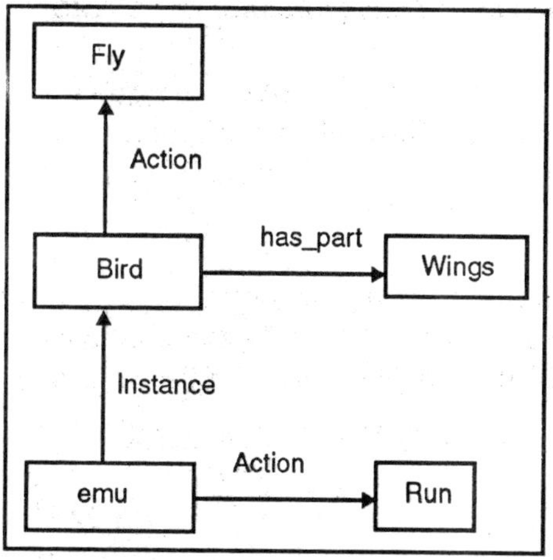

Fig. A Semantic Network for a Default Reasoning

In making certain inferences we will also need to distinguish between the link that defines a new entity and holds its value and the other kind of link that relates two existing entities. Consider the example shown where the height of two people is depicted and we also wish to compare them. We need extra nodes for the concept as well as its value.

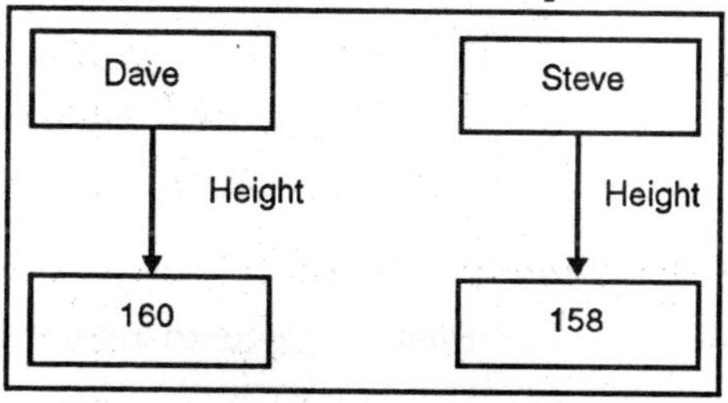

Fig. Two Heights

Special procedures are needed to process these nodes, but without this distinction the analysis would be very limited.

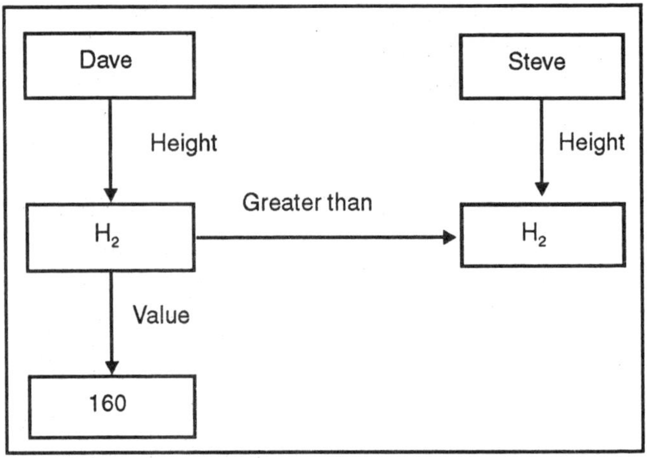

Fig. Comparison of Two Heights

Entities, attributes, and attribute values are the components of semantic nets, as illustrated in the previous section.

The relationships between these three components are shown again here to illustrate how they may be recursively applied to incorporate greater and greater amounts of detail about the "highest level" entity being described.

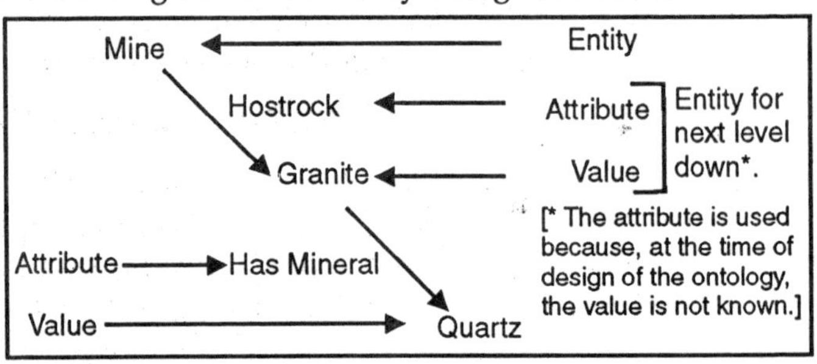

Referring Attributes

Sometimes we find that we need to refer to an already existing entity, effectively as an attribute of another entity -

for example when we want to say that a mine has a "fold", and the fold occurs in a granite which hosts the mine, we may represent the information in this way.

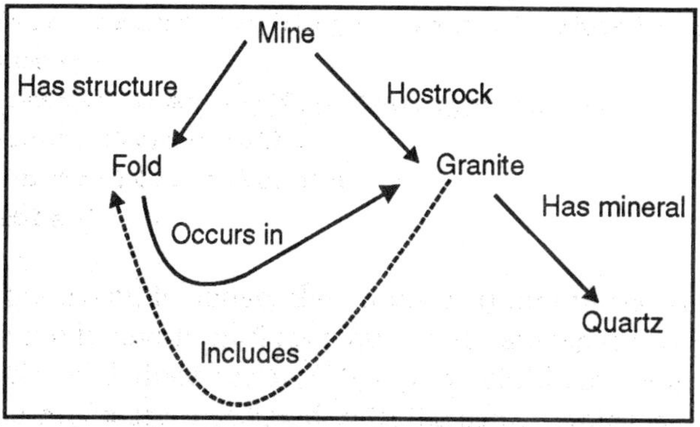

In such a situation, the value domain of the attribute "occurs in", which is a reference to another entity (the granite), is the collection of entities already existing in the semantic net, whose class is appropriate for the context (in this case, class = hostrock).

To implement this functionality, LegendBurster does the following:

- Allows the user to create "Referring Attributes" with the Ontology Editor, whose allowable target entity classes have to be specified during the attribute creation procedure. Its inverse attribute also has to be named at this time.
- Presents to a user entering a referring attribute into a description all qualifying entities which already exist on the semantic net (object or query), ahead of taking as input one or more of the qualifying entities as targets.
- Writes the target entity(s) node numbers into the referring attribute's value field, and an appropriately informative label into its label field (usually the value of the target entity), and then does the same for the target entity(s) with regard to the inverse attribute.

In this way the required link is effectively established. Arrows are suffixed to attribute/value pairs when they are displayed to the user on screen or in print to flag the presence of in-coming (<-) or out-going (->) links, as shown in the example on the left. (The sense of whether these are incoming or outgoing is determined by the semantics of each link.)

Reified Attributes

When an expression of fact requires reference to an association of attributes, a commonly used knowledge engineering technique, called "reification", converts the multi-attribute relationship into a "thing" with its own identity, and makes the attributes which are part of the relationship into attributes of the newly-created "thing".

Examples of such a situation in a geological context would be a contact between two rocks, or an alteration assemblage (involving minerals and other attributes: example).

On the "Create Attribute" screen, LegendBurster's Ontology Editor allows the designation of an attribute as a "Reified Attribute", in which case it will behave, and be treated, in the following manner:

- At the time a reified attribute is created, an entity with the same name as the reified attribute will be created
- After creation of a reified attribute, the user will need to input values for the attribute domain. The number of values input would depend on the maximum number which might be needed in any descriptions or queries, given consideration of (3) below. Values should ideally have a first part which remains constant, and might be the same as the attribute name, and a second part which is ideally an increasing number or letter (examples: "assemblage 1", or "contact A").
- Each time a reified attribute value is used when describing a map object or a query, that value is removed from the list of values available for any future attribute/value pairs of the same domain that may be entered. This ensures that every reified

attribute is given a unique name. Although this name will not be used by the system during any comparisons with other map objects or queries, its unique identity is crucial to resolving which parts of a description match which parts in any other description or query.

- During the comparison of queries to map objects, all reified attributes (entities) of the same class are compared with all the equivalents in the compared object - and paired up based on quality of match. in other works, after the best matching pair is found, they are "paired", their matching scores are calculated, and they are removed from consideration. Then the next-best matching pair is sought, and so on. When an unequal number of reified attributes is processed, the attributes which would have produced the poorest matching scores are left unpaired.

Value Attributes

Value Attributes are attributes related to an entity, not because of the class it belongs to, but because of its value in the class (effectively, because of its sub-class).

When LegendBurster is called on to provide the possible attributes for any entity (during instance description, or query definition), it takes into account both the class of the entity, and its value (sub-class).

Example: We may define a class of entities in our domain of interest to be "geological structures", with sub-types "faults" and "folds". Since all structures have the attribute "age", faults, as well as folds, would have an attribute "age". However, faults have many attributes that folds do not have, and vice versa.

In LegendBurster, we would call these "value attributes", because they exist for a geological structure depending on whether its value (sub-class) is "fault" or "fold". Value attributes are described in greater detail, with screen-shots from the Ontology Editor in the "Working with Attributes" section.

EXTENDING SEMANTIC NETS

Here we will consider some extensions to Semantic nets that overcome a few problems (see Exercises) or extend their expression of knowledge.

Partitioned Networks Partitioned Semantic Networks allow for:

- Propositions to be made without commitment to truth.
- Expressions to be quantified.

Basic idea: Break network into spaces which consist of groups of nodes and arcs and regard each space as a node. Consider the following: Andrew believes that the earth is flat. We can encode the proposition the earth is flat in a space and within it have nodes and arcs the represent the fact (Fig. 15). We can the have nodes and arcs to link this space the the rest of the network to represent Andrew's belief.

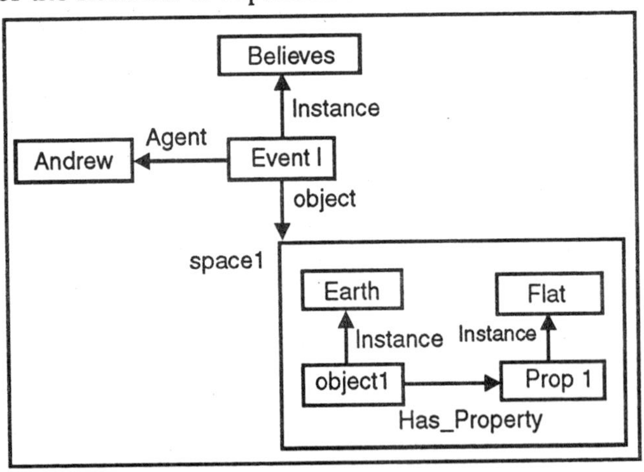

Fig. Partitioned Network

Now consider the quantified expression: Every parent loves their child To represent this we:

- Create a general statement, GS, special class.
- Make node g an instance of GS.
- Every element will have at least 2 attributes:
  - A form that states which relation is being asserted.
  - One or more forall or exists connections -- these

represent universally quantifiable variables in such statements *e.g.* x, y in parent(x) :child(y) loves(x,y)

Here we have to construct two spaces one for each x,y. We can express variables as existentially qualified variables and express the event of lovehaving an agent p and receiver b for every parent p which could simplify the network (See Exercises).

Also If we change the sentence to Every parent loves child then the node of the object being acted on (the child) lies outside the form of the general statement. Thus it is not viewed as an existentially qualified variable whose value may depend on the agent. So we could construct a partitioned network as in Fig.

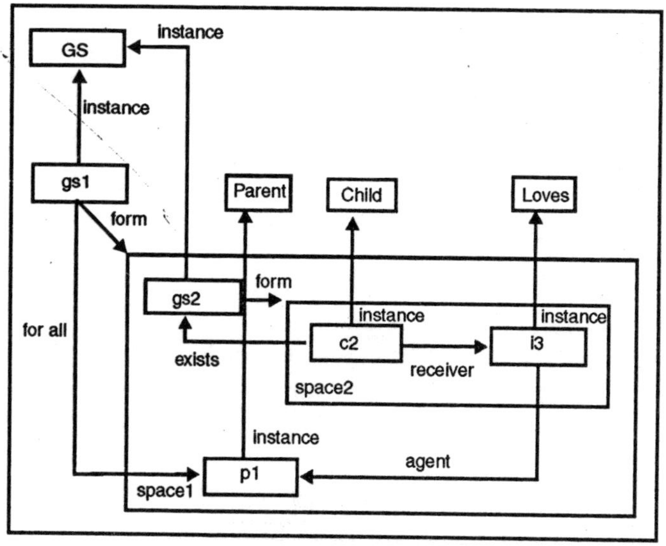

Fig. Partitioned Network

MINSKEY FRAMES

CASE OF FRAME SYSTEMS

Minsky's early formulation of frames as conceptual structures with default values was rather vague, it was accepted and made both more precise and logically expressible in different formalisms: Winograd himself used similar ideas in KRL, KL-ONE family of semantic networks developed a theory of default values, Hayes 1979 translated the idea of frame into logical formalism; after these results the idea of frame and frame-nets has become a common tool in A.I. and has been described in most textbooks of LISP or of introduction to A.I. I will give a highly abstract characterization of it, in order to make some theoretical points.

In early semantic networks, such as Quillian 1967, in order to understand the meaning of a word it is necessary to go through the entire net (*e.g.* to check all the activated nodes to compare the meaning of two different lexical items); after the discussion of the idea of frame and of default value, the situation seems changed.

Let us consider the concept of "tiger". A frame for "tiger" may be seen as a set of slots with default values, such as

- is a : mammal
- has legs 4 (1-4)
- eats: meat Vegetables
- has fur: yellow-black stripes white-black stripes, yellow
- lives in: the jungle Zoo, Circus

The first slot is an ISA arch, which links the concept to its immediate superconcept in the net. Each other slot is given a default value, but it may have other alternative values (the ones after the), which are activated depending on incoming information. In this way we can express the idea that there is no set of necessary and sufficient conditions for something to be a tiger (Wittgenstein's ideas on family resemblance predicates are quoted by Minsky as one of his sources in devising the idea of a frame). *E.g.* a tiger may become vegetarian, may have white and black stripes (if it is an albino tiger), may have three legs (if it has been wounded), but it still is a tiger.

Frames are part of a frame system, where each value of a slot may be [connected with] another frame. However, the default representation provided by the frame can be understood as a fixed meaning given to the lexical item representing the concept; this meaning is supposed to be the one that best represents the average use of the expression in the linguistic community. But other uses and other meanings may be attached to the same expression: other properties, instead of the default properties, may be the values of the slots of the frame. We may have them already enclosed in a set of possible values (*e.g.* the stereotypical table has four legs, but it may have also three legs: in the "legs" slot there will be a default value "4", but different values are allowed). The information of the context will help to decide which values to choose.

This does not amount to say that default values and the other possible values embedded in a frame representation are what is common to all speakers: probably there is no set of information which is the intersection of the information available to all speakers belonging to a linguistic community. But certainly meaning - average use - is determined by the majority, as influenced by experts and their definitions.

In case of conflict people defer to experts. Therefore, a certain stability in the definition of meaning reflects the practice and the needs of a linguistic community. Frames with default values are stable structures; the availability of alternative values for each slot of a frame is what gives new life and flexibility to the idea of meaning.

We might say that the idea of frame brings out the difference between a general objective representation of a concept and different ways of approximating it; as Frank 1995 claims, different combinations of the values of a frame may be considered somehow "private combinations", which are built upon a more stable "lexical content" (the "stable information represented in the mental lexicon").

We do not necessary need to speak of "mental" lexicon here; we just need to distinguish between different, idiosyncratic ways of understanding a concept, on the one hand, and the stable function of concepts in interpersonal intercourse, on the other. We need stable concepts specific enough to be used as starting point for different uses of the expression which is used to express them; a set of default values which is intended to give the stereotype is a good approximation to this kind of stability. The stereotypical definition of a concept may be intended as representing the meaning of the predicate used to express the concept.

But, even if we accept that a stable, stereotypical definition of meaning is given by the interplay of average use and deference to experts, it is still unclear to what extent individual frames depend on the overall system. As we have already remarked, we find the idea of global connections at the origin of semantic networks: in Quillian's perspective differences in meaning between two lexical items were individuated with the differences of all the connections activated with other nodes of the network, starting from the set of links immediately defining the items.

From this point of view, in order to understand the meaning of an item, and compare it with another, we need to run the entire data base. But this sounds very uncomfortable Although this idea ("spreading activation") seems fascinating, there is something strange: intuitively we do not need to understand the entire system of lexicon in order to understand a sentence like "Peter killed the tiger"; we need to know just a few things about tigers and killing.

This intuitive attitude is reflected in the restrictions that are imposed on artificial systems: if we are building a frame system, we must take care that individual steps in its computations do not involve the whole system, on pain of combinatorial explosion. A technical requirement deriving from the finite nature of our machines leads to restrictions on our representation of meaning. In A.I., we have at least two strategies for dealing with this problem:

- One strategy consists in making a difference between conceptual definitions and factual information. This kind of research is somehow an attempt at recovering a viable distinction between sentences (or inferences) that are necessary to define meaning and sentences that are not; it is an attempt at performing the role of the distinction between analytic and synthetic sentences, which had been so effectively criticized by Quine. Obviously, this attempt must face formidable difficulties. KL-ONE systems, for instance, have proposed a distinction between the assertional and the definitional; however, they do not explain the distinction but rather presuppose it (see Marconi 1994). Moreover, the KL-ONE distinction between definitional and assertional remains rather vague and does not represent aprincipled distinction.

A similar strategy had been already envisaged by McCarthy in his early work. In his "Advise taker" project he defined the concept of "immediate inference": in order to understand a situation we do not need to make explicit all the inferences from the relevant premises, but only their immediate consequences, beginning with the inferences which require just one step in the deductive process. The idea is barely sketched; however, it does point to the necessity of controlling the risk of combinatorial explosion of inferences derivable from a single premise.

What do we count as "principled"? Priciples which define the distinction between two kinds of inferences might derive from the needs of implementation. If machines are limited artefacts (as we are limited agents), we need, at least for computational economy or computational necessity, to distinguish basic semantic information from factual idiosyncratic information, or basic information about the literal meanings of words from information about different applications.

If we abandon the principles behind the analytic-synthetic distinction, we may still find some pragmatic principles which justify the distinction between two sorts of inferences, the one defining basic uses of words, the other defining occasional applications of them.

A philosophical attitude of this kind is well followed in the practice of A.I.: any "viable" (=compatible with an A.I. systems) representation of meaning as inferential role is bound not to include all (or most) possible inferences. Many A.I. programmes may be considered as attempts to respect this restriction in defining meaning and understanding. A clear example is the work of Norvig 1989, who designs an algorithm computing a limited set of proper inferences quickly, without computing all types of inferences. Proper inferences are defined as plausible, relevant, and easy. Quick computation of a small set of proper inferences yields a partial interpretation, which can be used as input for further processing.

- Another strategy consists in defining, with some degree of arbitrariness, a set of relevant contexts: if we are speaking of tigers and refer to somebody shooting a tiger, we need some idea of what happens in big-game hunting, but we do not need to know anything about skiing or going to a restaurant. This strategy is reflected in the practice of partitioning a semantic network into an organised, hierarchical structure, where superconcepts control sets of concepts under their nodes.
- Hereditary aspects, widely discussed in the literature do not entail that in order to understand the meaning of a lexical item you need to go through the entire net: the path of hereditary relations is followed inside a specific semantic field, and what happens in other semantic fields is not at all relevant to understanding or defining the meaning of the items in the field under consideration. Information about birds (*e.g.*, that penguins don't fly) is not relevant to understanding what a tiger is.
- Shank's scripts are another classic example of this kind of strategy. The idea of a script (think of the famous script "restaurant") is just the idea of encoding a certain amount of information in a single unit, somehow autonomous and not depending on other information.
- High level representation such as scripts are treated in formalisms which use, to a certain extent, a top-down representation of knowledge, where procedures (demons) are used to activate the script

or scenario relevant to a given situation (the first to think of a connection between frames and procedures.

In both cases frame systems can be seen as representing the average use of words in a language. They might include links to experts' knowledge: part of commonsense knowledge about the world is the acknowledgement that experts exist for most of our fields of interest. Admitting a link to scientific definitions of each term is a representation of such an ability to defer.

This representation must presuppose individual sites for scientific definitions, and the availability of such sites to people looking for more precise information and definitions. In both cases, what counts as semantic competence is relatively fixed.

We must assume some "idealisation" of the speaker, which does not amount to claiming that speakers share exactly the stereotypical meaning, the set of properties stereotypically defined. If the representation of meaning is the representation of the practice of a language in a community, the stereotype is the set of features which are the most constant in this practice.

6

Knowledge Based Expert System

OVERVIEW

Knowledge-based expert systems, or simply expert systems, use human knowledge to solve problems that normally would require human intelligence. These expert systems represent the expertise knowledge as data or rules within the computer.

These rules and data can be called upon when needed to solve problems. Books and manuals have a tremendous amount of knowledge but a human has to read and interpret the knowledge for it to be used. Conventional computer programmes perform tasks using conventional decision-making logic -- containing little knowledge other than the basic algorithm for solving that specific problem and the necessary boundary conditions.

This programme knowledge is often embedded as part of the programming code, so that as the knowledge changes, the programme has to be changed and then rebuilt. Knowledge-based systems collect the small fragments of human know-how into a knowledge-base which is used to reason through a problem, using the knowledge that is appropriate.

A different problem, within the domain of the knowledge-base, can be solved using the same programme without reprogramming. The ability of these system to explain the reasoning process through back-traces and to handle levels of confidence and uncertainty provides an additional feature that conventional programming don't handle.Most expert systems are developed via specialized software tools called shells. These shells come equipped with an inference mechanism (backward chaining, forward chaining, or both), and require knowledge to be entered according to a specified format.

They typically come with a number of other features, such as tools for writing hypertext, for constructing friendly user interfaces, for manipulating lists, strings, and objects, and for interfacing with external programmes and databases. These shells qualify as languages, although certainly with a narrower range of application than most programming languages.

The expert system is a major application of AI today. Also known as knowledge-based systems, expert systems act as intelligent assistants to human experts or serve as a resource to people who may not have access to an expert. The major difference between an expert system and a simple database containing information on a particular subject is that the database can only give the user discrete facts about the subject, whereas an expert system uses reasoning to draw conclusions from stored information.

The purpose of this AI application is not to replace our human experts, but to make their knowledge and experience more widely available.An expert system has three parts: knowledge base, inference engine, and user interface. The knowledge base contains both declarative (factual) and procedural (rules-of-usage) knowledge in a very narrow field. The inference engine runs the system by determining which procedural knowledge to access in order to obtain the appropriate declarative knowledge, then draws conclusions and decides when an applicable solution is found.

An interface is usually defined as the point where the machine and the human "touch." An interface is usually a keyboard, mouse, or similar devices. In an expert system, there are actually two different user interfaces: One is for the designer of the system (who is generally experienced with computers) the other is for the user (generally a computer novice). Because most users of an expert system will not be computer experts, it is important that system be easy for them to use. All user interfaces are bi-directional; that is, are able to receive information from the user and respond to the user with its recommendations. The designer's user interface must also be capable of adding new information to the knowledge base.

ROLE OF PROGRAMMERS

Are computer programmes that are derived from a branch of computer science research called Artificial Intelligence (AI). AI's scientific goal is to understand intelligence by building computer programmes that exhibit intelligent behaviour.

It is concerned with the concepts and methods of symbolic inference, or reasoning, by a computer, and how the knowledge used to make those inferences will be represented inside the machine. Of course, the term intelligence covers many cognitive skills, including the ability to solve problems, learn, and understand language; AI addresses all of those.

But most progress to date in AI has been made in the area of problem solving -- concepts and methods for building programmes that reason about problems rather than calculate a solution. AI programmes that achieve expert-level competence in solving problems in task areas by bringing to bear a body of knowledge about specific tasks are called knowledge-based or expert systems.

Often, the term expert systems is reserved for programmes whose knowledge base contains the knowledge used by human experts, in contrast to knowledge gathered from textbooks or non-experts. More often than not, the two terms, expert systems (ES) and knowledge-based systems (KBS), are used synonymously.

Taken together, they represent the most widespread type of AI application. The area of human intellectual endeavor to be captured in an expert system is called the task domain. Task refers to some goal-oriented, problem-solving activity.Domain refers to the area within which the task is being performed. Typical tasks are diagnosis, planning, scheduling, configuration and design. Building an expert system is known as knowledge engineering and its practitioners are called knowledge engineers.

The knowledge engineer must make sure that the computer has all the knowledge needed to solve a problem. The knowledge engineer must choose one or more forms in which to represent the required knowledge as symbol patterns in the memory of the computer -- that is, he (or she) must choose a knowledge representation. He must also ensure that the computer can use the knowledge efficiently by selecting from a handful of reasoning methods.

Building Blocks of Expert Systems

Every expert system consists of two principal parts: the knowledge base; and the reasoning, or inference, engine. The knowledge base of expert systems contains both factual and heuristic knowledge.

Factual knowledge is that knowledge of the task domain that is widely shared, typically found in textbooks or journals, and commonly agreed upon by those knowledgeable in the particular field.

Heuristic knowledge is the less rigorous, more experiential, more judgmental knowledge of performance. In contrast to factual knowledge, heuristic knowledge is rarely discussed, and is largely individualistic. It is the knowledge of good practice, good judgment, and plausible reasoning in the field. It is the knowledge that underlies the "art of good guessing."

Knowledge representation formalizes and organizes the knowledge. One widely used representation is the production rule, or simply rule. A rule consists of an IF part and a THEN part (also called a condition and an action). The IF part lists a set of conditions in some logical combination.

The piece of knowledge represented by the production rule is relevant to the line of reasoning being developed if the IF part of the rule is satisfied; consequently, the THEN part can be concluded, or its problem-solving action taken.

Expert systems whose knowledge is represented in rule form are called rule-based systems. Another widely used representation, called the unit (also known as frame, schema, or list structure) is based upon a more passive view of knowledge.

The unit is an assemblage of associated symbolic knowledge about an entity to be represented. Typically, a unit consists of a list of properties of the entity and associated values for those properties.Since every task domain consists of many entities that stand in various relations, the properties can also be used to specify relations, and the values of these properties are the names of other units that are linked according to the relations.

One unit can also represent knowledge that is a "special case" of another unit, or some units can be "parts of" another unit. The problem-solving model, or paradigm, organizes and controls the steps taken to solve the problem. One common but powerful paradigm involves chaining of IF-THEN rules to form a line of reasoning.

If the chaining starts from a set of conditions and moves towards some conclusion, the method is called forward chaining. If the conclusion is known (for example, a goal to be achieved) but the path to that conclusion is not known, then reasoning backwards is called for, and the method is backward chaining.

These problem-solving methods are built into programme modules called inference engines or inference procedures that manipulate and use knowledge in the knowledge base to form a line of reasoning. The knowledge base an expert uses is what he learned at school, from colleagues, and from years of experience. Presumably the more experience he has, the larger his store of knowledge.

Knowledge allows him to interpret the information in his databases to advantage in diagnosis, design, and analysis.Though an expert system consists primarily of a knowledge base and an inference engine, a couple of other features are worth mentioning: reasoning with uncertainty, and explanation of the line of reasoning.

Knowledge is almost always incomplete and uncertain. To deal with uncertain knowledge, a rule may have associated with it a confidence factor or a weight. The set of methods for using uncertain knowledge in combination with uncertain data in the reasoning process is called reasoning with uncertainty.

An important subclass of methods for reasoning with uncertainty is called "fuzzy logic," and the systems that use them are known as "fuzzy systems." Because an expert system uses uncertain or heuristic knowledge (as we humans do) its credibility is often in question (as is the case with humans). When an answer to a problem is questionable, we tend to want to know the rationale.

If the rationale seems plausible, we tend to believe the answer. So it is with expert systems. Most expert systems have the ability to answer questions of the form: "Why is the answer X?" Explanations can be generated by tracing the line of reasoning used by the inference engine. The most important ingredient in any expert system is knowledge.

The power of expert systems resides in the specific, high-quality knowledge they contain about task domains. AI researchers will continue to explore and add to the current repertoire of knowledge representation and reasoning methods.

But in knowledge resides the power. Because of the importance of knowledge in expert systems and because the current knowledge acquisition method is slow and tedious, much of the future of expert systems depends on breaking the knowledge acquisition bottleneck and in codifying and representing a large knowledge infrastructure.

Knowledge Engineering

Knowledge Engineering is the art of designing and building expert systems, and knowledge engineers are its practitioners. Gerald M. Weinberg said of programming in The Psychology of Programming: "'Programming,' -- like 'loving,' -- is a single word that encompasses an infinitude of activities" (Weinberg 1971).

Knowledge engineering is the same, perhaps more so. We stated earlier that knowledge engineering is an applied part of the science of artificial intelligence which, in turn, is a part of computer science.

Theoretically, then, a knowledge engineer is a computer scientist who knows how to design and implement programmes that incorporate artificial intelligence techniques. The nature of knowledge engineering is changing, however, and a new breed of knowledge engineers is emerging. Today there are two ways to build an expert system.

They can be built from scratch, or built using a piece of development software known as a "tool" or a "shell." Before we discuss these tools, let's briefly discuss what knowledge engineers do.

Though different styles and methods of knowledge engineering exist, the basic approach is the same: a knowledge engineer interviews and observes a human expert or a group of experts and learns what the experts know, and how they reason with their knowledge.

The engineer then translates the knowledge into a computer-usable language, and designs an inference engine, a reasoning structure, that uses the knowledge appropriately. He also determines how to integrate the use of uncertain knowledge in the reasoning process, and what kinds of explanation would be useful to the end user.

Next, the inference engine and facilities for representing knowledge and for explaining are programmed, and the domain knowledge is entered into the programme piece by piece.

It may be that the inference engine is not just right; the form of knowledge representation is awkward for the kind of knowledge needed for the task; and the expert might decide the pieces of knowledge are wrong. All these are discovered and modified as the expert system gradually gains competence.

The discovery and cumulation of techniques of machine reasoning and knowledge representation is generally the work of artificial intelligence research. The discovery and cumulation of knowledge of a task domain is the province of domain experts. Domain knowledge consists of both formal, textbook knowledge, and experiential knowledge -- the expertise of the experts.

Tools, Shells, and Skeletons

Compared to the wide variation in domain knowledge, only a small number of AI methods are known that are useful in expert systems. That is, currently there are only a handful of ways in which to represent knowledge, or to make inferences, or to generate explanations.

Thus, systems can be built that contain these useful methods without any domain-specific knowledge. Such systems are known as skeletal systems, shells, or simply AI tools. Building expert systems by using shells offers significant advantages.

A system can be built to perform a unique task by entering into a shell all the necessary knowledge about a task domain. The inference engine that applies the knowledge to the task at hand is built into the shell. If the programme is not very complicated and if an expert has had some training in the use of a shell, the expert can enter the knowledge himself.

Many commercial shells are available today, ranging in size from shells on PCs, to shells on workstations, to shells on large mainframe computers. They range in price from hundreds to tens of thousands of dollars, and range in complexity from simple, forward-chained, rule-based systems requiring two days of training to those so complex that only highly trained knowledge engineers can use them to advantage.

They range from general-purpose shells to shells custom-tailored to a class of tasks, such as financial planning or real-time process control. Although shells simplify programming, in general they don't help with knowledge acquisition. Knowledge acquisition refers to the task of endowing expert systems with knowledge, a task currently performed by knowledge engineers.

The choice of reasoning method, or a shell, is important, but it isn't as important as the accumulation of high-quality knowledge. The power of an expert system lies in its store of knowledge about the task domain -- the more knowledge a system is given, the more competent it becomes.

Bricks and Mortar

The fundamental working hypothesis of AI is that intelligent behaviour can be precisely described as symbol manipulation and can be modeled with the symbol processing capabilities of the computer. In the late 1950s, special programming languages were invented that facilitate symbol manipulation. The most prominent is called LISP (LISt Processing).

Because of its simple elegance and flexibility, most AI research programmes are written in LISP, but commercial applications have moved away from LISP.In the early 1970s another AI programming language was invented in France. It is called PROLOG (PROgramming in LOGic). LISP has its roots in one area of mathematics (lambda calculus), PROLOG in another (first-order predicate calculus).

PROLOG consists of English-like statements which are facts (assertions), rules (of inference), and questions. Here is an inference rule: "If object-x is part-of object-y then a component-of object-y is object-x."Programmes written in PROLOG have behaviour similar to rule-based systems written in LISP. PROLOG, however, did not immediately become a language of choice for AI programmers.

In the early 1980s it was given impetus with the announcement by the Japanese that they would use a logic programming language for the Fifth Generation Computing Systems (FGCS) Project. A variety of logic-based programming languages have since arisen, and the term prolog has become generic.

APPLICATIONS OF EXPERT SYSTEMS

The spectrum of applications of expert systems technology to industrial and commercial problems is so wide as to defy easy characterization. The applications find their way into most areas of knowledge work.

They are as varied as helping salespersons sell modular factory-built homes to helping NASA plan the maintenance of a space shuttle in preparation for its next flight. Applications tend to cluster into seven major classes.

Diagnosis and Troubleshooting of Devices and Systems

This class comprises systems that deduce faults and suggest corrective actions for a malfunctioning device or process. Medical diagnosis was one of the first knowledge areas to which ES technology was applied, but diagnosis of engineered systems quickly surpassed medical diagnosis. There are probably more diagnostic applications of ES than any other type.

The diagnostic problem can be stated in the abstract as: given the evidence presenting itself, what is the underlying problem/reason/cause?

Planning and Scheduling

Systems that fall into this class analyse a set of one or more potentially complex and interacting goals in order to determine a set of actions to achieve those goals, and/or provide a detailed temporal ordering of those actions, taking into account personnel, materiel, and other constraints. This class has great commercial potential, which has been recognized.

Examples involve airline scheduling of flights, personnel, and gates; manufacturing job-shop scheduling; and manufacturing process planning.

Configuration of Manufactured Objects

Configuration, whereby a solution to a problem is synthesized from a given set of elements related by a set of constraints, is historically one of the most important of expert system applications.

Configuration applications were pioneered by computer companies as a means of facilitating the manufacture of semi-custom minicomputers (McDermott 1981). The technique has found its way into use in many different industries, for example, modular home building, manufacturing, and other problems involving complex engineering design and manufacturing.

Financial Decision Making

The financial services industry has been a vigourous user of expert system techniques. Advisory programmes have been created to assist bankers in determining whether to make loans to businesses and individuals.

Insurance companies have used expert systems to assess the risk presented by the customer and to determine a price for the insurance. A typical application in the financial markets is in foreign exchange trading.

Knowledge Publishing

This is a relatively new, but also potentially explosive area. The primary function of the expert system is to deliver knowledge that is relevant to the user's problem, in the context of the user's problem.

The two most widely distributed expert systems in the world are in this category. The first is an advisor which counsels a user on appropriate grammatical usage in a text. The second is a tax advisor that accompanies a tax preparation programme and advises the user on tax strategy, tactics, and individual tax policy.

Process Monitoring and Control

Systems falling in this class analyse real-time data from physical devices with the goal of noticing anomalies, predicting trends, and controlling for both optimality and failure correction. Examples of real-time systems that actively monitor processes can be found in the steel making and oil refining industries.

Design and Manufacturing

These systems assist in the design of physical devices and

processes, ranging from high-level conceptual design of abstract entities all the way to factory floor configuration of manufacturing processes.

DOMAIN EXPLORATION

EXISTING SYSTEMS

Many donor-driven information systems are overly ambitious, overly complex and over-designed. Initiatives are often planned and implemented from scratch, overlooking the fundamental organizational processes and institutional incentives that drive information use.

They can also ignore the influence of potential "losers" who may subsequently resist implementation. Oversights generally fall into two categories: attempts to create new systems of communication rather than enhancing those systems which are already in place and accepted, and failures to recognize the ways in which the existing policy environment will affect the intervention.

Experience shows that the most effective systems for providing specific information to specific users are simple and modest, and build on existing communication and data collection systems.

There is a danger that the current focus on Internet-based information systems in developing countries will undermine rich and effective existing information networks. Through a better understanding of existing systems, project designers can enhance communications technology in ways that are relevant and appropriate to the users.

Designers should also attempt to gain support from internal 'champions' who are advocating change take care not to disrupt local cultural values, and offer incentives to individuals for contributing information.

EXPERTISE TRANSFER SYSTEM

The Expertise Transfer System (ETS) has been in use in Boeing for more than three years. Hundreds of prototypical knowledge-based systems have been generated by ETS. The system interviews experts to uncover key aspects of their problem-solving knowledge. It helps build very rapid prototypes (typically in less than two hours), assists the expert in analysing the adequacy of the knowledge for solving the problem, and creates knowledge bases for several expert system shells (S.1, M.1, OPS5, KEE, and so on) from its own internal representation (Boose, 1984, 1985, 1986).

The tools in ETS are now part of Aquinas, a much larger system. Aquinas was developed to overcome ETS's limitations in knowledge representation and reasoning. Due to these limitations, ETS was usually abandoned sometime during the knowledge acquisition process. Typically project approaches were explored or feasibility was assessed for several days or a week, and then development continued in some other expert system shell. While the use of the tool in this way saved substantial time (typically 1 or 2 calendar months from a 12- to 24-month project), it was desirable to explore new approaches for making the system more powerful.

TASKS AND TOOL SETS

Aquinas is a collection of integrated tool sets. They share a common user interface (the dialog manager) and underlying knowledge representation and data base. Each set of tools addresses a general knowledge acquisition task and embodies sets of strategies that support the task:

Elicit Distinctions

Gaines has characterized knowledge acquisition as "the modeling of events enabling adequate prediction and action." In this view, a distinction is the primitive concept underlying the representation of knowledge and the formal theory of modeling.

Systems that acquire problem-solving knowledge seek to establish qualitative and quantitative distinctions that lead to effective prediction and action, while weeding out distinctions that are redundant or inconsequential. Eliciting distinctions with Aquinas

Personal Construct Psychology

George Kelly's personal construct theory provides a rich framework for modeling the qualitative and quantitative distinctions inherent in an expert's problem-solving knowledge. ETS (Expertise Transfer System) is a set of tools used by the expert to elicit, analyse, and refine knowledge as rating grids.

In a rating grid, problem solutions - elements - are elicited and placed across the grid as column labels, and traits of these solutions - constructs - are listed alongside the rows of the grid Traits are first elicited by presenting groups of solutions and asking the expert to discriminate among them.

Decompose Problems

Experts building large knowledge bases face the task of decomposing their problem in ways that enhance efficiency and clarity. In our previous work using ETS, the difficulty of representing complex problems in a single rating grid became clear.

First, a single rating grid can represent only "flat" relations between single solutions and traits. No deep knowledge, causal knowledge, or relationship chains can be shown.

A second limitation was that only solutions or traits at the same level of abstraction could be used comfortably in a single grid. Finally, large single grids were often difficult to manipulate and comprehend.

Problem Decomposition Strategies in Aquinas

Hierarchical tools in Aquinas help the expert build, edit, and analyse knowledge in hierarchies and lattices. These hierarchies allow the expert to break up complex problems into pieces of convenient size and similar levels of abstraction. Hierarchies in Aquinas are organized around solutions, traits, knowledge sources and cases.

Nodes in the four hierarchies combine to form rating grids. In the most simple case, the children of a node in a solution hierarchy supply the solutions along the top of a grid;

the children of a node in a trait hierarchy supply the traits down the side of a grid. Rating values within the grid provide information about the solutions with respect to each trait. In eliciting knowledge for complex problems it is sometimes difficult for the expert to identify conclusion sets whose members are at similar, useful levels of granularity.

For instance, in an engine diagnostic system, the expert may include the repair solutions:

- Engine
- Battery
- Ignition coil
- Electrical system

"Engine" and "electrical system" are at more general levels of structural and functional abstraction than "battery" and "ignition coil."

Mixing more general and more specific solutions in the same rating grid causes problems during trait elicitation, since traits useful in differentiating "engine" from "electrical system" problems are not necessarily those useful in discriminating "ignition coil" from "battery" problems.

Solution Hierarchies

Solutions are grouped in specialization hierarchies within Aquinas. This structure aids experts in organizing large numbers of solutions that may exist at different levels of abstraction.

For example, a solution class named "vehicle" is a superclass (parent or prototype) to "car" and "truck" subclasses. The "car" class can serve in turn as a parent to a class of specific car models or to a particular instance of a car.

Trait Hierarchies

Characteristics of a particular level in the solution hierarchy can be structured in trait hierarchies. For instance, in a knowledge base for a Transportation Advisor, the solutions exist in hierarchies of vehicles. Each level in the solution hierarchy has a trait hierarchy that contains information needed to select solutions at that level. A trait hierarchy attached to the "vehicle" abstraction level of a solution hierarchy, for instance, may contain information about general use type, relative speed, cost, and so forth for the types of vehicles in the hierarchy. The "car" subclass is attached to a car trait hierarchy that contains information useful in selecting a particular car.

Expert Hierarchies

Expert hierarchies represent multiple knowledge sources as structured groups. Each node in the expert hierarchy may represent an individual, an aspect of an individual, a group, or an independent knowledge source.

Information from multiple experts may be independently elicited and analysed, then weighted and combined to derive joint solutions to problems. Analyses can be performed that show similarities and differences among experts.

Experts each have their own solution and trait hierarchies, which may or may not overlap those of others. Each expert's unique problem-solving strategies and information are preserved.

Case Hierarchies

Case hierarchies define subsets of the knowledge base appropriate to solving a particular class of problems. For example, in a knowledge base of information about vehicles, a user may want to include different knowledge for selecting a vehicle for going over land than for going over water. A land case and a water case may be created, each drawing on a subset of the expert pool knowledgeable in those areas.

Additional levels may be created for short or long land trips, cost considerations, and so on. A hierarchy of cases allows the knowledge base to be developed, modified, and maintained based on specific classes of situations. Eventually the lower leaves in case hierarchies become specific consultation instances when the knowledge is tested and used to solve a specific problem.

From Hierarchies to Rating Grids

A rating grid is built by combining values associated with nodes in each of the four basic hierarchies. Relationships between nodes do not have to be strictly hierarchical; lattices may be formed when more than one parent points to the same child.

The expert defines the current rating grid by selecting appropriate nodes in the hierarchies. In a sense, each rating grid is four dimensional. Any two of these dimensions are shown at once as rows and columns in a given grid.

Usually solutions and traits are shown, but sometimes it is useful to show other combinations. For instance, a grid could display the ratings of several experts across the top with particular solutions down the side.

The associated trait and case nodes would be shown to the side of the grid. Often the ratings displayed summarize or generalize information from different nodes in the hierarchies.

Techniques for Defining and Exploring Hierarchies

Strategies for helping the expert build and refine hierarchies in Aquinas include laddering, cluster analysis, and trait value examination. Some of these strategies will be demonstrated in the section describing the Programming Language Advisor.

COMBINING UNCERTAIN INFORMATION

A major limitation of most current knowledge engineering tools is that they do not allow experts to specify how specific pieces of information should be combined. Most tools either tend to use fixed, global numeric functions to compute values or restrict the expert to purely symbolic representations of uncertainty.

Ideally, flexibility and comprehensibility could be achieved by allowing experts to specify how information should be combined locally either by selecting from a set of commonly accepted combining functions or by defining their own method. In Aquinas, uncertain knowledge, preferences, and constraints may be elicited, represented, and locally applied using combinations of several different methods. These methods may be classified into three main types: absolute, relativistic, and probabilistic.

Absolute Reasoning

Absolute (categorical) reasoning involves judgments made with no significant reservations. It "typically depends on relatively few facts, its appropriateness is easy to judge, and its result is unambiguous".

For example, in selecting a programming language, users may be able to say with certainty that they would be interested only in languages that run on an Apple Macintosh or that they will not consider a language that costs more than $400, regardless of other desirable characteristics. Experts can also build these types of absolute constraints into the knowledge associated with an Aquinas rating grid.

Relativistic Reasoning

Unfortunately, not all judgments can be absolute. Many involve significant trade-offs, where information and preferences from several sources must be weighed. Even if criteria for the ideal decision can be agreed on, sometimes it can be only approximated by the available alternatives. In these cases, problem-solving information must be propagated in a relativistic fashion.

Aquinas incorporates a variety of models and approaches to relativistic reasoning, including MYCIN-like certainty factor calculus, fuzzy logic and the Analytic Hierarchy Process.

Probabilistic

Future versions of Aquinas will have more complete models for the elicitation and analysis of probabilistic information including Bayesian and other approaches. Users may also define their own methods for combining and propagating information. The availability of different inference methods within a single workbench allows users and experts flexibility in adapting Aquinas to the problem at hand. Methods are currently selected based on the cost of elicitation, the precision of the knowledge needed, convenience, and the expert's preference.

Future research will suggest heuristics for helping experts select appropriate methods and designs for particular types of questions. These heuristics will be incorporated into the Aquinas dialog manager.

Bibliography

Benny, Raphael and Krishnamoorthy C. S.: *Automating Finite Element Development using Object Oriented Techniques,* India: Cambridge University Press, 2002.

Bruce, Hendrickson and Robert, Leland: *Algorithms and Software for Partitioning Meshes,* New Jersey: Engelwood Cliffs, 2000.

Coplien, James O.: *Advanced C++, Programming Styles and Idioms,* UK: Addison Wesley Publishing Company, 2002.

David, G.: *Linear and Nonlinear Programming,* UK: Addison–Wesley Publishing Company, 2004.

Davis, T.A.: *Data-Management Services for Parallel Application,* Florida: University of Florida and Rutherford, 2000.

Dennis, J. E.: *Quasi-newton Methods, Motivation and Theory,* UK: SIAM Review, 2001.

Duff, I.S.: *Object Oriented Finite Element Programming: Theory and C++ Implementation for FEM Objects C++ 01,* Switzerland: Elmepress International, 1998.

Fletcher, R.: *Practical Methods of Optimization,* India: John Wiley and Sons, 2002.

Helmut, Kopka and Patrick W.: *A Guide To LATEX,* UK: Addison Wesley, 1993.

Henricson, Mats: *Programming in C++, Rules and Recomendations,* Sweden: Ellemtel Telecomunication Systems Laboratories, 2003.

Herbert, Schildt: *C++, The Complete Reference,* UK: Osborne McGraw Hill, 1998.

Jendele, L.: *Numerical Modelling of Moisture, Heat and Pollutant Transport in Partially Saturated Porous Media using Object Oriented Programming*, Scotland: University of Glasgow, 2005.

Jonathan, Richard Shewchuk: *An Introduction fo the Conjugate Gradient Method without the Agonizing Pain*, Pittsburgh: Carnegie Mellon University, 2004.

Joshi, Mahesh: *Object-Oriented Programming, Systems, Languages and Applications*. Minnesota: Univesity of Minnesota and IBM , 2002.

Karypis, George: *Analysis of Multilevel Graph Partitioning*, Minnesota: Univesity of Minnesota and Army HPC Research Centre, 2001.

Kenneth J. Perano and Nielsen, Paul E.: *A C++ Class Template for Self–Describing*, California: Sandia National Laboratories, 2006.

Kevin, Dowd: *High Performance Computing*, Morris Street: O'Reilly and Associates, 2005.

Kumar, Vipin: *A Performance Study of Diffusive vs. Remapped Load–Balancing Schemes*, USA: NASA Ames Research Centre, 2000.

Kumar, Sumit: *Multilevel Algorithms for Multi–constraint Graph Partitioning*, Minnesota: Univesity of Minnesota and Army HPC Research Centre, 2002.

Nath, Rajiv: *A Survey of General-purpose Computation on Graphics Hardware*, Minnesota: Univesity of Minnesota, 2002.

Makles, Kevin: *Large Scale Finite Element Computations on Parallel Computers: Application to Elasto–plastic Problems in Geomechanics*, UK: Clarkson University, 2000.

Margaret, A.: *The Annotated C++ Reference Manual*, New Jersey: AT and T Bell Laboratories, 2001.

Olton, Mark: *Beowulf Class Parallel Computer "GeoWulf": Design, Construction and Testing. Progress Report*, California: University of California, 2001.

Petersson, Hans: *Computer Added Learning of the Finite Element Method CALFEM*, Sweden: University Sweden, 2003.

Prakash, G.: *Computer Methods in Applied Mechanics and Engineering*, Minnesota: Univesity of Minnesota and IBM , 2002.

Robert, B.: *Numerical Methods for Unconstrained Optimization and Nonlinear Equations*, New Jersey: Engelwood Cliffs, 2000.

Schloegel, K.: *Language Oriented Programming Computer Science Department*, UK: Univesity of Minnesota, 1998.

Stephen, Wolfram: *Mathematica, A System for Doing Mathematics by Computer*, UK: Addison–Wesley Publishing, 2005.

Stroustrup Bjarne: *The C++ Programming Language*, UK: Addison–Wesley, 2002.

Thomas, Zimmermann: *Object Oriented Finite Element Programming: Theory and Smalltalk V Implementation for FEM Objects PC 01*, Switzerland: Elmepress International, 2004.

William, T.: *Numerical Recipes in C, The Art of Scientific Computing*, New York: Oxford University Press, 2006.

Index